Project
Governance

Contributions to Economics

www.springer.com/series/1262

Patrick S. Renz

Project Governance

Implementing Corporate Governance
and Business Ethics
in Nonprofit Organizations

With 33 Figures and 6 Tables

Physica-Verlag

A Springer Company

Series Editors

Werner A. Müller
Martina Bihn

Author

Dr. Patrick S. Renz
Lucerne School of Business
Zentralstrasse 9
P.O. Box 3140
CH-6002 Luzern
Switzerland
patrick.renz@gmx.net

Library of Congress Control Number: 2006938886

ISSN 1431-1933
ISBN 978-3-7908-1926-7 Physica-Verlag Heidelberg New York

Physica-Verlag is part of Springer Science+Business Media

springer.com

© Physica-Verlag Heidelberg 2007

The use of general descriptive names, registered names, trademarks, etc. in this publication does not imply, even in the absence of a specific statement, that such names are exempt from the relevant protective laws and regulations and therefore free for general use.

Typesetting: Camera ready by the author
Production: LE-TeX Jelonek, Schmidt & Vöckler GbR, Leipzig
Cover-design: Erich Kirchner, Heidelberg

SPIN 11948254   134/3100YL - 5 4 3 2 1 0   Printed on acid-free paper

What our mind can wring from muddles
eventually benefits the stuff of life;
even if sometimes it is only thoughts,
they dissolve within that greater blood
that keeps flowing farther...

And if it's feeling: who knows how far it stretches
and what it yields within that pure space
in which an extra bit of light and heavy
sets worlds in motion and realigns a star.

Rainer Maria Rilke, 1924
Translation from German: David Oswald, 2005

Preface

Is governance an area reserved for the company board only? Are governance matters of interest only for the board of directors?

What is the bottom-up perspective on governance tasks?

And what is the relevance of governance for the nonprofit sector, specifically for development aid and development projects?

A development project in Bangladesh, which focused on the economic development of small and mid-size enterprises (SMEs), lies at the root of the above questions. A major multi-donor project, providing major management challenges in the midst of development aid challenges in one of the world's poorest countries, provided the opportunity to analyze the relevance of management and governance issues in development projects: A research project from the University of St. Gallen accompanied the start-up and the first 20 months of project operation on the ground.

The research results are presented in this book. Departing from the identification of a governance gap, the book suggests the concept of *project governance* for development projects, which operationalizes governance concerns and assures good management of development projects: *A project governance that considers strategic orientation, holistic control and integrated, ethically reflected management,* and contributes to development projects so as to *increase their impact, their efficiency and their accountability.*

The research project and the development of the project-governance concept would not have been possible without the countless contributions of numerous colleagues, friends from all over the world, and above all from my family – in fact people from four different continents and four religions have contributed in some way! My deepest gratitude goes to all of them. Particular thanks also to SwissNGO, to Prof. Dr. Peter Ulrich and Prof. Dr. Martin Hilb from the University of St. Gallen, and several professors from the University of Dhaka for their generosity of allowing this empirically oriented research, and for facilitating and supporting it with great interest.

I want to make special mention of my parents, Helen and Dr. Stephan Renz, who were always there to critically question my initial findings, but also supported me in periods of thirst. I want to thank my sisters Dr. Monika Renz and Helen Renz as well as my friend Dr. Jürg Muffler and Prof. Dr. Beat Sitter-Liver for their fundamental inputs in giving birth to the idea of such a dissertation in the first place. I would like to express particular thanks to my sister Dr. Ursula Renz for her concise, razor-sharp insights and her empathic inputs and support from a philosophical perspective. Additional thanks go to all of the following persons: To my friend PD Dr. Moshe Mresse for his tireless support as a sounding board and a highly creative challenger. To Mathias Weis and Dr. Afreen Huq, herself an associate professor, for reading through the entire book and providing first-class input from an academic perspective as well as from Bangladesh and the development world. To my friends David Howard and Dorothea Baur for providing critical and very constructive inputs from the perspectives of science as well as practical project management. To Victor Jans, Vinay Kalia, and Dr. Peter Krepper for their candid suggestions on specific chapters of the book. And to Anita Schneider for her patience and great support in improving the graphics and the layout. Special thanks go to the AVINA Stiftung Schweiz for their generous support in publishing this book.

Not to forget the friends and loved ones in the background who gave me loyal support or provided whatever piece was needed to complete the puzzle: Andria Mitchell, Jürg Stricker, Béatrice Horn, Miriam Schütt-Mao, Prof. Dr. Abdul Moyeen, Dr. Helmut Barz, Dr. David Oswald, and Dr. John Peck.

I also wish to acknowledge those many needy and humble persons whose lives are at the very root of development, represented by the many Bangladeshi men, women, and children whom I met and who inspired me not only to deliver results from the development project but also to develop viable concepts of project governance.

Dr. Patrick S. Renz   Zürich / St. Gallen / Dhaka, October 2006

Visit our website at www.aidgovernance.com or send your feedback or question to info@aidgovernance.com. I welcome all governance related stories you care to share.

Executive summary

This book is based on the hypothesis of a governance gap. Such a gap impacts the successful and meaningful implementation of development goals in development projects.

The author, an experienced manager of senior rank as well as on the project level, first describes this gap from a multi-perspective review of existing theory, in particular of corporate governance and nonprofit governance, project management, and the development sector. Inclusion of the ethical perspective corroborates that this governance gap also involves a shortcoming on ethical reflections, an 'ethics gap'.

A case study conducted during nearly two years in a major development project in Bangladesh confirms this hypothesis. Based on several management models developed by scholars at the University of St. Gallen, governance-related organizational theories and the insights gained from roughly 400 case examples, the author develops a Model of Project Governance. This is a process-oriented system by which projects are strategically directed, integratively managed and holistically controlled, in an entrepreneurial and ethical way.

This book identifies six modules constituting the key responsibilities of project governance: They are system management for the systemic understanding of the project environment. Mission management spells out the core governance tasks in the area of strategy, structure and organizational culture. Integrity management suggests a process model to assess and resolve challenges threatening the integrity of the project. The process model was developed drawing on a combination of discourse ethics and recognition ethics based on the insights gained from the analysis of 130 relevant case examples. Its novelty lies in bridging the tension between theory and practice. The module of extended stakeholder management shows how a broad identification and continuous joint monitoring of mutual claims and expectations can be achieved, ultimately enabling a truer cooperation in development cooperation. Risk management provides, again relying on system understanding, a complete as possible risk identification and integrative risk management cycle. Audit management, finally, proposes a more holistically controlled audit setup for development projects.

The author concludes that the closing of the governance gap that is described, by means of the suggested Model of Project Governance, not only supports a more efficient and accountable implementation of development objectives but also becomes an implicit part of the objective for true development cooperation.

Table of contents

Table of figures

Table of tables

1 Objectives and approach

1.1 Why a book on project governance

Governance is about 'checks and balances,' about 'direction and control.' From the organizational perspective it is usually associated with the top leadership of an organization. We call it corporate governance in a corporate context, nonprofit governance for the context of nonprofit organizations, and so on.[1]

But is governance relevant for the company board only? How are governance concerns broken down and operationalized for the rest of the organization?

'Direction and control' is relevant not only at the top, but throughout the entire organization: Risk management, for instance, as a typical board responsibility, is only effective if risk management exists on the operational level and if it is integrated throughout the entire organization.

The question is *how governance concerns are implemented within the organizational units*. This is of particular interest when some of those organizational units have a high level of autonomy, such as a development project, a remote subsidiary, or a joint venture involving several stakeholders. Corporate or nonprofit governance concerns will need to be broken down; and vice versa, operational concerns will need to be looped back to the normative and strategic top leadership.

A look at the relevant literature leads one to deduce the hypothesis of a *governance gap*.[2] The literature hardly describes how corporate governance

---

[1] The terms nonprofit organizations (NPO) and non-governmental organization (NGO) are often used synonymously. There is no consistent distinction between them in literature or practice. See Renz & Pucetaite (2005: 3f) for a description of this phenomenon. Schwarz (2005: 29) presents a comprehensive overview of the broad usage of the term NPO, without, however, referencing the term NGO. Also, Nonprofit Governance refers to the governance of NPOs as well as NGOs, and there is no such thing as "Non-governmental Governance". This book therefore uses NGO and NPO synonymously.

[2] See Chapter 2.2.

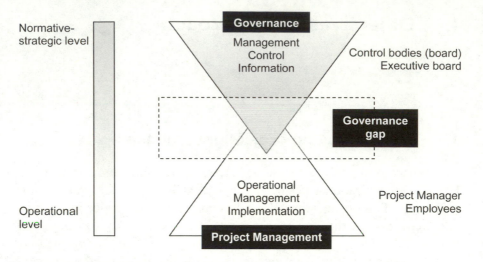

Figure 1. The governance gap[3]

concerns impact the *operation*, or how the operation of a project, for instance, is embedded within the corporate or nonprofit governance concerns. This governance gap is illustrated in Figure 1.

Case study research confirms the existence of such a governance gap. The research project leading to this book captured, during two years in a major development project in Bangladesh, any managerial situation falling out of a normal context, and anything worth logging in protocols. Posterior analysis has shown evidence of a gap in governance: The vast majority of the logged-in situations describe a problem (and sometimes a solution to the situational problem) arising from the existence of such a governance gap. These problems can be grouped among the following categories:[4]

- Gaps in a systematic understanding of the 'system' or the context, such as a lack of intercultural sensitiveness (in 25% of the gap-relevant protocols);

- Gaps in the direction of the project or – at the opposite extreme – micro-management (19%);

---

[3]   Enhanced from Erfurt 2004: 47, Wunderer 1995: 20 and Tricker 1984: 175. See also Schedler's description of "two rationalities" in the context of public management needing 'translation,' between a "political rationality" and a "management rationality" (2003).

[4]   Numerous examples are included in this book.

- Cases of ethical randomness (37%);

- Gaps in a reflected and continuous management and monitoring of *stakeholders* (12%);

- Gaps in *risk* management and in the *audit* area (7%).

It is not surprising that classical concerns such as audit and risk management score the lowest: They have traditionally received a lot of attention, but they are still appearing. The main challenge is to understand what exactly the nature of these governance problems is in the other categories, and what a good concept for overcoming this governance gap might be.

A thorough search for bridging this governance gap makes it clear that some type of *middle governance* is needed, a *project governance* in the case of project-intense environments, and subsidiary governance in the case of subsidiaries, joint-venture governance etc. This is illustrated in Figure 2.

This book suggests that some form of project governance is necessary for any development project, independent of its size and content.

Now that one can see why the topic of project governance – for overcoming a governance gap – is a desideratum, we can take up the next chapter, which defines the particular objective this book is trying to reach.

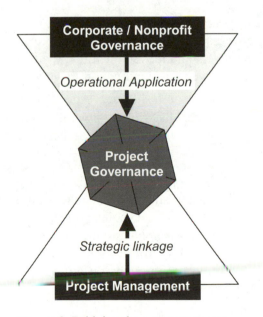

Figure 2. Bridging the governance gap

1.2   Objectives and target audience

What should such project governance look like? The objective of this book, which in the nature of things is exploratory, is to develop a model describing 'good project governance' using the example of a development project. The specific objectives are:

1. To develop the *foundations and the shape* of a concept for *project governance*. The research draws on the context of development projects characterized by the particularities of development policies, by the sometimes extreme context of local realities in the development country and by the interdisciplinary, intercultural and ethical challenges of its mission. The project governance concept should be pragmatic and supportive to the project manager, the top management, and other stakeholders. For all these reasons, specific instruments and processes should be defined. These should be generically valid, independent of the size and content of a project; the only thing which may differ from project to project is the organizational setup.

2. To contribute to a successful implementation of corporate or non-profit governance, as well as business ethics, by *delivering solutions on an operational level*.

3. To contribute to the relevant *research* into the governance of organizations, by identifying governance issues and solutions prevalent on lower-ranked hierarchy levels and raising them to the attention of the debates on corporate governance and nonprofit governance (i.e. the higher level).

4. To identify areas of additional research that would hopefully contribute to an ongoing and fruitful debate between practitioners and academia.

By including numerous case examples, this book aims also at sensitizing the reader to the broad variety of possible governance issues, and to what it means to 'direct and control,' in other words *govern*, complex projects.

The research scope is limited as follows: This exploratory research does not focus on either corporate governance or nonprofit governance aspects per se, i.e. the level of top management. The focus falls on governance aspects – like the direction and control functions – *at the level of a subordinate organizational unit*, the project.

Similarly, this book does not look at or judge current development policies or the quality of development objectives or approaches. Rather, it looks into how they can be *brought into practice* within a systemic under-standing of the development context.

As the title indicates ("Project Governance – implementing Corporate Governance and Business Ethics in Nonprofit Organizations"), resolving the governance gap requires a multidisciplinary perspective. The broad and multidisciplinary perspective may also attract readers from a variety of backgrounds:

Primarily, this book addresses and lends support to all actors in the non-profit sector, by specifically focusing on development aid with the aim of achieving better aid efficiency, accountability, and transparency. Secondly, it addresses the reader, practitioner or researcher with a deeper interest in both corporate governance and nonprofit governance, illustrating why gov-ernance concerns specifically need operational attention. Thirdly, it speaks to ethicists, in particular from business or development ethics, by trying to bridge the often-lamented gap between theory and practice in bringing ethi-cal considerations down to the operational level. Finally, it is also for those project managers of all types, regardless of the industry, who are looking for enhancements to the traditional craft of project management.

With this we turn to the approach of the book.

1.3   Approach

This chapter outlines how the above objectives are being approached, first through the overall approach, then a presentation of the research method-ology, and finally by briefly introducing the concrete case study project.

1.3.1   Overview and structure of the book

The topic of project governance is novel in character. As the objective is not only to describe the governance gap but also to develop a solution for bridging it, an exploratory approach is best. This book pursues such an approach with the following structure (see Figure 3):

This first chapter summarizes the identified problem (the governance gap), suggests the idea of project governance as a solution, shows how this problem is approached, and clarifies terminology.

Chapter 2 takes up the question whether a need for project governance really exists. A look from various angles and theoretical perspectives con-firms the hypothesis of a *governance gap,* which is the chief basis for mak-ing a case for project governance.

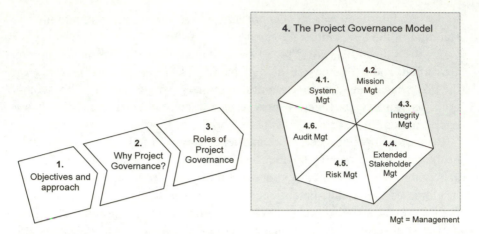

Figure 3. Structure of the book

The next question is what such project governance should look like and what roles it should take (Chapter 3). Looking at governance-related organizational theories allows one to identify a number of basic *governance roles* that such project governance should play. Finally, in order for a governance board to fulfill these roles (i.e. put them into practice), *six* concrete *governance key responsibilities,* or major tasks, are identified.

Chapter 4 introduces these key responsibilities (or governance modules): System Management, Mission Management, Integrity Management, extended Stakeholder Management, Risk Management, and Audit Management. Using a combined analytic and synthetic process, this book draws on the current status of the literature, the current best practices, and the findings from the case research. For each key responsibility, a model is developed and/or adapted, illustrated with concrete examples from the research case at hand.

The book concludes with a summary, the research limitations, and the implications and recommendations for practice and further research.

1.3.2   Practical research – research methodology

Practical research needs not only to confirm the existence of the governance gap but also chiefly needs to indicate possible ways for resolving this gap, ideally through providing numerous illustrating examples. The novel nature of the objectives outlined in Chapter 1.2 translates into the following research requirements:

1. A scientific model for a (strategically positioned) Project Governance in general, and applicable in development projects in particular, does not now exist. The primary focus is therefore an *exploratory* development of theory in the form of a project governance model.

2. The number of influencing disciplines is high, and the novelty of the research objective also grows out of the combination of those disciplines. The exploratory nature of the research will therefore require a *combined deductive – inductive* approach. Practical *case examples* illustrating issues need to be inserted continuously into the presentation, thereby allowing observers to verify approximate solutions early in the game.

3. The research area lies at the intersection of different cultures and religions, in the midst of social challenges and ethical questions. The research methodology therefore ought to allow one to *capture data of high qualitative depth*, along the lines of ethnographical research projects; otherwise, there is an imminent risk that relevant data will go unrecognized and leave one far from understanding the whole extent of the research problem.

4. Considerations of internal, external, and construct validity and reliability are to be made and presented as part of any 'good' scientific research.

The key points of the selected research methodology are summarized below. A more detailed description can be found in Annex 2: Research Methodology.

As a suitable research strategy, a case study approach was deemed the most appropriate for fulfilling the above requirements.

Data collection was performed through participant observation allowing an exploratory approach and resulting in data of high qualitative depth. This allows studies of "cause and effect,"[5] resulting in a high degree of internal validity. The case study research accompanied the development project DRIVER[6] during the project startup and during the first twenty months of project operation. The collected data consists of 397 events, incidents or observations which were collected in line with Eisenhardt's requirements for successful field notes.[7] Data triangulation helped to maxi-

---

[5] Scandura & Williams 2000: 1252.

[6] For a description of the development project, see Chapter 1.3.3: The case study – an introduction to DRIVER.

[7] See 1989: 539.

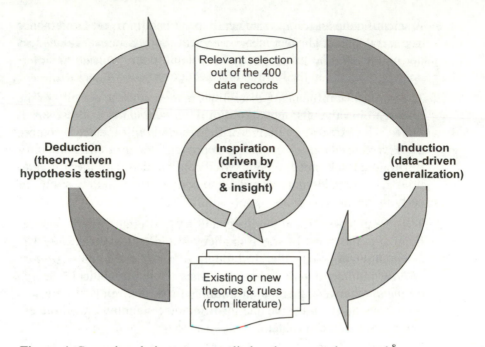

Figure 4. General analytic strategy applied to the case study research[8]

mize the construct validity; additionally, a variety of key informants and the separation of data collection and data analysis into different phases have complied with Bernard's "ethical imperative"[9] for the participant observer.

For data analysis a general analytic strategy was chosen as stipulated by Yin and detailed by Langley (see Figure 4). Several data bases served the need of "examining, categorizing, tabulating, [and] testing"[10] the data provided by the case study. This again helped to maximize research reliability.

Out of the roughly 400 cases, around 80 have been included in this book. They are distributed among the chapters as illustrations, allowing the reader more clearly to follow the thought process (see table of case examples). A high number of rather negative examples may give the impression that the project serving as a case study may not have been successful, but the contrary is the case (the project was extended and nearly doubled in budget). From a scientific perspective, the orientation toward negative

---

[8]   Terms in bold letters from Langley 1999: 708.

[9]   Bernard 2000.

[10] Yin, 2003: 109.

examples, however, has a higher heuristic value: 'Bad stories' have a better pedagogical effect than 'plain successes'.

Readers familiar with the case may identify mistakes in the examples. None of them is intended. It is clear, however, that many details had to be summarized and simplified, in order to concentrate on the essence and to present it to the reader in a comprehensive form. All names of persons and institutions were altered so as to allow an optimal choice of examples and an exploration in depth.

In summary, the research methodology of a case study with participant observation for data collection has yielded data of high quality and depth, resulting in high internal validity. It is exactly this depth that made it possible to develop a comprehensive project governance model in the first place. Its statistical generalization may be the subject of further research.

The next chapter gives a brief overview of the specific case study.

1.3.3   The case study – an introduction to DRIVER

1.3.3.1 Objective of the development project and the development approach

The research focused on the start-up and first twenty months of operation of the development project DRIVER. This was a multi-donor funded initiative that contributed to the first Millennium Development Goal (MDG #1), which is to eradicate extreme poverty and hunger. The approach chosen was an economic development approach targeted at small and mid-size enterprises. DRIVER would work as a market facilitator helping SMEs to become more productive and competitive, thereby creating more income and jobs with the expectation that this would help to reduce poverty.

While it is not within the scope of this book to assess the above goal hierarchy or judge the value of market facilitation compared to irrigation projects, for instance, the reader is encouraged to bear in mind the complexity inherent in such goal hierarchy as it impacts the complexity of project management.[11]

---

[11] The complexity arises from the following concerns among others: (1) The logic of the goal hierarchy is *complex*, theoretically and practically. The approaches are young and disputed. (2) Causality: Is there a proven causality between the layers? (3) Attribution: How can economics in a market be *attributed* to the activities of the project? These are also typical questions discussed at the level of development policies, or as part of the fundamental ethical debate on 'good' development (See, for instance, Ulrich P. 2004, Kesselring 2003, Stiglitz 2002, Sen 1999, Goulet 1995, Rawls 1971).

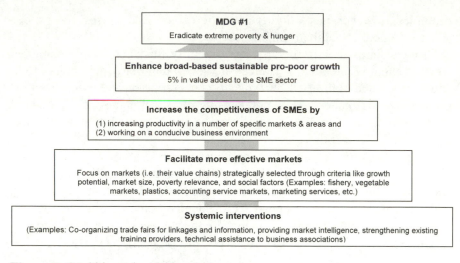

Figure 5. Goal hierarchy and break-down

The intention of the three donor agencies that had joined up for DRIVER was to make a substantial impact. The project size, therefore, was major; it is in fact currently the largest of its kind worldwide: A staff of over 50 employees, with over 100 local subcontracts, a time horizon of five years, and a budget of ca. 30 million US$.

1.3.3.2 Formal organization

The organization was set up as outlined in Figure 6. The intention with this chart is not that the reader grasp its details, for it might be called a 'chaos draft'. To appreciate the richness of the case study, a few points should, however, be borne in mind: The funding donors were three European donor agencies, each with a decentralized coordination office in Dhaka, but with largely differing autonomy levels among them. Project implementation was mandated to SwissNGO, headquartered in Switzerland. SwissNGO subcontracted one part to GerCon, headquartered in Germany and with regional support offices in Dhaka and Katmandu. SwissNGO was entirely responsible for the project unit in Dhaka (DRIVER), but during the first three months a GerCon Manager acted as an interim manager. The organization chart also shows a number of key stakeholders, such as the government-focused policy steering committee. The roughly 100 local subcontractors are not shown on the chart.

Without going into some of the outcomes of this research, it can be said that this organizational setup is either too complex or else requires extraordinary discipline.

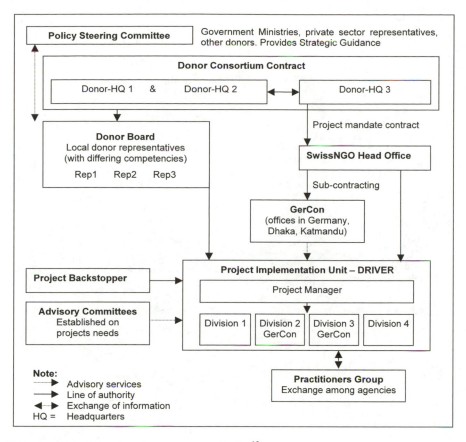

Figure 6. Organizational setup as per design[12]

1.3.3.3 Informal organization

The structural complexity of the formal organization can best be under-stood when complemented with a picture of the informal organization and bilateral channels (see Figure 7). This perspective lets one see how many deviations from the formal organization occurred.

The high number of informal lines suggests that the formal organization is in fact too complex, and that the extra discipline required to follow it is not on hand. This book accordingly proposes that such complex structures should be streamlined and supported by a model of *project governance* based on a sound groundwork of carefully delineated roles and responsibilities.

---

[12] As per original project appraisal document and project document (DRIVER 2002, 2004).

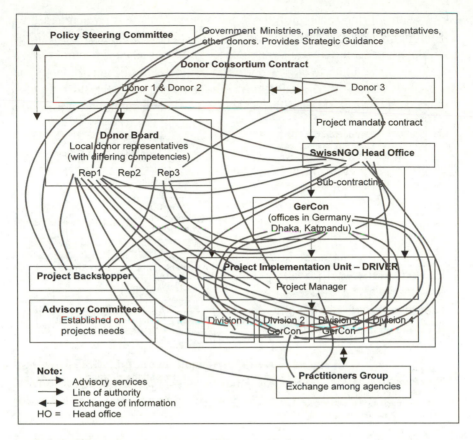

Figure 7. Informal organization and bilateral channels

Beyond questions of organization, readers will also want to assess the project's achievements. Were its objectives reached? In objective terms, project impact on market development projects can usually be assessed only around 2 years after the major project interventions. An earlier assessment cannot make valid statements about the scale and sustainability of impact. Therefore, DRIVER tried to identify early indicators. By the time the research project ended, the project had shown encouraging early indicators and had acquired good reactions from the markets and a wide geographical coverage, to the extent that other donors wanted to join and overall funding nearly doubled.[13]

---

[13]   Fortunately, this expansion was postponed, because it would have overtaxed the organizational capacities of the implementing NGOs. In the meantime, the project's time horizon has been extended by 4 years.

After this brief review of the book's structure, the chosen research methodology and the presentation of the concrete case, we now turn to the terminology used throughout this book.

1.4   Terminology

This chapter clarifies the terminology, in particular looking at the definition of 'project' and the understanding of 'governance' from various angles. Finally, the term 'project governance' will be defined, including the distinction between project management, project governance, and corporate / nonprofit governance.

1.4.1   What is a project, and what are development projects?

This book relies, with a slight enhancement, on a recent and general definition of projects by Gomez et al., who define projects as "*singularly executed endeavors within a fixed period of time, of particular complexity and containing interdisciplinary tasks.*"[14] This further comprises "target specifications [on] content, quality, costs, effort, deadlines."[15]

Practitioners will probably critique one point in this definition, the "fixed period of time". In practice that period often turns out to be relatively flexible, not just because of possible project delays but also because a prolongation or shortening of the project may be indicated. However, the important aspect about time in a project definition is that a project *has a beginning and an end*, because otherwise it is no longer a project.

Therefore, the following definition of projects will be adopted throughout this book:

Project
A project is a singularly executed endeavor with a certain scope, quality and a financial frame, with a beginning and an end, of particular complexity and interdisciplinary in character.

---

[14]   Gomez et al. 2002: 32 (translation and emphasis Renz).

[15]   Idem.

This generically valid project definition already yields a first possible governance issue: It looks as if a project is a self-contained organizational unit. The above definition induces the (only partially correct) assumption that the project design and approval are preceding stages and possibly independent of the "singularly executed endeavor"; in other words, the project is the result of an approved project design which – additionally – is most probably based on an approved overall strategy. Independently of whether a project design and initial approval are (intended) parts of the definition of projects, it becomes obvious that there is more than the (narrowly) defined project. This 'more' has to do with its embedding, its steering, and its context. These are questions at the heart of the governance issues described later on.

How can projects be understood in the context of *development*? Development projects are one of the key vehicles for achieving the objectives of development cooperation. According to the Swiss Agency for Development and Cooperation (SDC, the German abbreviation being DEZA), these objectives are "to improve the living conditions of the most deprived people on our planet."[16] The currently most prominent development objectives are the Millennium Development Goals (MDGs), which all United Nation Member States have pledged to meet by 2015. The MDGs define eight concrete objectives ranging from halving extreme poverty to providing universal primary education and promoting gender equality.[17] A huge number of international and local actors, relying on either government or private initiative, contribute in many ways towards these development goals. What do these actors do specifically – that is, 'what is being done concretely'?

In a simplified view, there are basically two distinct implementation vehicles for development aid: The creation and execution of a *development project,* and support for the efforts of a specific government through *budgetary means*, where the respective donor basically funds part of a governmental budget line.

For example, the Swiss Agency for Development and Cooperation (SDC), a rather small agency in its field, was engaged in around 1,000 projects in 2004.[18] The reader may note at this point that while some 'economies of scale' certainly play their part, in terms of knowledge and organizational execution such a high number of projects none the less cre-

---

[16] SDC 2004: 4.

[17] See Annex 1: The UN Millennium Development Goals (MDGs) for a summary.

[18] SDC 2004.

ates – *because of the singular character* of projects – elevated demands on the actors involved, especially with respect to execution.

There is another term similar to 'development project,' namely 'development program'. While in principle a program is thought of as a synergetic set of projects, the distinction in practice is not that clear-cut. For instance, in the case study a project may itself consist of various components, hence, the terms 'project' and 'program' are often used interchangeably. For reasons of scientific conciseness, this book focuses on the more precise project context, whereas many of its statements may also be valid for programs or similar organizational constructs.[19]

We may now turn to clarifying the term 'governance'.

1.4.2   Governance: A multi-facetted term

Governance has its roots in the Greek word 'kybernan' or Latin 'gubernare', to steer. The *Oxford English Dictionary* defines governance as the 'action or manner of governing'. Further, to govern is defined as '[t]o rule with authority, esp. with the authority of a sovereign; to direct and control the actions and affairs of (a people, a state or its members), whether despotically or constitutionally; to rule or regulate the affairs of (a body of men, corporation); to command the garrison of (a fort)'.

The term *governance* has undergone an explosive expansion in usage mainly in *two domains*, the political and corporate ones:

1. *Good governance* has become a development catchphrase promoted by the United Nations (among others) with respect to the (political) ruling of a state, mainly as the priority agenda item within development efforts. This *political* domain of governance is defined by Neumayer as follows: Governance is "the respect for political, civil and human rights of citizens; accordance with the rule of law; the provision of effective, non-corrupted public services; and the use of public resources in an accountable and transparent way, with the aim of promoting general social welfare."[20]

2. *Corporate governance* focusing on business organizations has been a prominent topic for several years, mainly as a response to recent corporate scandals and cases of major fraud. A more neutral term than corporate governance would be *organizational* governance,

---

[19] See also Chapter 5.4 for recommendations on further research.

[20] 2003: 8.

which also encompasses nonprofit governance, hospital governance etc. – i.e. any governance of an organization outside of government. When elaborating the concepts of project governance, this book resorts to the concepts of *organizational governance* rather than political governance (although, content-wise, the project might be confronted at some point with political governance as part of its scope).

The above definition in the *Oxford English Dictionary* underlines two key dimensions which are usually understood as constituting the essence of governance: The setting of *direction* and the exercise of *control*. These two criteria of direction and control, however, do not sufficiently reflect the dimensions of governance. The *Oxford English Dictionary,* by also mentioning the qualifying criteria 'despotically or constitutionally' (which establish a continuum with extremes rather than a dichotomy), raises the question of review: Who may qualify governance as being either despotic or constitutional, and on the basis of which underlying value scheme? Haberer incorporates in his definition of corporate governance the "[…] *optimal* firm direction and firm control,"[21] which implies that there is a judgment of 'appropriateness' to context-specific conditions involving a *valuation*.

While there is certainly "no single definition or model [of governance] which is universally recognized or applicable,"[22] this book adopts Hilb's multi-perspective understanding according to which he defines corporate governance "as a *system* by which companies are *strategically directed, integratively managed* and *holistically controlled,* in an *entrepreneurial and ethically reflected* way, and in a manner appropriate to each particular context."[23] This definition is sufficiently broad and open so that it can also be applied to the context of nonprofit organizations and to their 'direction and control'. Nonprofit governance is then defined as follows:

Nonprofit Governance

Nonprofit governance is a system by which nonprofit organizations are strategically directed, integratively managed and holistically controlled, in an entrepreneurial and ethically reflected way, and in a manner appropriate to each particular context.

---

[21] Haberer 2003: 3 (emphasis Renz).
[22] Davies 1999: 3.
[23] 2005: 9 (emphasis Renz).

At this point, it is useful to take a holistic look at an organization and understand how corporate or nonprofit governance integrate structurally and functionally into an organization. To this end, the distinction in several management levels and leadership functions as suggested by Hans Ulrich and Probst will help.[24] They suggest a distinction into upper, middle, and lower management[25] and a split of leadership functions into normative, strategic, and operational ones. This systemic view is illustrated in Figure 8. The key point is that all three functions are relevant on all three levels; What differs is their prevalence. Corporate / nonprofit governance, for instance, is located on the upper management level.[26] With H. Ulrich and Probst corporate governance would primarily have a normative, then a strategic, and finally an operative leadership function.[27]

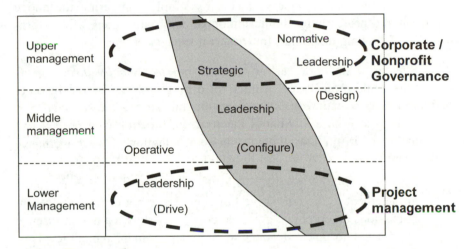

Figure 8. Management levels and leadership functions: Locating corporate / nonprofit governance[28]

---

[24] See Ulrich H. & Probst 1995.

[25] With Ulrich H. & Probst, this book adopts a broad and *inclusive* understanding of management, where for instance corporate governance bodies are (substantial) part of the upper management.

[26] The terms 'upper' and 'top' management are used synonymously in this book.

[27] The expectations towards governance roles are examined more in detail in Chapter 3. As a side remark this graphic leads one to an interesting question: Did the corporate governance crisis take root in an overemphasis of operational "driving" and strategic orientation, while the content of normative leadership was ignored?

[28] See Ulrich H. & Probst 1995: 277, 283 and Steinle 2005: 18.

Figure 8 also allows one to illustrate the location of project management which is on the lower management level, obviously. With this we can turn to the definition of project governance.

1.4.3   Defining and positioning project governance

The perspective on different management levels as seen in Figure 8 implies that middle management plays a transparent hinge-point role. While this would not be incorrect as a preliminary assumption, deeper analysis of recent theoretical contributions[29] and empirical evidence from the case study,[30] however, points out the *de facto* existence of a vacuum, a governance gap.

This becomes readily understandable by simply comparing the above definition of a project with the definition of corporate / nonprofit governance. The following dilemmas, for instance, appear:

- Strategy-wise: How can governance be *strategically directing* affairs while projects are characterized by their *singularity?* In other words, how can *singular* projects fit into an *overall* strategy? Or, looking at Figure 8, what is the strategic function of a project and how does it interplay with the strategic function of the governance board?

- From a *normative* perspective: What is the contribution of lower management to the normative function? Have not exactly the recent discussions on corporate governance already shown a major absence of reflected normative leadership on the upper management level?

- The control-aspect: How can projects be holistically controlled if they are singular and of *particular* complexity, i.e. of situational and variable complexity?

Looking at the first point, most people would probably agree that projects in general – despite their singularity – *must* be strategically oriented, and hence that there is a need to constructively resolve the dilemma outlined. The constructive and process-oriented resolution of such dilemmas, through the bridging of a vacuum, lies at the core of this book. Project governance aims at bridging or linking the levels. This is illustrated in Figure 9:

---

[29]   See Chapter 2.2.

[30]   See Chapter 1.1 and Chapter 4.

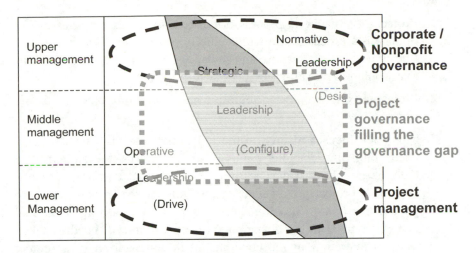

Figure 9. Positioning project governance

That there is a need for research illuminating the interplay and differences *between management levels* is also corroborated by Bruch, Vogel and Krummaker, who state that current findings on differences between management levels are "very limited."[31]

At this point, the reader might also get a first grasp of why this is called a g*overnance* gap: The gap seems to exist mainly in *governance-prevalent* roles, i.e. the normative and strategic functions. This is no surprise given the newness of the corporate (and even more the nonprofit) governance discussions.

With this we now can define what project governance is. Drawing on Hilb's definition of 'corporate governance' and the above definition of a 'project', the term project governance is defined as follows:

Project Governance

Project governance is a process-oriented system by which projects are strategically directed, integratively managed, and holistically controlled, in an entrepreneurial and ethically reflected way, appropriate to the singular, time-wise limited, interdisciplinary, and complex context of projects.

It is useful here to draw attention to a number of key points:

---

[31]   Bruch, Vogel & Krummaker 2006: 304 (translation Renz).

1. Project governance is process-orientated, for in as much as development is a process, a project is chiefly processual. This fact underlines the value of learning and pedagogy over predefined solutions that would provide all-embracing answers.

2. Project governance is an integrative and integrating element, as per Figure 9.

3. This book focuses mainly on the functional side of project governance, following Chandler's maxim to first clarify the strategy and then the structure. It can be said, however, that corporate governance, like project governance, is institutionalized in some form of governance board. Situational aspects such as multi-organizational contexts typical in the development cooperation will need be taken into consideration in the concrete institutionalization of a project governance board.

4. This book will further elaborate on the roles and structure of such a board, as well as on its difference from the ubiquitous steering teams.

5. Finally, project governance is not project management, nor is it nonprofit (or corporate) governance; rather, it is the linking pin between them, aiming at resolving what this study will subsequently describe as the governance gap between project governance and nonprofit (or corporate) governance.

This chapter has given an overview of why project governance is an important topic. The approach and the context of the specific case study for the empirical research was described. Finally, the terminology used in this book was clarified. The next chapter will analyze the specific need for project governance in more detail.

2 Is there a need for project governance?

This chapter analyzes the need for project governance in depth: Is there really a case for project governance? What are the perspectives calling for such project governance? These questions will be explored in Chapter 2.2. Before doing so, however, a pair of more fundamental question needs to be answered: Is there any management needed at all in development? Does sustainable development need management? These questions lie at heart of Chapter 2.1.

2.1 Management in development projects: Sense or nonsense?

> 太上，下知有之。其次，親之譽之。其次，
> 畏之。其次，侮之。信不足焉，有不信焉。
> 悠兮其貴言，功成事遂，百姓皆謂我自然。

> *A leader is best when people barely know he exists, not so good when people obey and acclaim him, worst when they despise him. But of a good leader, who talks little, when his work is done, his aim fulfilled, they will say, 'We did this ourselves.'*

> Laozi, 604-531 BC. Daodejing, ch. 17[32]

Laozi points out a crucial modal point of leadership, or more general of management: Is management something which is best when it is not perceived? If yes, then why is it needed? And what – in particular – is the need for management in development cooperation? Is there not a fundamental paradox at work – managing vs. developing?

---

[32] Translated by Bynner (1944).

2.1.1 'Managing' a development project: A paradox?

Does a project which aims at inducing change in a *sustained and self-motivated* way – for instance in developing the local economy of a poor region – need management? Managing involves the setting of objectives and inducing motivation in the managed personnel. Sustainable development involves distributed ownership and self-motivation. How can such managerially 'induced motivation' be compatible with 'self-motivation'?

'Local involvement' and 'ownership' are the buzzwords which apparently resolve this contradiction, but still the apparent paradox describes a key challenge in development: How can somebody *be convinced to own* a certain development effort? And who, based on reasonable legitimacy, should undertake the task of convincing them?[33]

On the other hand, from a Western perspective,[34] questions around 'correct and appropriate' spending of development money are more controversial than ever. In today's on-line societies, with their increased awareness of natural and human catastrophes, and also with the increased visibility of both achievements and under-achievements on the UN development agenda, the public and political pressure for efficiency and effectiveness of development money is bound to increase. Therefore, the debates about the sense and form of management in development projects are more relevant and real than ever.

2.1.2 The need for management in development projects

Flatter organizations, delegation and empowerment down the hierarchy, and increased teamwork ('we did it ourselves'!) all may give the impression that hierarchy, and with it management, is disappearing. Flatter organizations, however, are an expression of an increasing *division of labor*

---

[33] This apparent contradiction is taken up by Kesselring, who identifies a 'suspicion of paternalism' inherent in development policy. He highlights the difficulty of determining that there is no 'tutelage' in the game. "Development processes which are kicked-off from outside need to be justified towards the target group. In the end, though, it is about more than justification, in fact being about acceptance by those concerned," and even then such acceptance must amount to more than "an attitude of obsequiousness under an authority" (2003: 104; translation Renz).

[34] In development slang, the western or northern countries refer to the 'more developed,' often donor countries; eastern or southern refers to recipient countries of development aid.

which again requires – in one form or another – coordination mechanisms: The complex structure resulting from an increased division of labor can be regarded as a "socio-technical system"[35] which, without structuring and ordering coordination, i.e. management, "would promptly fail and dissolve into nothingness."[36] From this, one can conclude that *any organizational structures*, such as a business or a development organization, "are and remain – despite all tendencies towards flatter organizational concepts – hierarchically organized structures"[37] (and hierarchy implies management!). Management, therefore, is changing its forms rather than disappearing, to such an extent that Malik even designates "management [to be] the most important societal function."[38] Or in the words of García Echevarría and del Val Núñez: "The division of labor is constantly changing: what does not change is the essential requirement of learning to manage people."[39]

What does this perspective on management mean for the sector of development aid? In development work, too, there is a division of labor: Governments allocate tax money to development aid, citizens pay taxes, governmental development agencies decide on allocation priorities, and implementation agencies bid for projects and implement them mostly in combination with local NGOs and development businesses bringing local expertise to the table.[40] In a hypothetical scenario, without any division of labor, the individual tax payer would need to run his[41] own development program: The tax payer would decide on his intention and the amount to allocate to development, would himself visit countries in need in search of opportunities, would run his own (mini-)project, and possibly somehow try

---

[35] Ulrich P. & Fluri 1995: 13 (translation Renz). For a detailed introduction to and definition of the term 'system,' see Chapter 4.1. System Management.

[36] Rüegg-Stürm 2005: 10.

[37] Ulrich P. 1999a: 230 (translation Renz).

[38] Malik 2002: 109ff (translation Renz).

[39] 2000: 140.

[40] As it does not add to the perspective on dividing labor, for the moment this study sets aside any question of how political and/or economic interests drive the set-up for such division of labor as well as the question of what the motivation behind involving local expertise may be.

[41] For ease of readability, this book usually tries to adopt gender neutral language. Where this is not possible, the male form, and in some instances both forms, are used. Regardless of gender, these usages always implicitly refer to both sexes.

to assess the impact. For most readers, this illusory scenario would be asking too much, with the result that "the resources of development [would] remain resources and never become development."[42]

Development projects represent such an 'organizational structure' within the division of labor for development work: On one side, they are that part of the labor which receives a mandate for implementation, while on the other side they are an on-site coordinating structure bringing different actors (stakeholders[43]) together and trying to join forces in structuring and ordering a socio-technical system.

Furthermore, a development project's internal structure represents a system organized around the division of labor. Without management, such a project 'fails' and risks falling apart, as illustrated by the following example:

Management vacuum

When Geoffrey – a grey-haired development expert – took over as project manager of a big development project from his predecessor, one of the core messages he spread in his large organization was the following: "This project has been set up for the good of Bangladesh. The project money is for you, the people of Bangladesh. You will have to decide what best to do with it." In principle his statement was correct, but it also ran the risk that "resources for development may never become development" if not coordinated appropriately.

Only weeks later, Geoffrey lost control of his coordination role. Several local key employees 'negotiated' up to 50% salary increases, threatening that they had received better job offers. It is Important to note that the project had already been offering competitive salaries. Not surprisingly, these arbitrary salary increases caused dissatisfaction and conflicts among the other staff. The system's peaceful social order was lost, and it risked falling apart. (Fortunately, Geoffrey's employer became aware of the management vacuum and terminated his contract within a few weeks).

---

[42] This phrasing follows Drucker's on the role of management: "Without leadership 'the resources of production' remain resources and never become production" (1999: 3).

[43] The term 'stakeholder' is defined and introduced in detail in Chapters 4.1. and 4.4.

This example illustrates the need for management through the crucial fact that there are certain tasks, such as salary management, which cannot be delegated. With no management at all, or with management that uses a *laisser-faire* approach, these non-delegable tasks induce problems of opportunism.[44] In such a situation, a development project risks failing to engage its resources in the best common interest unless it is properly coordinated, which is to say managed.

In summary, any organization is built on some type of division of labor and therefore requires coordination mechanisms. The same is true of the development world, whose organizations and development projects need coordination through some type of meaningful management. That the form of such management requires particular attention has become obvious from the apparent paradox of managing in a paternalistic-free development context. This book proposes a solution on the operational level in the form of project governance, as being necessary for each development project regardless of its size and content. The next chapter analyses in greater detail the reasons behind the need for project governance.

2.2 A case for project governance: Various perspectives calling for project governance

> *"There is Microeconomics and Macroeconomics. There is almost no "Middle Economics." There is no – or only a little – economic theory of society and of social organizations [...]. Yet in the years since World War One [...] all developed countries have become Societies of Organizations."*
>
> Peter Drucker, 2005

The main intent of this book is to both introduce and operationalize a concept of project governance. In analogy to Peter Drucker's "Middle Economics," the concept of Project Governance works to fill the middle layer between Corporate (or Nonprofit) Governance and Project Management.

---

[44] Peter Ulrich refers to this as a responsibility gap, see Ulrich P. 2002: 118. According to Ulrich, management has a role to play in providing guiding principles and values which help overcome episodes of opportunism like the one in the case example.

This chapter looks at the following questions: What is new about project governance, and why there is a present and growing need for project governance, with a particular focus on development projects?

Only by addressing these questions can one analyze the need for project governance and the gap which it aims to close. We shall examine the issue from the following four perspectives: The project management perspective, the corporate governance perspective, the development sector perspective, and the ethical perspective.

2.2.1 Project management needs project governance: Reasons and differences

One could argue that project governance is part of project management, referring in particular to the *strategic* tasks of the project manager. Additionally, there are often steering committees overseeing the activities and progress of the project. Isn't that enough?

A review of the project management literature helps one to understand the current state of art. The generally extensive and mature literature on project management can be divided into four categories:

1. Basic literature on organization and management in general, introducing project organization as one specific *organizational form*.[45]

2. Numerous *best practices for project management* and practical how-to guides of all colors and qualities. One of the most prominent guides is the Project Management Book of Knowledge of the Project Management Institute (PMI).[46] Most of the practical literature oscillates around the traditional project management skills ('knowledge areas' in PMI terms), along the different project phases ('process groups' in PMI terms). See Table 1 for an overview of the knowledge areas and process groups.

3. Literature on *one specific project management topic*, such as risk management.[47]

---

[45] See, for instance, Thommen 2002, Lennertz 2002, Grün 1992.

[46] For the Project Management Book of Knowledge (or PMBOK Guide), see PMI 2004. Comprehensive overviews can also be found in Kupper (2001) and Harrison & Lock (2004). Furthermore, see Führer & Züger (2005), Fiedler (2001), Lester (2000) or Bainey (2004).

[47] See, for instance, Gassmann, Kobe & Voit on high-risk projects (2001).

Table 1. The knowledge areas of project management according to the Project Management Institute (PMI)[48]

Process Groups / Knowledge Areas	Initiating	Planning	Executing	Controlling	Closing
1. Project Integration Management					
2. Project Scope Management					
3. Project Time Management					
4. Project Cost Management					
5. Project Quality Management					
6. Project Human Resource Management					
7. Project Communication Management					
8. Project Risk Management					
9. Project Procurement Management					

4. *Sector specific* project management, for instance for IT projects or civil construction projects.[49] Under this category fall also a number of project management best practices from national *development* agencies, such as the PEMU or to a certain extent the PCM method.[50]

Most project management literature looks at the core function of (operational) project management. Both the strategic orientation and the answers to concrete constitutional questions about projects are lacking or under-represented. The term "project governance" or concepts like those devel-

---

[48]   Adapted from PMI 2004: 38.

[49]   Interesting insights on IT Project Management can be found in Gómez et al. (2002) or Buchta, Eul & Schulte-Croonenberg (2004).

[50]   For PEMU (German acronym for Planning, Evaluation, Monitoring, and Implementation of the Swiss Agency for Development and Cooperation SDC), see SDC 1996. For PCM (Project Cycle Management of the EuropeAid Cooperation office), see PCM 2004.

oped by this research project (such as project mission management or integrity management) are new and do not appear in the scientific literature. This lack of strategic embedding of project management illustrates the governance gap from the project management side as shown in Figure 1 in Chapter 1. From the literature perspective, there is extensive coverage of governance, mainly corporate governance aspects, which we will look at later; and there is also extensive literature coverage on operational project management from the bottom up. The interface between both represents the gap which project governance aims to close.[51]

With this much said, the earlier question posed about the relation of *steering committees* can be answered: While the establishment of project governance is a responsibility of the governance level, steering committees in practice are often constituted bottom-up by the project management. Kupper, for instance, recommends the project manager "to just nominate" his project steering team in cases where there is no "institutionalization from the top."[52] Why is this well-meant advice problematic? Because it works well only for smaller and in-house projects. It signifies, however, an (often tacit) delegation of responsibility for strategic compliance and direction-giving to the project manager, who – particularly in "singular, complex and interdisciplinary endeavors" – should instead be able to rely on the best possible strategic support and backing.

The project governance case reported in this book gives the officers at both levels, in governance as well as project management, the leverage and concrete tools to institutionally resolve the governance gap. Project governance assures the best possible backing for the project manager, while properly establishing the strategic and constitutional influence from stakeholders.

Issue	Proposition by Project Governance
How can a project manager be supported in a fundamentally strategic way beyond the help that comes on the executional level?	*The strategic and integrative nature of project governance bridges the governance gap, going beyond standard project management methodologies.*

---

[51]   See also Ganske 2004: 40ff on combining internal and external governance.

[52]   2001: 51 (translation Renz).

2.2.2   Corporate governance operationalized through project governance

The previous chapter – from a *project management* perspective – has stressed the need for linking a project with the *strategic and normative sphere* of the organization, i.e. the need of the "bottom" to be strategically and normatively linked and to have constituted accesses to the upper levels.[53] This chapter looks at the reverse or top-down perspective, under the two headings of strategy operationalization and information asymmetry.

2.2.2.1 Strategy operationalization

There is no doubt that top management has a genuine interest in assuring that established directions and strategies are *operationalized,* i.e. deployed down the hierarchy. As noted earlier, the fundamental roles of corporate governance are direction giving and controlling.[54] Nationally legislated acts of regulation (such as Sarbanes-Oxley in the US) in fact mainly focus on the board's *controlling* responsibility.

However, being legally responsible, and giving directions and enabling them to happen are quite different things. "Recent studies of the management of multinational corporations have found that headquarters had difficulties in controlling the activities of subsidiaries in their worldwide operations."[55] This difficulty in establishing *and maintaining* a strategic navelstring is even more pronounced in project-intense environments, where the operations are executed mainly through projects. How can a head office assure, within a variety of singular, complex and changing projects, that it is not 'the tail that wags the dog,' and that an undesirable, un-*control*-able self-dynamic develops within the projects themselves?[56]

---

[53] See also Figure 2 and Figure 8.

[54] For a more detailed discussion of governance roles, see Chapter 3.

[55] Engwall 2003: 172 referring to the studies of Forsgren, Holm & Johanson (1995) and Forsgren, Holm & Thilenius (1997).

[56] Rollins & Lanza highlight a total absence of project focus on internal control under the Sarbanes-Oxley Act: The emphatic understanding of internal controls (adopted from the COSO report – Committee of Sponsoring Organizations of the Treadway Commission) "makes no mention of reviewing projects as part of their internal control reporting framework." Moreover, as "most [controlling] professionals are not trained in project and program management, […] many companies will go without reporting project fraud until after it is too late." (2005: 8).

The kind of corporate governance discussion that is best known to date has established the needs and responsibilities only of the top management levels. Departing from this base line, the project governance proposed here uses an in-depth understanding of the needs and roles of governance (see Chapter 3.1) to translate them into a project governance system (Chapter 3.2) aimed at bridging the gap between governance and operations in project-intense environments.

Issue	Proposition by Project Governance
How – in a project intense organization – can strategy operationalization be supported?	*A system linking governance and operation, based on the roles of governance, carries governance concerns to the operational level, creating a handshake between governance and operations.*

An immediate counter-argument at this point might say that there is no need for project governance, as these responsibilities are being fulfilled by the respective middle management or program managers. The insights gained from the research of this case study, however, indicate that while the *organizational form* may be partly up and running, still its *functions are not systematically* in place. Following Chandler's rule that "structure follows strategy,"[57] the book at hand focuses first on a systematic deduction of the content (strategy) of project governance and only then deals with structural implementation.

2.2.2.2 Resolving information and knowledge asymmetry

Business cycles have become progressively faster (shorter cycles for product development and marketing, faster competition, etc.). At the same time, organizations have become flatter through "delayering and empowerment."[58] Authority is delegated simply in order to run the increasingly complex business models. This empowerment or delegation is not finally a reaction to a growing *information asymmetry:* The top level decision makers lack sufficient information, insight and understanding to take relevant

---

[57] 1972.

[58] Grant 1996: 120. See also Johnson 1992.

decisions in a timely manner, and hence delegate decisions to the organizational level where the relevant information can best be found.

The information asymmetry or *"the information gap,"*[59] however, has not been removed. It probably still exists for those decisions which – for instance for legal reasons – cannot be delegated. This is the case with decisions on the ultimate "direction and control," as regulated in the new laws related to corporate governance. Consequently, the information asymmetry remains, but possibly at another level (see Figure 10).

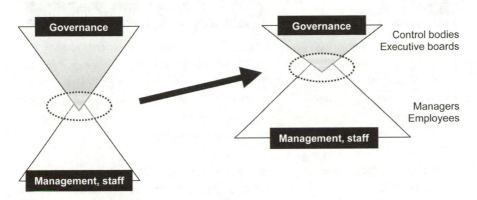

Figure 10. The move towards flatter hierarchy – information asymmetry is only shifted, not removed

This is supported by Rechkemmer, who concludes that top management (i.e. the governance level) "often consider their provision with information as insufficient and sub-optimal."[60] The reader may well wonder how, based on what (actual) *information*, top management can take decisions and exercise appropriate control functions.

This concern is exacerbated by the needs of today's increasing 'knowledge economy,' which creates a *"knowledge asymmetry."*[61] This can be illustrated as follows: "When managers know only a fraction of what their subordinates know and tacit knowledge cannot be transferred upwards, then [...] hierarchy is inefficient."[62] With respect to the governance level, this refers to an asymmetry in the *understanding of the organization and of*

---

[59]   Rechkemmer 2003 (translation Renz).

[60]   2003: 14 (translation Renz).

[61]   See Shapiro 2005 and Sharma 1997.

[62]   Grant 1996: 118.

the business the organization is engaged in. In their recent book *Back to the drawing board,* Carter and Lorsch claim that "strange to say, but [board members] often don't have a robust understanding of how money is made. They don't know the leverage points and what really drives profitability."[63] Also, the missing understanding cannot be compensated through an information machinery "providing information of their need to [the top management] following the queen-bee principle."[64] They will "continue to struggle to absorb the information thrown at them."[65]

Issue	Proposition by Project Governance
How can information and knowledge asymmetry between operation and governance be appropriately resolved?	*Project governance represents a meaningful, value-adding link between project management and (corporate) governance. It institutionalizes a targeted information flow that enables the building of necessary knowledge.*

Assuring the provision of relevant information, and building appropriate knowledge and understanding, are ultimately the responsibility of the board. It is not only a truism that "ignorance is no excuse"[66]; some governance laws or codes even specify that the responsibility for information provision rests with the responsible governance boards.[67]

The concept of project governance systematically contributes towards resolving the issues of information and knowledge asymmetries because it proposes a system for *strategically directing* and *holistically controlling* projects involving both operational and governance level in a number of responsibilities and processes. Hence, it institutionalizes meaningful information flows that enable the building of necessary knowledge.[68]

---

[63] 2004: 153.

[64] Rechkemmer 2003: 53 (translation Renz).

[65] Carter & Lorsch 2004: 153.

[66] Mueller R.K. 1993, as cited in Monks & Minow 2004: 207.

[67] See Rechkemmer 2003: 14.

[68] Project Governance and CGIFOS, a corporate governance information and early detection system proposed by Rechkemmer (2003), are based on the same information asymmetry. Project governance, however, is a wider concept which comprises the information and knowledge from CGIFOS in one of its components, extended stakeholder management. See Chapter 4.4 for more details.

In principle, project governance represents a diversification of governance research, which is also a desideratum pointed out from an academic perspective by various scholars: Hilb's situational approach suggests approaches along the lines of different organizational types and ownership forms.[69] Conger, Lawler and Finegold also suggest that we redesign the board concept by differentiating it, that is, by introducing new structural governance forms such as venture capital boards, partnership boards, advisory boards, and so forth.[70] It is the outlook of this study that the project governance proposed here can make a contribution to this debate.

In summary, strategy operationalization and information asymmetry are two relevant concerns of corporate governance which are also reflected in current academic debate. This accounts from a theoretical perspective, for the desideratum of project governance to provide a solution for both strategy operationalization and information asymmetry.

2.2.3   The need for project governance in the development sector

The previous two chapters have shown that there is room for action from the operational as well as the strategic perspectives on organizations. Do these points also hold true for the development sector? What is different? Can a need for project governance also be recognized in the development sector?

In what follows, four particularities of the development sector will be examined more closely, always in the light of the question whether they substantiate a desideratum for project governance:

1. Discussions on aid effectiveness and accountability, and the related public pressures, are taken up.

2. Analysis is devoted to certain typical project characteristics (such as singularity) to determine why they are particularly pronounced in development projects, and to what extent this fact may affect the need of governance.

3. The problematic of 'who owns a development project' will be analyzed.

4. Finally, a number of earlier findings are projected into the development sector: The previous chapter has identified two needs from the corporate governance perspective, strategy operationalization, and

---

[69]   2005: 17ff and 36ff.

[70]   2001.

information and knowledge asymmetry, which substantiate the desideratum for project governance. In this chapter, those findings are reviewed with a view to the question of whether they also hold true in the context of nonprofit governance.

2.2.3.1 Effectiveness, accountability[71] and public pressure

A particularity of the development sector in general is its involvement with increased public attention and pressure. The profile of development work is also heightened through the (welcome) existence of the MDGs and its respective progress reports. Additionally – and in contrast to some of the outcries following corporate scandals – the development sector faces a permanent groundswell of noise calling for more *effectiveness and accountability*. The NZZ, a leading Swiss newspaper, editorializes that Africa is being paralyzed by money, and that "the black continent doesn't need more, but less help."[72] Apparent mismanagement by donors and recipients as well as corruption are the grounds often voiced in such arguments. A World Bank poll reports that 58% of opinion leaders in industrial countries "believe that most foreign assistance is wasted due to corruption."[73] Despite contrary voices which argue that "inefficiencies [are] not proven,"[74] the development sector seems to recognize the issue through the recent *Paris declaration on aid effectiveness* in which the "ministers of developed and developing countries responsible for promoting development and [the] heads of multilateral and bilateral development institutions […] resolve to take far-reaching and monitorable actions to reform the way [they] deliver and manage aid."[75]

While the Paris declaration targets mainly the macro-level of development efforts (such as the need for national development strategies, more predictable aid flows or the need for donor alignment), and certainly represents an impressive declaration of intent, it remains unclear how the issues

---

[71] The author is aware of the debate on accountability and aid effectiveness. (See Lee 2004 for a comprehensive introduction on accountability). The argumentation in this subchapter is independent of the exact definition of accountability or effectiveness. See also the introduction of differentiated responsibility in Chapter 4.3 based on discourse ethics.

[72] NZZ 09.07.2005: 29 (translation Renz).

[73] World Bank 2003: 7.

[74] Kappel & Zürcher 2004.

[75] 2005: 1.

of effectiveness and accountability could actually be addressed on the operational level. This opaque lens onto the operational level also accounts for the frustration of taxpayers "who hardly can check [themselves], whether in Burundi or Mali what was supposed to be reached was in fact reached."[76]

Issue	Proposition by Project Governance
Pressure for aid effectiveness and accountability	*Aimed at improving effectiveness and accountability, project governance provides an integrative and holistic governance system, giving a face to operational opaqueness.*

Project Governance through its systemic, holistic, and integrative approach *gives a face* to this operational opaqueness. It contributes to what Mc Donnell and Solignac from OECD demand, namely "new approaches to communicating development realities and complexities."[77] It is also part of the solution for the NZZ's request for "a coherent and formulable system to monitor the usage of public means beyond the admittedly obvious checking of receipts."[78]

2.2.3.2 Typical project characteristics are particularly pronounced in development projects

In hardly any other sector are the particularities of projects as pronounced as in the development sector. For instance, with respect to '*particular complexity*':[79] A development project often builds on vague grounds where the highest-level objectives ("eradicate extreme poverty") are pursued with young development approaches, and in the absence of mature best practices as their foundation (quite often development projects develop their own approaches on-the-go). And this is not to mention the intercultural challenge, which adds to further complexity.

The '*singularity*' of development projects takes shape from *pioneering* in new fields and geographies, which imply *high exposure, vulnerability,* and *loneliness* in crisis periods, i.e. they represent *extreme conditions* in general. This *per se* is not surprising; on the contrary, a development project

---

[76] NZZ 23.08.2005: 7 (translation Renz).

[77] 2005: 5.

[78] 23.08.2005: 7 (translation Renz).

[79] See earlier definition of *project*.

sets out precisely to improve economic and/or socio-cultural 'under-developments'. The question then rather is whether a development project is appropriately armed and equipped.

To what extreme situations a development project may be exposed is illustrated in the following example from the case study:

The police raid

It was a quiet morning, but one that would shake the foundations of our ambitious small and medium-sized business development project. I was as yet clueless when I rushed to the reception hall, following an urgent call from my head of administration. What I saw left me dumbstruck: Five armed police officers had taken over the hall and were surrounding my staff; amidst the general commotion and frantic discussions in Bangla, I caught sight of a stocky man I didn't recognize; his head was bandaged and he was carrying a child, but he still managed to wave his arms about aggressively.

I inquired what the matter was. One of the police officers held out a crumpled piece of paper with a grim look on his face: It was a warrant to arrest three of my staff for attempting to murder and rob the gesticulating stranger.

This reeked of a frame-up. I was aware that there had been a fight previously, something to do with one man hankering after another's wife, apparently – but surely not attempted murder. Was the arrest legal? Could the police simply burst onto the scene and haul our staff off unhindered (a scenario often involving torture)? Was this warrant, this crumpled piece of bumph, genuine? Were the officers simply keen to "make a bit on the side" – and was this yet another bad-joke episode from the Bangladeshi police, which a Bangladeshi paper had branded the most corrupt organization in the world's most corrupt country? All these thoughts were rushing through my mind at the same time.

This was followed by hours of tactical stalling and dozens of desperate phone calls: I called my main donor representative, innumerable security attachés at my donors' embassies, higher-ranking police officials, trying in various ways to let the matter percolate beyond the confines of the reception hall. But to no avail. The three members of my staff were marched off. We were left with a profound sense of helplessness and a feeling of being at the mercy of our environment; we were angry, too, at the lack of support from the project's donors and at their well-meant avuncular advice. Ahead of us lay a very long way out of this mess.

This example illustrates the particular law-and-order issues inherent in the development context, and with them the vulnerability and loneliness to which a project may be exposed. Precisely because of such extreme conditions faced by development projects, the tools of the traditional project management craft (such as the nine task areas of the PMI) are not enough: A successful execution of development projects needs a systemic embedding that provides for the *best possible support on all levels*. A systematic project governance would institutionalize such a support.

Issue	Proposition by Project Governance
The typical project characteristics are particularly pronounced in development projects (pioneering, high exposure, vulnerability, and loneliness in crisis periods, with intercultural challenges).	*Project governance offers the institutionalization of a systematic embedding in the project context, allowing one to draw on the best possible support.*

2.2.3.3 Who owns the project? About multi-owners and stakeholders

Twenty years ago, a development project was mandated by a (governmental) donor agency (such as USAID, the Swiss Agency for Development and Cooperation SDC, the British Department for International Development DFID etc.) and implemented by an international NGO (such as Care, Helvetas, Swisscontact etc.), with the collaboration resembling a typical principal-agent relationship.

Today's setup looks different, and in fact more realistic: Stakeholders such as the government of the developing country, the target group, and multinational donors become upfront partners in the development efforts.[80] Projects often receive financial or in-kind contributions from several sources. With all these various inputs, immediately the question arises: Whose responsibility is it to steer and control the project? The relationship between project management and governance is more complex than a one-to-one relationship. The governance gap as described above widens and becomes multifaceted, as shown in Figure 11.

---

[80] See also the 'Partnership Commitments' of the Paris Declaration on Aid Effectiveness (2005: 3).

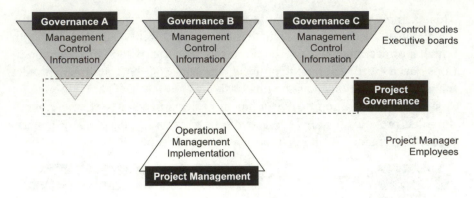

Figure 11. Project Governance in a multi-organization environment[81]

On these grounds, the need for project governance is even more obvious than in an environment of one-to-one relationships. Our initial question – Who owns the project? – thereby acquires a much more far-reaching extent, and can now be rephrased as follows: Who should be involved in the project governance, and with this involvement whose governance should prevail: The donor(s), the implementation NGO's, the government's or any other actor's? In order to answer this question, one must go on to ask *whose development* the project is aiming at.[82]

Stakeholder management is only part of the answer. Projects in fact do manage stakeholders, as recommended by numerous relevant best practices.[83] Stakeholder management, however, needs to be revisited with a view to the empowerment of development stakeholders and "partnership commitments."[84]

Emerging from these considerations, we can conclude that the multi-organizational context of development projects forces open a systematic project governance. The respective governance roles, and the way in which the actors are involved, will be further elaborated later (see Chapters 3 and 4.4).

---

[81] The very nature of graphics is to simplify. The above figure simplifies matters in that the governance of the various actors involved looks the same. While the concrete governance form certainly varies between organizations, the graphic retains its validity in representing strategic and 'entitled' influences from various organizations.

[82] See Chapter 2.2.4 below on ethical considerations.

[83] See footnote 404.

[84] Paris Declaration on Aid Effectiveness 2005: 3.

Issue	Proposition by Project Governance
Multi-ownership and increasingly strategic orientation of stakeholders	*The strategic orientation of project governance allows to bridge with multi-ownership, on strategic level.*

2.2.3.4 Nonprofit governance and project governance: Differences and integration

In Chapter 2.2.2, we have seen that from the *sector-neutral* perspective of corporate governance, project governance facilitates strategy operationalization and helps resolve information and knowledge asymmetry. This chapter takes up the question of whether these findings are also valid from the perspective of nonprofit governance (i.e. within the development sector). To this end, the state of the art of *nonprofit governance* is looked at first of all. Then the issues of strategy operationalization and information, in particular knowledge asymmetry, are reviewed.

Nonprofit governance – the state of the art

Nonprofit governance is only about to emerge as a factor: "Only recently has 'Nonprofit governance' become the standard *term* for the directing and controlling functions of organizations acting for worthy causes."[85] Content-wise however, in contrast to corporate governance "next to nothing has been said about the governance of nonprofits."[86] Public voices call for more professionalism in the governance of nonprofit organizations, and scholars make more differentiated demands that "[g]overnance in the charity sector needs to become more strategic"[87] or that there be a "backlog demand in the management of NPOs,"[88] particularly the need for "increased management orientation"[89] on several levels within NPOs.

Simply said, nonprofit governance refers to the governance of nonprofit organizations (NPOs) or non-governmental organizations (NGOs).[90] These

---

[85] Hilb 2005: 42 (emphasis Renz).

[86] Eldenburg et al. 2001: 4.

[87] Davies 1999: 61.

[88] Schwarz 2005: 59 (translation Renz).

[89] Schwarz 2005: 61 (translation Renz).

[90] See Footnote 1 on the term NGO and NPO.

terms, however, comprise a broad spectrum of organizations, from hospitals, professional associations and sport clubs to development organizations or political parties. Accordingly broad, therefore, are the requirements of nonprofit governance.

The *Freiburg Management model for NPOs* by Peter Schwarz et al.[91] is a systematic introduction to the management of nonprofit organizations *in general* (including a chapter on "cooperative governance.")[92] Without diminishing the high-caliber contributions to research and practice in this area, it can be said that its general character primarily builds on the nature of *national (nonprofit) associations*; hence its applicability to the NGOs or NPOs *in the development sector* and to their (nonprofit) governance is limited. Certain other scientific contributions on nonprofit governance are recent, scarce, and often narrow in focus.[93] Other very recent developments include the Swiss Foundation Code, being 22 "recommendations for the establishment and management of grant-making foundations,"[94] and the Swiss NPO-code, a code of corporate governance standards for big social and humanitarian nonprofit organizations based in Switzerland; this code draws on Voggensperger et al.,[95] and represents a preliminary stock-taking of nonprofit governance.

Strategy operationalization

In the context where the 'hit topic' of corporate governance "has so far hardly touched the scenery of nonprofit-organizations"[96], and where researchers still ask for "increased management orientation"[97], an interesting question arises: How much are nonprofit boards strategically oriented anyway? Does the call for efficient strategy operationalization make sense as long as increased strategy orientation of the board is itself a desideratum?

Both questions point to a greater rather than lesser *distance from operation* (for the governance gap as described in the general context of corporate

---

[91] Schwarz et al. 2002, Schwarz 2005.

[92] 2005: 222ff (translation Renz).

[93] See, for instance, research on health and hospital governance by Alexander & Weiner 1998, Eldenburg et al. 2001, Herman & D.O. Renz 1998.

[94] Hofstetter & Sprecher 2005: 1.

[95] 2005.

[96] Rhinow 2005: 11 (translation Renz).

[97] Schwarz 2005: 61 (translation Renz).

governance, see Figure 1 in Chapter 1.1). Against this background, project governance would seem not only to support the operationalization of established strategies, but it would also serve as a bottom-up 'strategy enabler' in the first place, by systematically reflecting on operational issues and bringing them to the attention of the managers responsible for (strategic) direction and control. The following example illustrates such a distance from operation:

A new strategy, based on what?

The nonprofit governance board of SwissNGO indeed showed commitment when initiating and participating in a revision of the fundamental strategy of the SwissNGO foundation. Without criticizing the strategy, however, I wondered about the basis on which their understanding of it was built. DRIVER was by far the biggest project of SwissNGO thus far to come along – accounting for close to 20% of the SwissNGO budget – and as such also a monumental risk. How come we were never visited by a SwissNGO board member, or invited to discuss the specifics of DRIVER? It would have been easy to combine it with one of the trips I made to Switzerland for personal reasons.

This example also serves to illustrate the next point, about information and knowledge asymmetry.

Resolving information and knowledge asymmetry

Nonprofit boards are often not remunerated, working strictly on a voluntary basis. Building (development and project) knowledge is therefore a particular challenge, i.e. the described information and knowledge asymmetry (see Chapter 2.2.2.2) becomes even more significant. It is hardly surprising that the members of nonprofit boards are often overwhelmed by the number of projects, and by the variety of countries they have hardly ever seen, and that they lack operational understanding. Phrases like "I am lacking that specific background, nor do I know the country in question, but in my opinion ..." cannot serve as responsibility-wavers. A system like project governance, functioning as both a transmitter and interpreter, will allow the board to cope with its tasks of 'checks and balances' and with an appropriate risk management.

We may conclude that the governance gap is particularly pronounced in project-intense nonprofit organizations. First, an increased strategic focus of the nonprofit board is a desideratum *per se*, without which the strategic direction of projects becomes illusory; and second, the information and knowledge asymmetry is at least as problematic as in business hierarchies, and perhaps greater. The project governance proposed here can strongly contribute to supporting the resolution of both issues.

Issue	Proposition by Project Governance
How can – in a project-intense nonprofit organization – the gap between nonprofit governance and operation be bridged or diminished; a gap characterized by a lack of strategic influence by the governance board and a pronounced information and knowledge asymmetry?	*A concept positioned in between nonprofit governance and operational level staff, based on the roles of governance, carries governance concerns to the operational level and in return provides 'business' insights necessary for a more strategic orientation of the nonprofit board.*

We have now examined four particularities of the development sector in trying to answer the question whether a need for project governance can also be recognized in the context of the development sector (after having seen such need from a more general angle). The analysis of all four particularities has revealed a particularly pronounced need for project governance.

2.2.4   Ethical considerations calling for project governance

The last few chapters have supported the desideratum for project governance from various angles: The project management, corporate governance, and development sector perspectives. This chapter finally investigates whether there are also ethical considerations calling for project governance.[98] First, ethical relevance on the level of development policies is taken up, and then again on the operational project management level, both reviews leading us to conclude that the governance gap also comprises some type of ethics gap.

---

[98]   The moral point of view adopted in this book is oriented on a combination of normatively critical, discursive reflections and forms of reciprocal recognition. This will be elaborated in Chapter 4.3.

Is development value-neutral? Already the question, what is 'good' development, implies the need for "normative background assumptions."[99] Indeed, development cannot be value-neutral: In analogy to Peter Ulrich's "magic triangle of reasonable economic acting,"[100] a similar *magic triangle of reasonable development* can be created, as illustrated in Figure 12. Reasonable development[101] needs to provide answers to two questions: (1) the question of sense, i.e. development for what (purpose), and (2) the question of justice and legitimacy, i.e. development for whom. Both questions contain normative dimensions requiring ethical reflections.

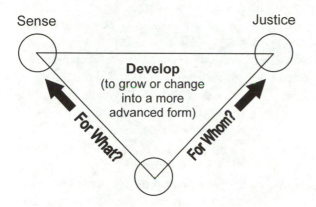

Figure 12. Magic triangle of reasonable development

Practitioners such as Walter Fust, the director of the Swiss Agency for Development and Cooperation, underline the importance of ethics in development: "The efforts for the 'common welfare' or for global 'public goods' are hardly possible without ethical impulses, without [a] moral centrifugal force, without moral energy."[102] The most important proof of this ethical relevance is the existence of the current Millennium Development Goals: they are strongly influenced by the merits of the ethically rooted capability approach as developed by Sen and Nussbaum.[103]

---

[99] Ulrich P. 2004: 3 (translation Renz).

[100] 2004: 4 (translation Renz).

[101] The Cambridge Advanced Learner's Dictionary defines *to develop* as 'to (cause something to) grow or change into a more advanced, larger or stronger form.'

[102] Fust 2004a: 47 (translation Renz).

[103] See Sen 1999, Nussbaum & Sen 1993. For a critical appreciation, see Kesselring 2003.

"Ethical impulses" and reflections are required not only on the "*high*" level of development policies but also on the "*bottom*" level where all the development projects are being implemented. Development projects face ethical challenges in the deployment of development policies, as well as in concrete integrity challenges arising from local realities in the field, such as corruption, hidden agendas, etc.[104] The following is a simple example:

A 'just' salary grid

The substantial size of our project required the hiring of around 50 people. When I arrived in Bangladesh, an interim manager had established a small number of work contracts. A professional compensation structure did not yet exist; a salary grid needed to be established benchmarking our conditions with employers who recruited similar people.

Once established, It turned out that our salaries for professional staff were reasonably within the range. The salaries of our support staff, however, i.e. cleaning and service personnel, were around a third of what comparable employers (such as international NGOs or multinational companies) were paying.

While some employers apparently were paying those low levels of salaries, we decided to adjust their salaries gradually upward – thereby not taking advantage of our strong position with less skilled labor.

This example illustrates a situation in which project management must undertake ethical reflections in order to make a decision. In a "modern democratic society of free and equal citizens,"[105] the legal environment and pressures on organizations to be "good corporate citizens" and assume "corporate social responsibility,"[106] provide some type of warranty against, for instance, arbitrary and immoral working conditions. In such a context work contracts are normally the expression of a "declaration of free will

---

[104] See Chapter 4.3 for more examples.

[105] Ulrich P. 2001a: 286 (translation Renz; a manuscript for an English edition was used by the author for some of the translations). See also Ulrich P. 1999b: 70.

[106] See, for instance, Ulrich P. 2001a: 393ff, in particular 462 and 423. See also the corporate social responsibility (CSR) initiative of the UN, and the UN Global Compact with its ten principles in the areas of human rights, labor, the environment, and anti-corruption (see www.unglobalcompact.org).

and the consent of the concerned [people] themselves,"[107] constituting "social contract[s] between autonomous agents."[108]

A development project whose objectives are to "improve the living conditions of the most deprived people,"[109] operates, however, in the context of a so-called LDC, a less developed country, or even one that must be described as least developed.[110] In such a context, the above contractual point of view is not enough to prevent from arbitrary treatment at the cost of the weakest. In fact, going a step further, one must ask if precisely such 'good' or ethically reflected resolutions of challenges are not also at the core of a development mission, particularly if such development wants to be successful in inducing *sustainable* changes?

These thoughts induce the following hypothetical question: Is there an 'ethics gap' similar to the earlier derived governance gap? Do concrete ethical reflections and discourses take place on all levels or "loci" (i.e. on the level of development policies as well as on the project level),[111] and is there a meaningful connection between the reflections and discourses of the different levels? The question targets the *institutional* aspect of ethics in development, dealing with *where* (location) and *by whom* (responsibility) such ethical reflections should be made. The hypothesis of an 'ethics gap' points more precisely to *a gap in the integrative institutionalization of the ethical discourse on development issues.* This differentiation becomes understandable by way of the following questions:

Examples illustrating the hypothesis of an 'ethics gap'

Are policy topics with ethical relevance, such as MDGs, the Paris declaration, the Washington Consensus, the Copenhagen Consensus... discussed on the project level at all? What would the impact and relevance be on the project level?

---

[107] Ulrich P. 1999a: 235 (translation Renz).

[108] Honderich 1995: 477.

[109] SDC 2004: 4.

[110] Based on social and economic criteria, the UN classifies countries in LDCs (less developed countries), LLDCs (least developed countries), and SIDS (small island developing states). In practice, LDC and LLDC are often used synonymously as 'least developed country'.

[111] See Ulrich P. 2001a: 285ff.

Are ethical dilemmas faced by the project personnel, such as corruption, hidden agendas, etc., discussed and analyzed, including some type of open ethical reflection?

Are experiences with ethical dilemmas from the project level shared with higher levels, and are ethical considerations of policy development explained to personnel at the implementation levels?

In line with the above examples, the case study examples were able to confirm the existence of such an ethics gap.[112]

Additionally, the following reflections corroborate the existence of an 'ethics gap':

1. With development policies on one side, and the daily realities from the field on the other side, a development project operates within a *tension of normative expectations* which are most likely to be divergent. By default, this puts an increased demand on the project unit to be capable and mature enough for ethical reflections in order to face this ethical responsibility. It would not be surprising if the majority of local project units were overtaxed by their ethical responsibility; this would in fact explain the *Realpolitik* and opportunistic relativism prevalent among development actors.[113]

2. As mentioned, the current MDGs are strongly influenced by the ethically rooted capability approach. To assess the success of MDG-related development projects hence also signifies to measure capability changes. While measuring capability changes "can work in practice,"[114] as proven by Patry in a recent case study, the development sector, however, is far from using such ethically reflective methods for capability measurements in a *majority* of projects. Independent of this shortfall in actual practice, it is unclear whether many projects would meet with the ethical skills for such assessments. These thoughts are another indicator of a possible 'ethics gap'.

---

[112] See Chapter 1.1.

[113] From the perspective of a discourse-oriented ethics as adopted in this book, there is a tragic factor in such relativism, in that the avoidance of assuming such discourse as one's ethical responsibility sooner or later compromises the legitimacy of the project or, even worse, the overarching development policy.

[114] Patry 2005: 44.

3. From an academic perspective, finally, various scholars point out that the positive evolution from the ethics approaches based on normatively critical reflections further requires an increased "closeness to the business practice,"[115] with the result of decreasing – for practitioners – argumentation gaps or "in-authentic arguments,"[116] or avoiding "insufficient ethical guidelines [...] for the middle managers." That this business view is also valid for development cooperation is supported by Kappel's statement that development cooperation needs to develop "pragmatic moderation- and mediation-instruments and strategies"[117] in order to facilitate effective dialogues on "habits of mind"[118] among development actors.

From all of the above considerations, an 'ethics gap' can easily be discerned; and the results of the case study presented later amply confirm it. How, then, can this gap be overcome?

From an ethical viewpoint, the desideratum can be formulated in such a way as *to support the project execution in its normative management tasks*. Establishing project governance can therefore be understood as the institutionalization of ethical responsibility, at least in closing the described gap and enabling the project to cope with its ethical challenges. In other words, the project governance proposed herein is desirable because it first of all *institutionally enables* (through direction and control) an ethical discourse to occur in the first place. Second, a well-designed project governance itself *leads an ethical discourse* beyond a corrective or functionalistic ethic,[119] for instance when managing stakeholders.

Issue	Proposition by Project Governance
How can the observed 'ethics gap' – in the form of a gap in an integrative and complete institutionalization of the ethical discourse on development issues – be overcome?	*Project governance, positioned between project management and the development policy level, constitutes such institutionalization of ethical responsibility.*

---

[115] Leisinger 2004: 25 (translation Renz).

[116] As observed by Kirsch in moral-practical board discussions (2004: 23, translation Renz).

[117] Kappel 2003: 6 (translation Renz).

[118] Idem.

[119] See Ulrich P. 2001a: 95ff, particularly 128

2.2.5 Conclusion

The interdisciplinary character of project governance has required us to look at a broad number of perspectives in order to analyze whether the desideratum of project governance is substantiated. The perspectives discussed above (project management, corporate governance, the development sector including nonprofit governance, ethical considerations) all confirm a need for a project governance in the form of a "process-oriented system by which projects are strategically directed, integratively managed and holistically controlled, in an entrepreneurial and ethically reflected way, appropriate to the singular, time-wise limited, interdisciplinary and complex context of projects."[120]

With this, we turn to identify possible roles of project governance.

---

[120] See definition in Chapter 1.4.3.

3   The roles of governance in development projects

A [governance] board should primarily be a door opener.

The board's role is to control the executive management.

The primary contributions of the board are the long-term vision and strategies....

Popular views on the role of governance

We have seen the need for comprehensive governance in development projects. What should such governance look like?

What are the fundamental roles attributed to such project governance?

What concrete tasks and responsibilities are derived from these roles? Answering these questions is the objective of this chapter.

To this end, the theoretical basis which is currently available will be examined, in particular with regard to organizational theories and their contribution to the governance debate.[121] How does the theory define the role of governance? The first chapter (3.1.) draws on various organizational theories,[122] summarizing their role expectation towards (organizational) governance. At the same time, possible shortcomings or downsides of the theories are outlined. The result is a synthesized view of various governance roles and their downsides applicable for development projects.

With a clarified understanding of the roles in hand, we will then look into the character of the tasks and responsibilities with which these governance roles can be put into practice. This examination will have us identify a number of concrete responsibilities of the governance body, the so-called

---

[121] In the absence of an existing theoretical debate on project governance (see Chapter 2), this study turns to the literature on corporate and nonprofit governance.

[122] With regard to the assumption that "there is no *single* competent and integrative theory or model to explain the roles played by governing boards," See Hung 1998: 101 (emphasis Renz).

key responsibilities. Chapter 3.2 therefore describes which key responsibilities are needed both to cover the governance roles and also to consider or overcome the possible downsides.

3.1 Organizational theories, governance roles and their relevance for development projects

3.1.1 Overview of selected organizational theories

In order to develop an "integrated and multi-theoretic point of view"[123] of possible governance roles, a set of organizational theories is considered. These will serve as a heuristic tool for the identification of key responsibilities in project governance. Hung presents a "valuable research typology,"[124] and provides a comprehensive overview of governance-related organizational theories (see Figure 13).[125]

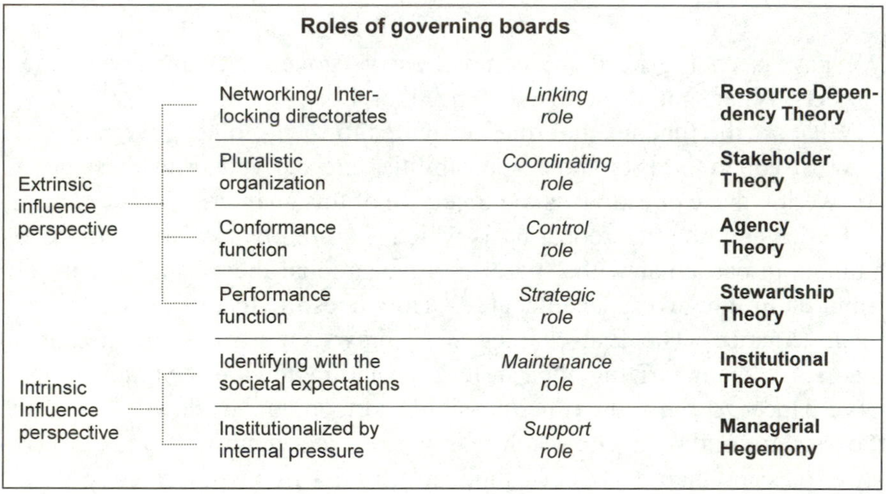

Roles of governing boards			
Extrinsic influence perspective	Networking/ Inter-locking directorates	*Linking role*	**Resource Dependency Theory**
	Pluralistic organization	*Coordinating role*	**Stakeholder Theory**
	Conformance function	*Control role*	**Agency Theory**
	Performance function	*Strategic role*	**Stewardship Theory**
Intrinsic Influence perspective	Identifying with the societal expectations	*Maintenance role*	**Institutional Theory**
	Institutionalized by internal pressure	*Support role*	**Managerial Hegemony**

Figure 13. A typology of the theories relating to roles of governing boards[126]

---

[123] Hilb 2005: 6, without emphasis.

[124] Hilb 2005: 6.

[125] Hung 1998: 105. See Kreitmeier 2001: 45. The author is aware of the limitations of such typologies, and also that there are additional theories. The objective of this chapter, however, is not to discuss these theories in detail, but to provide comprehensive guidance in establishing the broad roles of project governance.

[126] Adapted from Hung 1998.

Hereafter, the roles as mentioned by Hung will be critically illustrated in the context of each organizational theory. All of the summaries of these six points below are nearly entirely paraphrases of ideas already established in the field. This book's contribution consists of sketching applications of these ideas into the context of development projects.

3.1.2   Resource dependency theory

Resource dependency theory assumes, as its name indicates, that organizations depend critically on access to, and control of, (external) resources; it denies the concept of "organizations as self-directed, autonomous actors pursuing their own ends."[127] These dependencies create external control situations which continually shape the managerial role, in the sense that "board members can play valuable roles in making resources available to, and in coaching, the CEO."[128] In this respect, boards are "seen as critical links, or an important linking instrument of the organization, to the external environment."[129]

The downsides of this perspective mentioned in the literature are the possibility of "interlocks"[130] or clientelism between organizations; in an extreme form, this may lead to "preserving class interests" through class coalitions, as observed by Mace in analyzing the group of top executives from the largest American corporations.[131] Interlocking dependencies can also take the form of (hidden) collusions if agendas behind the interlocking parties are not revealed to those concerned.

Resource dependency is certainly applicable to development cooperation, and in several ways. First of all, development projects (through their implementation agencies) depend crucially on the resources funded by donors. Hodge and Piccolo have found empirical evidence that the level of dependency correlates with the level of involvement by the boards of non-profit agencies.[132] A similar direct dependency can be assumed at the level

---

[127] Pfeffer & Salancik 1978: 257.

[128] Hilb 2005: 6.

[129] Hung 1998: 104.

[130] See Pfeffer & Salancik 1978: 161 – 166, Hung 1998.

[131] Mace 1971.

[132] Hodge & Piccolo revealed a correlation between the level of how much the boards of non-profit agencies are involved with the CEO and the dependency of the non-profit agency on external funds (2005). See further Wood 1996: 15ff.

of a possible project governance board. Secondly, resource dependency theory can play an important role in development *'cooperation,'* at least for that type of development work which tries to improve a cause in *sincere joint collaboration* with other partners such as the development country – in these cases "the action" is to a certain extent "externally constrained and situational."[133] Such development crucially depends on the respective contributions of resources from the different parties. Therefore, the governance of development projects also has a *linking role*, and at the same time an *arbitration or negotiation role* for preventing too great a dependency: Interlocks should not end in deadlocks.

3.1.3   Stakeholder theory

The classical stakeholder theory by Freeman defines a stakeholder as "any group of individuals who can affect, or is affected by, the achievement of a corporation's purpose."[134] Possible stakeholders are employees, customers, providers, government, banks, environmentalists, and so forth. With respect to the role of governing boards, the stakeholder approach "expects the board to negotiate and compromise with stakeholders," thereby supporting a *"coordinating* role of the governing board."[135]

The main critique of the classical stakeholder view is that it puts strategic calculations above normative considerations: Stakeholders are considered based only on their "actual effective power"[136] or "threat potential" and not on their "legitimate claims" or expectations (stemming from "special rights out of contractual agreements [...] or general moral rights"). Based on discourse-based stakeholder interactions,[137] Peter Ulrich proposes an "ethically critical stakeholder value approach."[138]

The idea of stakeholders is particularly important in development *cooperation,*[139] even to the extent that there is no truly sustainable development

---

[133] See Pfeffer 1982.

[134] Freeman 1984: vi.

[135] Hung 1998: 106.

[136] Ulrich P. 2001: 442 (translation Renz).

[137] See Ulrich P. 2001. See also Kirsch describing the stakeholder approach as a "survival model" characterized by "functional appropriateness of actions," whereas a higher developed model (the "progress model") would be characterized by "authentic appropriateness of actions" (1997: 643).

[138] See Rüegg-Stürm 2005: 18ff.

[139] See also the ethical considerations on 'development for whom' in Chapter 2.2.4.

progress without an ethically critical consideration of stakeholders. Moreover, it is precisely through stakeholder theory's challenging dilemmas –
such as "who is the customer, the beneficiary or the donor?"[140] – that one
gains a platform for broader considerations. Project governance has more
than a *coordination role* to play: Normative reflections need to assure that
an on-going stakeholder discourse serves as a "license to operate"[141] for
any given development project.[142]

3.1.4   Agency theory

Agency theory is the most dominant theory behind today's corporate governance legislation. Agency theory is "directed at the ubiquitous agency
relationship, in which one party (the principal) delegates work to another
(the agent), who performs that work."[143] Based on the metaphor of a contract, agency theory tries to resolve relationship problems "in which the
principal and agent have partly differing goals and risk preferences,"[144]
thereby aiming at reducing agent or managerial opportunism. Such problems at their origin arise from the separation of ownership and control.[145]
Agency theory assumes a form of "homo oeconomicus, which depicts
subordinates as individualistic, opportunistic and self-serving."[146] According to Hung, governance takes on the role of *control*, surveying the *conformance* of the organization.

Agency theory is critiqued for exclusively considering the needs of top
executives and shareholders, but not the justifiable needs of other possible
stakeholders. It "ignores group interactions,"[147] "institutional embeddedness,"[148] and the entire "panoply of inter-personal relationships and

---

[140] This is in fact a prevalent dilemma: SwissNGO, for instance, refers to its funding donors as "customers which need to be satisfied."

[141] Post, Preston & Sachs 2002: 229.

[142] As we will see, such a discourse can take various forms depending on the
concrete circumstances, from real discourses to fictitious ones involving a political responsibility, as described in Chapter 4.3.

[143] Eisenhardt 1989: 58.

[144] Eisenhardt 1989: 59.

[145] Bearle & Means 1932.

[146] Davis, Schoorman & Donaldson 1997: 20.

[147] Hung 1998: 106.

[148] Aguilera & Jackson 2003: 448.

power."[149] Agency theory is also considered "inadequate to build trust"[150] because it can not "account for key differences across countries."[151]

To what extent, then, can agency theory be applied to the governance of development projects? The implementation of a development project is mostly delegated from one or various donors (principals) to an implementation 'agency'. Therefore, parallel issues arise in the development-project context. The 'separation of ownership and control' applies somewhat differently, however: On one side, the *feeling* of ownership needs to exist among more than just the funding donors, because for the project to succeed other key stakeholders, including beneficiaries and the governments of development countries, need to "buy in"[152]; on the other hand, development work is so complex and multifaceted that an implementation agency is less in control of the results than a business organization can be.[153] It must also be said that the typical incentive systems prevalent in business principal-agent relationships need to be replaced by other mechanisms: "Steering instruments [...and] elements of systematic controlling and reporting-system"[154] become more important.

What are the implications for the design of project governance? First, the control role is certainly at least as important in development projects as in business, but at the same time it is certainly more complex than for business organizations. The project's mission needs to be monitored, understood, and controlled in a *broader* context. Similarly, audit and risk management practices, two key control tools, are probably more complex in the development area. Second, the control role needs to be complemented by other governance roles, such as extended stakeholder management,[155] for instance, thereby strengthening the principal-agent relationship on grounds beyond those of monetary incentives. Project governance has to

---

[149] Tricker 1994: 56.

[150] Caldwell & Karri 2005: 249. See Roth 2005, Arjoon 2005.

[151] Aguilera & Jackson 2003: 448.

[152] Or as the director of the Swiss Development Agency SDC puts it: "Implementation agencies [!] must not only be the executors [say agents] of the policy as decided by SDC" (Fust 2004b: 137). In rough terms, he is referring to the importance of a political process when considering various stakeholders instead of one single principal.

[153] See the complexity of the goal hierarchy in Figure 5.

[154] Schwarz 2005: 146 (translation Renz).

[155] See Chapter 4.1. and 4.4. on the particularities of stakeholders in the development context.

consider the need for a *deeper functionality* in the traditional control roles (to control the more *multifaceted* development missions, to manage audits and risks) while assuring the incorporation of other key roles.

3.1.5 Stewardship theory

Stewardship theory offers the major alternative to the assumptions which support agency theory, namely that human beings are "individualistic, opportunistic, and self-serving"[156]; it depicts subordinates as "pro-organizational, trustworthy" and "collective-serving." With respect to governance, stewardship theory suggests that top managers act in the "best interests"[157] of the organization "even when financial incentives and monitoring systems are not in place to ensure that this is the case." The role of governance has a *strategic* focus and a *performance* function, concentrating on "guiding the management to achieve corporate mission and objectives."[158]

Stewardship theory is criticized for having too optimistic an idea of human nature, in assuming rational and legal behavior.[159] That is, it does "not reflect the interplay of power, conflict and ideology."[160] Furthermore, a certain "passive element"[161] may be attached to the involvement of the board: While "the support of the management by the board can [in principle] make sense," the influence of the board on the inner-organizational elements is not foreseen, however, under the stewardship theory. From this passivity perspective, governance would rather play a supporting than a strategic role.[162]

At first glance, stewardship theory qualifies quite well for non-profit organizations.[163] Social entrepreneurs, playing the "role of change agents within society," are also an example of "good stewards of the resources that others have entrusted to them."[164] It would also be overly optimistic,

---

[156] Davis, Schoorman & Donaldson 1997: 20.

[157] Hilb 2005: 6.

[158] Hung 1998: 107.

[159] Tricker 1994.

[160] Hung 1998: 107.

[161] Kreitmeier 2001: 49 (translation Renz).

[162] Kreitmeier 2001: 49.

[163] Idem.

[164] Hitt, Ireland & Rowe 2005: 33.

however, to claim that all human beings in development work are 'good stewards.'

The role of governance for development projects hence lies in assuming the role of strategic direction and support, and strengthening managerial 'entrepreneurship.' Like other theories, stewardship theory also has certain downsides which need to be considered, most notably power and ideology issues.[165]

3.1.6 Institutional theory

Some of the theories discussed above lack consideration for the wider context in development projects, for instance the particularities of cultures or in general the (wider) organizational environment as a factor in "providing meaning and stability to social organizations."[166] With respect to agency theory, for instance, Aguilera and Jackson argue that it "fails to sufficiently explore how corporate governance is shaped by its institutional embeddedness."[167] Institutional theory[168] can help to understand governance "in the context of social and cultural constraints imposed on organizations."[169] Governance gets a "*maintenance* role [in …] identifying with the *societal* expectations of organization."[170]

As Hung points out, a downside of institutional theory may well be a lack of explicit strategic attention, resulting in strategic passivity once the organization is perceived as over-embedded in its context.[171]

With respect to development cooperation, the institutional embeddedness of a development organization is of particular importance, because a development project usually tries to exert influence outside its own boundaries. Observing the project's environment allows one to see whether it succeeds in inducing changes, or whether it fails, for instance

---

[165] For instance, the recommendations of IFAC combine conformance and performance, the two fundamental roles of agency and stewardship theory (2004, see also Davis, Schoorman & Donaldson. 1997).

[166] Hung 1998: 104.

[167] 2003: 448.

[168] Aoki 2001. See also Furubotn & Richter 1998, Coase 1988, Meyer & Rowan (1977).

[169] Hilb 2005: 6.

[170] Hung 1998: 105.

[171] Idem.

when benefited SMEs keep on producing low-design products, a case in which a project may turn into a non-sustainable goal pursued for its own sake. In cases where the institutional environment simply does not exist (after catastrophes like a tsunami), then a development project may itself constitute an important piece of the wider environment. Even then, constant observation of the progress of the institutional context is of key importance. Therefore, understanding the "complexity and diversity of overall institutional arrangements across the economies as an instance of multiple equilibria of some kind"[172] is a vital practice. It is the task of project governance in development projects to assume this role of "maintenance in identifying with societal expectations," which stems precisely from its *societal embedding.*

3.1.7   Theory of managerial hegemony

Hung further indicates that "institutional force exerted on a governing board from within the organization can be explained in terms of *managerial hegemony.*"[173] In such situations, the board simply serves as a 'rubber stamp,' with strategic decisions being dominated by the professional managers. An attitude of not getting involved unless there is trouble certainly characterizes boards previous to the recent wave of corporate scandals.[174] In the words of Drucker: "The board of directors is an impotent ceremonial and legal fiction."[175] Within such a perspective, governance exercises only a *supporting role*, if not one of the rubber stamp.

What can be learned from proponents of managerial hegemony for the governance of development projects? Is this avenue a pursuable governance option? In fact, managerial hegemony is also a reality in development projects, often in the form of a paternalistic project manager; the existence of the governance gap described in previous chapters favors exactly this kind of hegemony. Established and well-functioning project governance takes all concerned stakeholders into consideration, for instance, thereby avoiding such one-sidedness. As is amply seen in the case of project governance, such managerial hegemony and the associated 'rubber stamp' role is certainly not a governance model desirable for development projects.

---

[172] Aoki 2001: 2.

[173] Hung 1998: 107.

[174] See Mace 1971.

[175] Drucker 1981: 107.

3.1.8   Synthesis: Governance roles relevant to development projects

A selected number of organizational theories have passed in review so that the reader might briefly identify their perspective on the role of governance. The shortcomings or downsides of these organizational theories have also been summarized. Finally, their suitability for the governance of development projects has also been assessed. From that survey, the reader can see that all except managerial hegemony contribute to a 'multi-theoretic' and 'integrated' perspective on governance roles for development projects. Table 2 summarizes the overview.

Table 2. Specification of roles and downsides needed to be considered for the governance of development projects

Organizational Theory	Governance roles relevant to development projects	Downsides
Resource Dependency	Linking role	Possible interlocks, Collusion and Class coalitions Deadlocks from dependency
Stakeholder Theory	Coordination role	Strategic vs. normative orientation
Agency Theory	Control role (Conformance)	Stakeholders not considered Ignores group interactions and power Not trust building Too legalistic focused No institutional embeddedness
Stewardship Theory	Strategic direction and support role (Performance)	(Too) optimistic idea of people Blind to interplay of power, conflicts, and Ideology Possibly passive governance
Institutional Theory	Societal Embedding role	Possibly strategic passivity
Managerial Hegemony	–	–

3.2   From governance roles to governance's key responsibilities

The last chapter has identified a number of fundamental governance roles, and has assessed their validity for the context of governance in development projects; the above graphic (Table 2), furthermore, summarizes which roles are best played by the governance of a development project. The same graphic also displays a number of shortcomings or downsides which should ideally be considered in the design of project governance.

In order for roles to turn into actions, specific tasks and responsibilities need to be identified: What are these tasks and responsibilities, how are they best bundled together in order to fulfill one or several of the specified roles, and how are shortcomings or downsides overcome?

In an inductive / deductive research process, as outlined earlier in Figure 4, the research project at hand has identified six key responsibilities. The analysis of the relevant data from the roughly 400 records (data-driven generalization), combined with a deductive literature review, has identified *six logical task-areas*, as the so-called *key responsibilities.* Some of them are known from corporate governance theories, while certain others are new, properly so in consideration of the development context and emphasis. The six key responsibilities, constituting the *modules of project governance* as identified by this research, are:

1. System management, assuming the societal embedding role.
2. Mission management, assuming the strategic direction and support role, as well as the control role.
3. Integrity management, assuming a role of normative guidance and as such lending support in downside issues.[176]
4. Extended stakeholder management, covering the linking role, coordination role and partially the control role.
5. Risk management, contributing to the control role.
6. Audit management, also contributing to the control role.

In a graphic perspective, we can imagine six shapes being laid on top of the summary Table 2 with the aim of covering the entire space of the columns 'governance roles' and 'downsides.' The result is shown in Figure 14.[177]

---

[176] See Chapter 4.3 for an exact definition of integrity.

[177] While graphics often express more than words can, they also have their limitations. In this graphic, which shows the basic influence of integrity management on other key responsibilities, such influence would, of course, go beyond what graphics help us to understand.

Subsequently, the six key responsibilities are described briefly. Chapter 4 will elaborate on them in detail.[178]

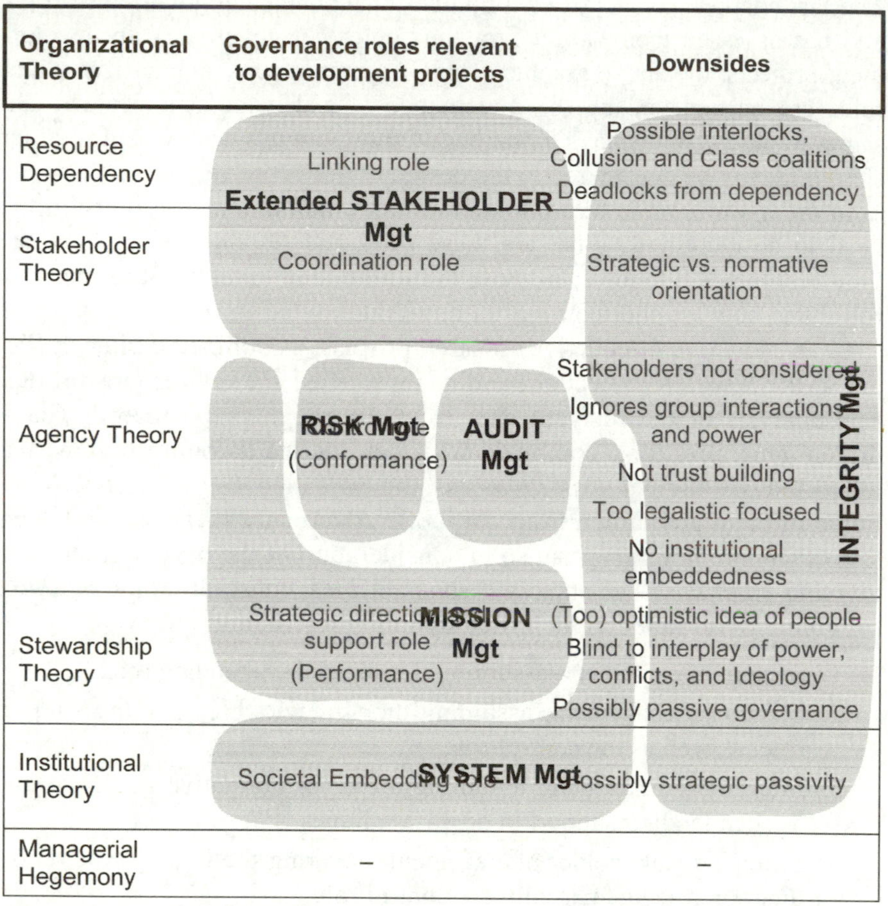

Organizational Theory	Governance roles relevant to development projects	Downsides
Resource Dependency	Linking role	Possible interlocks, Collusion and Class coalitions Deadlocks from dependency
	Extended STAKEHOLDER Mgt	
Stakeholder Theory	Coordination role	Strategic vs. normative orientation
Agency Theory	RISK Mgt (Conformance) AUDIT Mgt	Stakeholders not considered Ignores group interactions and power Not trust building Too legalistic focused No institutional embeddedness INTEGRITY Mgt
Stewardship Theory	Strategic direction MISSION support role Mgt (Performance)	(Too) optimistic idea of people Blind to interplay of power, conflicts, and Ideology Possibly passive governance
Institutional Theory	Societal Embedding Role SYSTEM Mgt	Possibly strategic passivity
Managerial Hegemony	–	–

Figure 14. From governance roles to key responsibilities of project governance

---

[178] One may debate whether to call the six modules Mission Governance and not Mission Management, for instance. While Chapter 1 tried to clarify definitions as clearly as possible, in reality the term 'management' in particular is used imprecisely. Current corporate governance practices suggest that 'risk management' (and not risk *governance*) ought to be a key governance task. This book consequently adopts the term 'management' in naming the governance responsibilities.

System Management assures institutional embeddedness. It serves to analyze and understand the specific development context through a systemic perspective, laying the groundwork for defining a possible development project as well as creating the know-how to understand the interrelationships and context of a project once it is up and running.

Mission Management combines a strategic, a support, and a control role. Based on a system understanding, mission management serves to identify the (strategic) mission for a project. It sets strategic objectives, outlines the fundamental implementation strategy, structure and – to a certain extent – the culture needed to achieve the project objectives or mission. Through mission management, the governance board further supports and controls the project along with the implementation of its mission.

The next key responsibility, *Integrity Management,* provides a normative foundation, firstly as a basis for certain other key responsibilities (for instance, for mission management, where defining the mission and 'setting' cultural elements involves normative reflections). Secondly, integrity management provides support for overcoming most of the summarized downsides of governance roles (Table 2): As the reader will readily observe, the majority of these downsides comprises a normative element. Integrity management constitutes an institutionalized space or platform where such normative issues, along with others, can be tackled.

Extended Stakeholder Management comprises the linking between the project and possible stakeholders along with a coordination role. Furthermore, it takes on a negotiation role, in the case of possible dependency interlocks or deadlocks. Extended stakeholder management assures that all possible concerned parties are considered by the project, and are possibly involved in the governance of the project as well. In order to further these aims, integrity management formulates a discursive foundation[179] to identify and assess stakeholders and their claims in an ethically reflected way.

Risk Management and *Audit Management,* finally, are both classic key responsibilities in governance. They stem principally from the control role which governance is expected to exercise over its project to assure its conformance to rules and laws and to manage possible risks pro-actively.

In summary, while Chapter 2 identified the need for project governance, this chapter has pursued the question of what such governance should look like and what roles it should assume. The review of the organizational theories relevant to governance has revealed a number of roles. At the

---

[179] The notion of 'discourse,' stemming from so-called 'discourse ethics,' will be properly introduced in Chapter 4.3.

same time, shortcomings, particularly the downsides of the respective theories, have been outlined. The next question was then what the concrete responsibilities and tasks of the project governance would be in order for governance to assume the roles that have been identified, and also for considering and avoiding the possible downsides. Six key responsibilities have been introduced, constituting the basic modules of the project governance concept. The next few chapters will describe these key responsibilities further, and give concrete guidance about how to set up a given instance of project governance.

4   The Project Governance Model

This chapter introduces the proposed Project Governance Model. It consists of six modules, which constitute the six key responsibilities as outlined in the previous chapter. Figure 15 shows the six key responsibilities, configured in the form of a diamond reflecting their integration with each other and, by way of its slightly rotated position, the dynamic character of project governance.

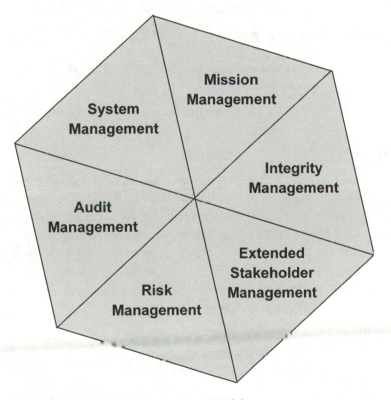

Figure 15. The Project Governance Model

Each chapter initially outlines the *objective* at which the particular key responsibility is aiming. Then, a number of development-specific *particularities* further shape the context in which that particular key responsibility stands. Subsequently, for each key responsibility, a suitable *model* is developed from theoretical foundations and best practices, and is then adapted to the context of development projects (in an analysis / synthesis process based on results and examples from the case study). Throughout, numerous case examples are inserted for concrete illustration.

While the theoretical grounding draws on a broad set of contributions, including insights gained from discussions with scholars of the University of Dhaka, several propositions developed by scholars at the University of St. Gallen turned out to be most suitable for the context of this book. First of all, it draws on the St. Gallen Management Model developed by Hans Ulrich and his collaborators;[180] secondly, it builds on the approach of "Integrative Economic Ethics" by Peter Ulrich;[181] finally, it draws on the "New Corporate Governance" concept developed by Martin Hilb.[182]

4.1   System management

> *It doesn't help to say, we are outside the system, we are inside.*
>
> The operations manager of SwissNGO[183]

4.1.1   Objectives of system management

As established in Chapter 3 on governance roles, system management lays the *systemic and systematic foundation* for (1) the *understanding and possible influencing of the wider environment* (or system), and (2) for the *managing of the project system*. Therefore, system management is the most basic key responsibility of project governance; the other key

---

[180] See Ulrich H. (1968/1970, 1984, 1978/1987); see further Rüegg-Stürm 2003 for the latest version of the St. Gallen Management Model.

[181] 2001a. See also 1999a, 2001c, 2002 and 2005.

[182] 2005.

[183] A point made during a workshop in 2005, aimed at introducing *systemic (!)* thinking in development projects. In other words it would be utopian (Greek: "without location") to believe that a development project can act *outside* its target system.

responsibilities build on the system understanding gained from system management.[184]

The systematic and systemic understanding of the wider environment is the basis for a sound identification of best development approaches that lead to the appraisal and possible creation of a development project. During its creation and existence, such a project is itself a system, or, more precisely, a "subsystem"[185] within the wider system.

Systems, independent of their complexity, are "compelled to rely upon *structuring influences* and *ordering forces*"[186] Without those structuring influences and ordering forces, a system "would promptly fail and dissolve into nothingness."[187] This condition supports the initially identified need for management: The inevitability of structuring influences and ordering forces "explains precisely why *leadership,* regardless of whom or how, is absolutely necessary."[188]

The systematic and systemic understanding of the wider environment (for instance of stakeholder interests) are the *basis* on which to establish these structuring forces and related structures of the sub-system called 'development project.' A system understanding also helps to understand the *borders* of one or several systems. In the case study project, exactly this understanding led, for instance, to the conclusion that the marketing work needed two 'faces,' namely so-called 'forward branding' (to the target audience) and 'backward branding' (to the donors; see case example in Chapter 4.4.3.4).

---

[184] It could be argued that system management constitutes an overarching heuristic, in other words, that it stands not only for a piece, i.e. one module, but for the whole. It is certainly true that the module system management as developed here delivers an overarching reference framework. The understanding gained from such a reference framework – like the reasons for social or economic nuisances – needs, however, to be verified and updated continuously; as such it is *part* of governance responsibilities. In practice, this referencing to an earlier established understanding is often lost; therefore, the purposeful positioning of system management *within* the key governance responsibilities attempts to prevent, precisely, this risk.

[185] Ulrich H. 1984: 20.

[186] Rüegg-Stürm 2005: 10.

[187] Rüegg-Stürm 2005: 10.

[188] Rüegg-Stürm 2005: 10. As a case in point, see the 'management vacuum' in Chapter 1, illustrating the 'dissolving' effect, or how a development project risks falling apart without appropriate managerial influences.

Finally, system understanding lays the groundwork for project evaluations, and it also constitutes a valid point of departure for risk management
and audit management (for instance in setting the borders for audits:
Should subcontracts also be audited?).

4.1.2   The particularity of system understanding in development: Sustainability, impact, and outreach

Successful development projects achieve positive results along the following three lines: Sustainability, impact, and outreach.[189] These objectives
are partially exclusive, i.e. they form a magic triangle that configures the
appropriate mix for making a project successful.

4.1.2.1 Sustainability, impact, and outreach in a system's context

The objective of a development project is to *impact* the target environment, i.e. to exercise "influence on the context, the societal or physical
environment."[190] This impact should occur in a *sustainable* way, so that its
effects continue after the project finishes. Therefore, the project needs (and
usually aims) to *systemically change* the target environment in order to
achieve this.[191] This target environment and the development project can
be understood precisely as a system being "an arranged whole built from
elements which stand in relation to each other."[192] It is even a *complex*

---

[189] *Sustainable* Development "is development that meets the needs of the present
without compromising the ability of future generations to meet their needs" (as
per generally agreed definition of the World Commission on Environment and
Development (the Brundtland Commission) from 1987. See www.un.org/esa/
sustdev). *Impact* refers to the "positive and negative, primary and secondary
long-term changes / effects produced by a programme/project, directly or indirectly, intended or unintended" (SDC 2002). *Outreach* usually refers to a variety of parameters, the most common being geographic outreach and scale (how
many are reached).

A simple example: Providing training in cattle breeding allowed 1,000
households (outreach) to increase their standard of living (impact) through
secondary income upon an on-going basis (sustainability).

[190] SDC 2002.

[191] In fact, such argumentation can be upheld for any type of project, not just development projects. Unsuccessful IT projects, for instance, may not have achieved
the promised cost savings (impact), may have to be prolonged indefinitely (lack
of sustainability), or do not support enough users (lack of outreach).

[192] Ulrich H. 1984: 50 (translation Renz). See also Rüegg-Stürm 2003, 2004.

system "as the system elements interact in manifold ways and as they stand in specific dynamic *relationship* to each other."[193]

Before the initiation of a development project, it cannot be assumed either that the understanding of such a (target) system exists or that it is readily available.[194] For development projects, which often enter new fields (strategy-, geography-, staff-wise etc.), such an understanding needs to be *built up*, both for project appraisal as well as for its execution. This is also why development projects prefer to see themselves as 'learning organizations,' and place emphasis on knowledge management and the dissemination of so-called 'best practices.'

4.1.2.2 Development projects as complex systems

One of the points made above can sustain a bit of emphasis, namely the system complexity of project development. Once a development project has started, it becomes part of the wider system and begins 'interacting' with elements of the target system. But the project itself also represents a system or a "subsystem"[195] of the target system, similar to enterprises as characterized by Peter Ulrich and Fluri:[196]

- A development project is also a "multifunctional system" fulfilling "functions for various parts of the environmental spheres" (participating in the labor market, influencing the social welfare system in case of a health project, etc.)

- It is a socio-technical system where "women and men transact processes in division of labor, with the help of technical means."

- In contrast to enterprises, a development project is not "an economically self-supported system," i.e. to maintain its existence it does not need to "produce profits." Instead, it aims at broader objectives and maintains a multitude of financing relationships which even *increase (system) dependencies,* such as the expectations of stakeholders. This results in the fact that development projects may have to deal with multiple and often contradictory values and strategies.

---

[193] Rüegg-Stürm 2003: 17 (translation Renz).

[194] Local actors and local NGOs have accumulated considerable know-how though often not in a systemic way. Still their involvement is crucial. The system understanding presented here, then, also allows one to qualify the know-how presented by local partners.

[195] Ulrich H. 1984: 20 (translation Renz).

[196] 1995: 31 (translation Renz).

This last point chiefly indicates the fact that development projects, taken in their entire context as systems, are at least as complex as enterprises if not *more complex*.

4.1.2.3 Why is system understanding relevant to management?

As we have seen, the structuring influences and ordering forces dictate the necessity for leadership or management. The following two restrictions, however, also become obvious:

1. It is clear that the wider system (i.e. the target environment) imposes considerable limits on attempts to control, guide or manage it; therefore, it is already an ambitious endeavor for any development project to *try to influence* such a wider system.

2. The managing of the narrower inner system, i.e. a development project itself, faces the same limitation as managing an enterprise: Both are "much less controllable, i.e. subjected to or open to the directing and designing influence of their managing bodies, than is generally accepted."[197]

System understanding thus provides a more realistic view to management, different from the perspective that a firm or development project is "exclusively a rational system which was consciously and intentionally planned in a given way."[198] The importance of system management therefore lies in the fact that it allows to lay the *systematic foundation for* both (1) the *understanding and possible influencing of the wider environment* (or system) and (2) *the managing of the project system.*[199]

4.1.3   Elements of system management

There are two constitutive elements of system management:

1. Systemic thinking as an integral part of the corporate or the project culture (the "software")

2. The existence and use of a system model (the "hardware").

---

[197] Malik & Probst 1984: 105. See also Rüegg-Stürm 2003: 19f.

[198] Malik & Probst 1984: 105.

[199] See Mann 2003 who views corporate governance as *systems*.

In drawing upon the St. Gallen Management Model, this book relies on an integrated and holistic management model which has proven its validity and practical applicability over several decades: Based on a sound understanding of system theory and cybernetics, the St. Gallen Management Model was developed by Prof. Dr. Dr. h.c. mult. Hans Ulrich and his collaborators and refined over more than 30 years; its current version has been issued by Prof. Dr. Johannes Rüegg-Stürm.[200]

A subsequent chapter will present the model in the context of project governance. Before that, however, we need to turn to the basics of systemic thinking.

4.1.4 Systemic thinking

Today, the importance of systemic or system-oriented thinking is broadly recognized. Still, even a widely acknowledged system cannot be effective unless the philosophy behind such a system is understood. Therefore, it seems advisable to review the five characteristics of systemic thinking identified by Hans Ulrich with a view to introducing concepts of system theories into the area of management:[201]

1. 'Holistic thinking in open systems'[202]

2. 'Analytical and synthetical thinking'

3. 'Dynamic thinking in circled processes' – i.e. more generally a *process*-oriented view

4. 'Thinking in structures and information processes'

5. 'Interdisciplinary thinking'

Systemic thinking needs to become a cultural element of the development project, a "philosophy of how to approach the solution of complex problems."[203] While this mental set in principle is relatively easy to understand, it requires – as any other element of culture does – substantial

---

[200] See Ulrich H. (1968/1970, 1984, 1978/1987); see further Rüegg-Stürm (2003, 2005) for the latest version of the St. Gallen Management Model.

[201] See Ulrich H. 1984: 49ff.

[202] Economies, for instance, are closed systems as long as their "entanglement with other spheres and appearances of the human society is not considered" (Ulrich H. 1984: 21).

[203] Ulrich H. 1984: 59 (translation Renz).

time to become part of daily work and life. One needs to *breathe life into the system model*.

Let us therefore look at examples of development approaches, reviewing their content in the light of systemic thinking.

Is the 'market development approach' holistic?

The project DRIVER of the case study was based on a relatively new development approach, the so-called market development paradigm.[204] One of its key elements is an in-depth understanding of the private sector environment. From a system perspective, one positive element is that the commonly used analytic models are broad, in that they consider a variety of stakeholders such as government and NGOs.[205] The approach runs short, however, in failing to provide a deep understanding of *interactions* between system elements. The societal and cultural environment is viewed only within an economic perspective. Normative or value-based interactions between system elements, and their continuous interdependent dynamics, are neglected.

This was acknowledged by the funding donors when they set up an additional division for the project DRIVER, responsible for normative topics such as gender orientation and socially and environmentally responsible business.

From an integrative and holistic system perspective, this example illustrates a shortcoming in the development approach. Additionally, the action taken represents a "corrective"[206] approach, by just annexing the structure instead of making the underlying market development approach more complete and integrative. In this way, such normative topics are made 'add-on' issues to the core project approach rather than being mainstreamed. For the sake of comparison, let us look at a strategy paper which outlines an alternate development approach:

---

[204] Formerly known as the BDS approach, standing for business development services approach.

[205] For further insights, see for instance the ILO website on small enterprise development.

[206] See also Ulrich P. 2001a.

Systemic improvement of the (business) enabling environments?

The strategy paper reads: "As a systemic approach we understand an approach that considers action and reaction between key stakeholders (market players) as well as their interaction with the wider (market) environment. It also takes into account the possibility and capacity for the stakeholders to contribute towards shaping the (market) system and the wider environment."[207]

The initiative of SwissNGO in catalyzing systemic thinking in development is remarkable: Without the comments in parenthesis (as per original text), the thinking appears to be holistic, addressing open systems. The parentheses however reveal that the final reference is to the market only, indicating that the thinking moves within a closed system.[208]

This book does not aim at criticizing development policies or approaches, a task which lies outside its scope. Examples such as the one above, however, show that some of the current analysis models fall short of framing a holistic, open, and interdisciplinary perspective. A system model needs to include the interactions between all levels of the environment, constituting interests, norms, and values important for the project context. The St. Gallen Management Model is indeed holistic, and so the next chapter will introduce it and analyze how it can be applied to development projects.

4.1.5   A system model

Systemic thinking based on the foundation of a holistic system-oriented model allows a project – in a first place – to *be configured* in the best possible ways according to the (local) system-specific circumstances, and secondly to *be managed* most effectively and efficiently, based on an enhanced system understanding.

This section will give a brief summary of the St. Gallen Management Model. For a detailed understanding, the relevant primary literature is recommended.[209] The basis for our review is the systemic understanding

---

[207] SwissNGO 2005: 3,

[208] See Footnote 202.

[209] In particular Rüegg-Stürm 2003, 2004, 2005. For a broader understanding, see also Ulrich H. & Krieg 1972, Ulrich H. 2001, Bleicher 1991, Gomez 1998, Müller-Stewens & Lechner 2005. For an overview of the development of the St. Gallen Management Model, see Schwaninger 2001 and Spickers 2004.

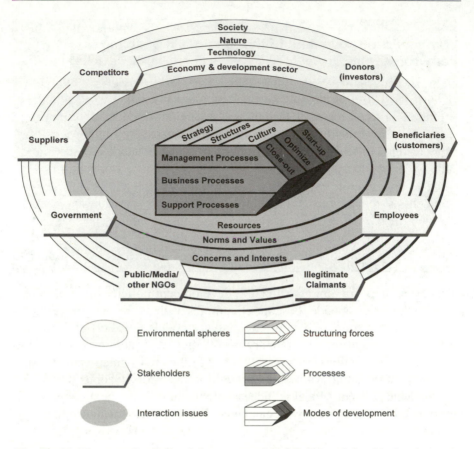

Figure 16. The new St. Gallen Management Model adopted for the development sector[210]

outlined above. There are six key areas or central categories within the St. Gallen Management Model (see Figure 16):

- Environmental spheres
- Stakeholders
- Issues of interaction
- Structuring forces
- Processes
- Modes of development

---

[210] Source Rüegg-Stürm 2005: 12 (development-specific adoption by the author).

These so-called basic categories relate to "the inner dimensions of management"[211] in the sense of "configuring, guiding (steering) and continuously developing purpose-oriented socio-technical organizations."[212] Rüegg-Stürm explains that "the term 'organization' is more broadly defined than enterprises," and hence that the model is valid for any "institution based on the division of labor."[213]

Hereafter, the six dimensions will be briefly described.[214] Their applicability to the management of development projects is illustrated with specific case examples.

4.1.5.1 Environmental spheres

The environmental sphere first of all covers society; secondly, it includes the perception of nature specific to society, technology application, and forms of value creation. Understanding these environmental spheres, and how they might possibly change, is particularly important for a development project, because it aims at making an impact.

One of the particularities of development work is that development projects are not supposed to aim at a goal which is an end in itself. Development projects always define themselves by their impact on their environments (compared to internally driven profit orientation). Hence, a continued understanding of the environmental spheres "to identify trends which are critical for success"[215] is crucially vital. Below, we list a number of particularly important aspects of the context for most development projects:

a) The environmental sphere 'society'

- Educational levels and willingness to perform
- Influences of religion
- Faces of poverty
- Questions of social status, position of women, treatment of minorities

---

[211] Rüegg-Stürm 2005: 11.

[212] Rüegg-Stürm 2003: 22 (translation Renz).

[213] Rüegg-Stürm 2003: 22 (translation Renz).

[214] See Rüegg-Stürm 2003, 2004, 2005 for a detailed description of the different spheres.

[215] Rüegg-Stürm 2005: 17.

- Social problems and conflict potentials
- Governmental norms and conditions
- Political forces and interferences
- Health system

Following are a number of examples of the societal factors which might possibly influence a development project in Bangladesh:

Example of societal influences in Bangladesh

With a population of 140+ million people Bangladesh is seven times more densely populated than Switzerland. If one hops on a bus with 10 people in Switzerland, in Bangladesh the comparable number would be 70.

Bangladesh is fascinating for its religious facets. Ramadan, for instance, is broadly observed, with reduced working hours for both fasting and non-fasting people (as in most Muslim majority countries). Traditionally, Ramadan is a time when people are supposed to do a lot of soul-searching and get to the spirit of giving/sharing, which then is supposed to improve the relationship between the 'haves' and the 'have nots.' But the Iftar (the breaking of fast) is not only a religious but also a social event – a reason for coming together, to meet and chat – perhaps, too, useful for networking.

Social recognition is very important, particularly as law and order are quite critical.[216] The minority 10% Hindus sometimes feel mobbed by default; also the acid-burn victims (somebody threw battery acid into their face, mostly women, for reasons of revenge) are a sad reality, as is the Rickshaw driver who committed suicide after he heard that his 11-year-old daughter was raped and lying in hospital.

The law and order situation is an engrossing topic. In my project alone, we were threatened by a number of law-and-order issues. Corruption in Bangladesh is nearly legendary, but that one also needs to pay off the official who comes to read the power consumption meter, so that

---

[216] *The Daily Star*, March 26, 2004: 1 carries the headline, "Free fall of law, order mocks government measures." The escalation of tension that came with the numerous bombings in the second half of 2005 is – very unfortunately – no surprise to the author.

he reads it *correctly,* was rather unexpected (see also example on corruption below).

An example which is amusing against the European background is that one of the best compliments one can receive is: "You must be doing well, you have gained weight!," because it connotes welfare and good health.

Particularly rewarding for me was the extremely deep gratitude expressed by certain Bangladeshi individuals, whether for help I gave or simply time we spent together. One woman, whom I referred to a sister project for a job, wrote numerous times to thank me: "Finally, my dream of working in the development sector where I could contribute much more to human development in this country has come true. I always gratefully remember your contribution and you may not believe this but I always say a little prayer."

As even these small examples show, an understanding of the environmental spheres needs to go beyond mere facts and figures, if it is ever to grasp, through impacts on daily life in its actual context and through anecdotal evidence, just how and where a development project might effectively intervene, and where not.

b) The environmental sphere 'nature'

- Availability of natural resources
- Potential of agro-sector and environmental issues, contamination
- Climate

One of the impressive factors in the case study was the natural environment and its faces in Bangladesh:

A fascinating countryside

The countryside beyond the big towns and large villages in Bangladesh are most fascinating, not to speak of the breath taking Sunderbans. One quickly comes to understand that Bangladesh is a country of water – and that the nearly yearly flooding is finally only a downside of Bangladesh's immense fertility, which is capable of feeding nearly its entire population on its own.

The immense agro-sector also has sad downsides: Vegetables, for instance egg-plants are at risk of receiving a finishing touch with a toxic color spray – in order to forestall thieves who harvest them while they are still immature. And the secretary general of the Bangladesh Frozen Food Export Association during our stay was trying to promote to European trade partners their "almost organic shrimp."[217]

c) The environmental sphere 'technology'

- Availability of process technologies, material supply
- Logistics, communication, and information technologies

The following example has to do with the availability of information technology:

Legal software

While it may be no news to insiders, the agreements to license Microsoft software for a multi-workplace office are not the easiest to understand. Not so in Bangladesh. Although it was impossible to purchase the official version of the Microsoft Exchange Server, which is key for email services, in Bangladesh pirated copies are available at the cost of a blank CD. Our project consequently had to first install pirated versions, wait two months for delivery of the officially and legally purchased software imported from Singapore, and then replace the pirated version again.

d) The environmental sphere' economy and development sector'

The fourth environmental sphere as described by Rüegg-Stürm needs to be enhanced in such a way that it looks not only at the economy, but at both the economy *and the* development sector. Not only current economic conditions, but also the currently on-going and planned development activities, need to be considered carefully. In countries where development has a

---

[217] *The Daily Star*, March 8, 2004: 6. According to the news report, the secretary general's claim [of producing almost organic shrimps] was immediately refuted by the Swiss *Charge d'affaires*, who said that there was no place for 'almost' with shrimp, which must be 'fully organic.'

long tradition, the development sector has become its own industry. Possible aspects of this sphere are:

- Macro-economic conditions
- Available infrastructure and respective barriers
- Labor market
- Methods of procurement for project needs

The following illustrates aspects from the case study with respect to both the economy and the development sector as an environmental sphere:

A vibrant economy and a vibrant development sector

Not only the yearly 5%-plus economic growth, but also the immensely busy areas around typical professional clusters, makes Bangladesh a vibrant economy.

Bangladesh is also unthinkable without the numerous NGOs and development organizations operating there. Following more than 30 years of development, there is hardly any international donor who is not represented in Bangladesh; young career-oriented Bangladeshi professionals consider a career in an international NGO the equal of one with a global business. Therefore, international businesses and international development organizations often compete on the labor market, obviously with competitive packages. Likewise, it has become a must for each international development worker to have some experience in Bangladesh on his résumé. Not surprisingly, there is quite an ambivalent attitude from the ruling government towards the well-established 'informal' sector: "Tough law to clip NGO wings soon"[218] or "diatribe against NGOs"[219] are headlines referring to the finance minister's speech in Parliament, "outperform[ing] himself in attacking NGOs" while characterizing the tricky environment. It cannot be denied that for certain people 'doing NGO' is equivalent to 'doing business.' Some doubtful infrastructure projects have certainly contributed to this double image – for instance, "another beautification project of a regional development bank" a local employee of mine would comment about the

---

[218] *The Daily Star*, March 26, 2004: 1.

[219] *The Daily Star*, March 8, 2004: 5.

replacement of the heavy road dividers with small imported bushes. A serious accident followed within days of the change. Or there is the "fountain of waste,"[220] the pleasant fountain at the exit of the international airport which none the less had to be demolished, since it had not been built correctly in the middle of the round-about and hence "was causing traffic congestions."

4.1.5.2 Stakeholders

Rüegg-Stürm defines stakeholders as "organized or not-organized groups of people, organizations and institutions, which are affected by the company's value-creating activities and sometimes also by value-destroying activities."[221] In the context of development projects, this definition needs to be modified in two respects. First of all, individuals too can constitute stakeholders, not only groups of people. In difficult legal contexts, for instance, the individual landlord of an office building – as subsequent examples will show – may resort to all sorts of illegal and physical intimidations if he feels unsatisfied, and thus cannot be ignored. Secondly, one must extend the understanding of relationship to include the fact that stakeholders are affected by, *or that they also affect,* value creation. This book defines stakeholders as follows:

Stakeholders

Individuals, organized or not-organized groups of people, organizations and institutions, which are affected by or do affect the development project's value-creating activities and sometimes also its value-destroying activities.

In comparison to a firm in its business environment, development stakeholders are even more crucially important, but also have a number of particularities:[222]

- Customers are not really customers in the business sense of the word, but rather people affected or concerned, as beneficiaries;

---

[220] *The Daily Star*, February 8, 2004: 17.

[221] Rüegg-Stürm 2005: 12.

[222] See also Chapter 4.4 on extended stakeholder management.

- Investors, i.e. funding donors, expect a different 'return on investment' than in business. The funds constitute a one-directional money flow which often orientates an NGO towards its donors, on whom their survival depends, and not towards their 'customers.' In fact, some NGOs call their donors 'customers';[223]

- these conditions often also attract parties, gravitating to funding sources, with blurred and sometimes illegitimate interests (called 'illegitimate claimants' in Figure 16);

- finally, the requirement for sustainability imposes greater expectations on the stakeholders of the system within which the project is positioned: The system's elements, and with it the stakeholders, are expected to change and improve the way they act, and interact, so that the catalyzing effect of the development project (and with this the project itself) becomes superfluous.

The importance of stakeholders is such that the project governance concept proposed in this book specifically contains a key governance responsibility called *extended stakeholder management*. The primary identification of stakeholders is made by way of the systemic understanding within system management; extended stakeholder management then concentrates on identifying them completely, assessing their claims and roles, possibly negotiating and creating interactions with them, and finally monitoring stakeholder interactions.

From the perspective of system management, the initial identification of stakeholders may already be a challenging task, despite a systemic understanding of the environment, as the following example illustrates:

Identifying political parties and forces

Gaining an understanding of political parties usually brings insights into local power games in a society. Bangladesh has been ruled for decades by two alternate parties: the Bangladesh Nationalist Party (BNP) and the

---

[223] Taken to an absurd extreme, this logic may sound as if the poor are the investors, putting poverty forward as an intangible stock capital, thereby helping NGOs to create a market and to attract customers who purchase development services. Though apparently absurd, it is unfortunately quite close to reality sometimes.

Awami League, currently in opposition. In a continuous struggle for power, every means is used. This became obvious when an attempt to prevent the creation of a 'political alternative' by former BNP members was made: The 'betrayers' where physically attacked ("our activists did what had to be done"[224]), the residence of one man was attacked with several bombs, a beverage factory was bombed and looted, tax officials started running tax audits at their enterprises, and customs officials forced the closure of several garment factories linked to the reformers.

One of our project's objectives was to improve the enabling environment, i.e. rules and regulations. In the light of what we knew about party politics (see above), we were faced with the question of what our project focus and profile should be when working with government on regulations.

We finally decided to focus on local regulations by working with local government bodies, staying out of the national skirmishes, and involving the central government in a consultative advisory board.

The call for sustainability in development work, and for systemic changes, has made it more difficult to identify the 'beneficiaries' of a project, because often the project does not work directly with them:

... and who are the beneficiaries?

Through a causal chain of effects our project aimed at contributing to the eradication of extreme poverty and hunger (the first millennium development goal). Our systemic approach – aimed at inducing sustainable system change – resulted, for instance, in the following intervention: We convinced fertilizer producers to provide training to retailers on better usage of fertilizer, because through market research we had found out that farmers did not know how to use it appropriately (too much, too little, untimely usage etc.). As a project we had no direct contact with the farmers, the beneficiary, or even all of the retailers. What impressed us in the short run were certain positive early indicators, which suddenly showed that some retailers felt more comfortable with their know-how, attracted more farmers looking for help, and sold their inventory faster.

---

[224] *The Daily Star*, March 14 & 16, 2004.

This example illustrates not only the difficulty of identifying the direct 'customers' or 'beneficiaries,' but also the dilemma that arises when one tries to analyze the impact of systemic change.

4.1.5.3 Issues of interaction

Between the project and its stakeholders, there are numerous exchanges and interactions on various, sometimes controversial issues. They can be of either a general or a material nature. Interaction issues represent the *content* of the relationship of an organization with its environment, its stakeholders. These issues "refer to what stakeholders bring to the company [...], or what of the [organization] they dispute."[225] Interaction issues fall into the categories of either intangible issues, such as (a) concerns and interests, and (b) norms and values, or of "tangible (material) elements"[226] such as (c) resources.

We have seen earlier that development projects are not *value-neutral*, because the concerns and interests, and the norms and values are *particularly* important in development projects.[227] Therefore, this book argues that *integrity management* be established as one of the key responsibilities of project governance. Integrity management takes up the interaction issues which system management has identified.[228] These interaction issues can also roughly be grouped into issues on the development *policy* level and on the *operational* level.

The following examples illustrate issues of interaction on the level of development policies:

- Attitude towards development cooperation: What is the attitude of the involved key stakeholders? Do donor agencies approach countries in need with a type of development paternalism? On the other hand, do beneficial stakeholders take development aid for granted?

---

[225] Rüegg-Stürm 2005: 22.

[226] Idem.

[227] See Chapter 2.2.4 for a discussion of the fact that normative decisions are involved in answering the two key questions 'development for what (purpose)' and 'development for whom (justice / legitimacy).'

[228] We could (artificially) distinguish between the *descriptive* character of system management, *identifying* possible interaction issues, and the *normative* discourse-oriented resolution character of integrity management. In practice, obviously, this distinction is artificial. Interaction issues will be tackled by system or integrity management, both key responsibilities of the project governance.

- Relativism in the development relationship:[229] Is there an unhealthy relativism in the relationship between key stakeholders that prevents a constructive discourse with "respectful consideration and carefully reasoned evaluation"?[230] Or is there a climate of reciprocal recognition and solidarity? The next example illustrates the issue of interaction in an environment where the development sector has become its own industry:

Development opportunity or a rip-off?

The company ChangeX, the Bangladeshi spin-off of an international NGO, approached several international donors and donor projects with a proposal to create an agriculture information platform and implement it in five existing cyber-cafés in rural Bangladesh. With this tool local farmers could access market data, information on crops, fertilizers etc. To me the proposal looked promising and complete, as it considered all the criteria which donors usually look at, like outreach, impact on poverty alleviation, rural focus, empowerment etc. However, the proposed budget was for 40,000 US$, of which the programming for the IT platform would be less than 10%, the rest being implementation cost. As a comparison: This corresponds to 650 monthly salaries of (still underpaid, but still privileged) garment workers. When confronted with the absurd financial figures, ChangeX referred to the high interest of other donors, not only trying to legitimize its claims but, even worse, to play them off against each other.

Examples of interaction issues on the *operational* level are:

- Salaries: What are the salaries a development project should offer, and how do local salaries stand in relation to the local labor market?

- Issues caused by unresolved individual objectives, such as those arising from micro-politics, hidden agendas, mobbing etc.

---

[229] Peter Eigen, founder of Transparency International, identified 'relativism' as one of the "worst liabilities which the western world committed" (speaking at the Sustainability Forum in Zürich on December 8, 2005).

[230] Rüegg-Stürm 2005: 22.

- Issues with corruptive practices interfering in the relationship.

- Transparency and confidentially: What is the level of transparency provided, and what is the level of confidentially kept?[231]

System management as such establishes a first point in time for consciously recording such interaction issues. A systemic understanding helps to assure that such issues are resolved at any point they arise during the performance of governance tasks.

4.1.5.4 Excursus: Intercultural collaboration

In today's globalization, working across cultures is a daily reality. The exchange or discourse between cultures is often, in the opinion of the author, guided in a rather naïve or incidental way. This "cultural blindness"[232] may be based on an over-simplified image of a universal human being but also, sometimes, on an opportunistic ignorance of possible differences.[233] Therefore, culture needs to be understood in a broad sense as including "almost anything and everything in the environment of human beings that is not immutably determined by nature."[234] Along with this sense, the understanding of issues in intercultural collaboration can hardly be reduced exclusively to understanding differences in ways of thinking.[235] Although styles of thought are an important element, still a deeper understanding of history and religion is needed.[236] Along these

---

[231] Traditionally, in development that is financed by public funds, the question of ownership of the results achieved as part of the development work is a difficult one to resolve. In principle, they are a public good, but in practice there are also good reasons for differentiating public from private claimants to ownership.

[232] Mäkilouko 2001: 73.

[233] Business organizations often 'resolve' the intercultural interface by assigning managers with respective experiences in both cultures. For development cooperation, this opportunistic way is not a solution; successful international development cooperation contains an open discourse as part of the cooperation. See also the chapter on integrity management.

[234] House, Wright & Aditya 1996: 538.

[235] See, for instance, Bachmann 2002.

[236] See, for instance, the five value pairs as outlined by Trompenaars & Hampden-Turner: Universalism vs. particularism, communitarism vs. individualism, neutral vs. emotional cultures, diffuse vs. specific properties, achievement vs. ascription orientation. (2003: 29).

lines, Bassam Tibi warns, for instance, of a naivety in the inter-religious discourse (stemming exactly from an oversimplified image of a universal being).[237]

One particularity of the approach presented in this book is that it tries to create sensitivity to differences, not in absolute terms ("That is how they are or think"), but in a procedural way by outlining the importance of a *process* or a discourse – such process being of particular relevance for successful development *cooperation.*

The last three system elements (structuring forces, processes and modes of development) constitute the 'inner circle' of a system view, i.e. the project *per se*. These three elements represent the whole managing and governing of a project, and are introduced briefly below.

4.1.5.5 Structuring forces

The structuring forces of an organization exist to supply "orientation, coherence and sense."[238] They consist of its orientating strategy, its coordinating structures, and its sense-making culture. Structuring these forces is obviously one of the key responsibilities of project governance – and as such also an element of *direction and control* of the mission for a development project. The particular importance of directing and controlling the project mission is considered with a proper *mission management* as a key responsibility. *System management* lays the foundation that provides the systemic thinking and understanding of context (i.e. the wider system), while mission management assures the on-going congruence of strategy, structure, and culture with the obtained results.

4.1.5.6 Processes

The fifth key area of the St. Gallen Management Model refers to processes that are classified in three categories, as management processes, business processes, and support processes. In the context of development projects, they signify the following:[239]

---

[237] Tibi 1991.

[238] Rüegg-Stürm 2004: 80 (translation Renz).

[239] See Rüegg-Stürm 2005: 54-55.

- *Business processes* concern the practical fulfillment of core development-related activities of the organization, which are directly concerned with creating 'customer' benefit.

- *Support processes* provide the infrastructure and the necessary internal services for the effective running of business and management processes.

- *Management processes* embrace 'the work of managing the firm' or the project – 'regardless of who might perform this.' As such, they comprise both project governance processes and project management processes.

What is the link between the structuring forces of strategy, structure and culture, and the outlined processes, particularly the management processes? The structuring forces represent constitutional elements, and as such they demonstrate a result-perspective, while the processes obviously bring in the procedural perspective – needless to mention their "circular interaction."[240]

4.1.5.7 Modes of organizational development

For 'normal' business organizations, the modes of development are 'renewal and optimization.' In the project context, the *renewal* mode has a modified meaning, given that projects by definition have a beginning and an end. The development version of the St. Gallen Management Model hence comprises three modes of development: Start-up, optimization, and close-out.

Do development projects also have development modes?

Starting up a project usually requires different skills than the on-going operation (or optimization). Also, the skills required of project closing are different to the extent that management usually leaves the project and a specialized team takes over to 'terminate' the project.

This observation confirms that a differentiation among modes of organizational development is also important for development projects. Lastly,

---

[240] Rüegg-Stürm 2005: 64.

such differentiation impacts the time horizon planned for a project. It also seems reasonable to assume that development projects have less flexibility in changing their time horizon than business projects. Considering the time horizon and different modes of development is essential in realistically timing the expectations one has for the project.

Thus far, we have gained an understanding of the St. Gallen Management Model as it might be adapted to development projects. How would we concretely put this understanding into practice?

4.1.6   How to "do system management"

The somewhat paradoxical term 'system management' has been chosen on purpose. We have seen that systems – being a complex set of interacting and related elements – are "much less controllable […and thus less manageable…] than is generally accepted."[241] Still, enterprises or other organizations work within systems and therefore have objectives or mandates to accomplish (otherwise, fundamental structuring forces are lacking and the organization "would dissolve into nothingness"). The task then is to *best understand the system* and continuously *try to influence* its moving towards established objectives. This continuous 'understanding' and 'trying to influence' are what this book understands as 'system management.'

"GEMINI" will resolve it all

The project appraisal document for our project was always referring to a so called GEMINI study as a basis for understanding the context in Bangladesh – i.e. the "system." A minor detail was that the study had still not been conducted. When during my interview for the job I was asked by the donors about my opinion on the project, I highlighted the risk that a lot would depend on this Gemini study.

It was finally conducted – a great census of the Bangladeshi SMEs, very useful on the level of general understanding. However, it did not replace the necessity for an understanding of the specific environment, the project stakeholders etc. which we then had to elaborate in parallel during the course of the project.

---

[241] Malik & Probst 1984: 105.

This example illustrates not only the importance of a system understanding, but also the difficulty associated with gaining a real and actionable system understanding. A big overall study may contribute perspective, but it cannot replace detailed work on the ground.

Like the other key responsibilities of project governance described later in the text, system management is an on-going governance task. It is not a one-time and never-again task – that would be a pity for the whole investment. It is not unusual that a project starts based on an immense effort of investigation, but afterwards the whole understanding and systemic thinking is lost or not passed on to the implementing team.[242] Project governance assures an on-going systemic and systematic management of a project with the support of a system model such as the one outlined above.

In summary, the key responsibilities within project governance for system management are:

- Promoting systemic thinking and the usage of a holistic and open system model as described above.

- System assessment and observation needs to be done as an on-going task. System management should assure that the different system elements are considered in all stages of the project, for instance at the time of the approval of the respective stage documents or reports by the governance board.

- Project governance may also define and observe certain thresholds, the passing of which would require a new system assessment and mission re-definition.

We now turn to the second key responsibility, mission management.

---

[242] See also footnote 184.

4.2   Mission management

4.2.1   Objectives of mission management

With the key responsibility of *Mission Management,* the governance board directs and controls the strategy, the structure and – to a certain extent – the cultural elements of a project. As established in Chapter 3 on organizational theories, mission management is the expression of the strategic, support, and control roles of governance.

The strategic, support, and control roles comprise an integrated and interactive function. With Gioia and Chittipeddi, it could be called a "sequential and reciprocal cycle of sense-making and sense-giving to expanding audiences,"[243] as illustrated in Figure 17.

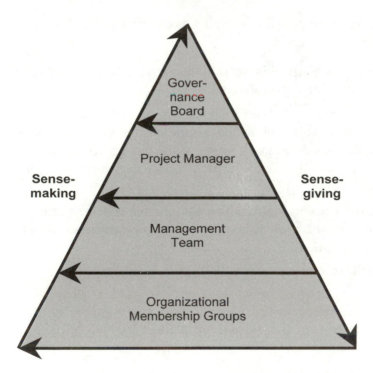

Figure 17. Governance function as a sequential and reciprocal cycle[244]

---

[243] Gioia & Chittipeddi 1991: 443.

[244] Adapted from Gioia & Chittipeddi, based on their ethnographic study of change management (1991: 443).

Though it is tightly integrated with project management, mission management is *not* project management, but rather the governance function of strategically directing, supporting, and controlling projects and their management.

4.2.2 Tasks of mission management

As seen in System Management, we can understand the organization (for instance of a development project) as the 'inner circle' of a system. The main system elements of this inner circle are three so-called 'structuring forces': strategy, structure, and culture (see Chapter 4.1.5). They lie at the core of Mission Management. Together with the governance roles of strategic direction, support, and control, as elaborated from organizational theories, they constitute the following matrix of tasks (see Table 3):

Table 3. The dimensions of the tasks of mission management

Project governance roles / Structuring forces	Strategic direction and support	Control
Strategy	X	X
Structure	X	X
Culture	X	X

These tasks will be elaborated below, following the structure of Table 3. As illustrated in the generic research process, they are the results of an analytic / synthetic process. Using the grounded theory approach, 115 relevant instances from the case study (including double counts) can be linked to the key responsibility of mission management. They serve to identify and illustrate the tasks as outlined in the following paragraphs, where numerous illustrative case examples are inserted.

4.2.2.1 The governance tasks within 'strategy'

With respect to the structuring force strategy, the role of mission management of strategic direction, support, and control materializes in the following governance tasks:

a) Establish the vision, the mission, the business principles, and the basic strategy

The governance board is responsible for establishing the basic foundations for the success of a project by "taking account of needs, concerns, interest, demands and moral values of all stakeholders" (see also Chapter 4.4 on extended stakeholder management, which explains the essential importance of stakeholders for development projects).[245] In this context, the term 'strategy' needs to be understood in a wider normative and sense-giving context, not in a narrow orientation for strategic action. This wider normative understanding comprises four elements: *Vision, mission, business principles, and basic implementation strategy.*[246]

The *vision* emerges from the systemic understanding of a concrete environment ('system'), while recognizing that there are opportunities which would possibly justify the 'raison d'être' of a development project. A vision needs to be sense-giving, motivating, and conducive to action.[247] The project in the case study arrived at its vision in the following way:

The vision of DRIVER

Our project had its own vision: "DRIVER is a leading market catalyst for measurably improving the competitiveness of the Bangladeshi economy. It envisions the growth of small enterprises based on vibrant and effective markets for business services. DRIVER is convinced that there will be more new, successful, and competitive SEs in Bangladesh by 2008. This will lead to greater opportunity for economic growth and poverty reduction."[248] While the good news is that DRIVER had its own vision, the bad news is that it was developed not by a working governance board, but by the project management itself (a couple of months into the project). A crucial aspect of any vision statement is its process

---

[245] Rüegg-Stürm 2005: 28.

[246] The development of these elements builds on inputs from several other key responsibilities of project governance: System Management delivers the understanding of the wider context, Integrity Management provides a discursive approach necessary for the sustained success of a vision and mission. This interdependency is proof of the integrative and holistic character of the project governance model.

[247] See Müller-Stevens & Lechner 2005: 235.

[248] DRIVER Project Document 2004: 8.

> of development, which per se has a lot of sense-giving, calibration and motivational value. For instance, we argued (constructively) for around two hours whether we should call ourselves 'a' leading or 'the' leading market catalyst (the boldness of which may stem from the fact that the project was the biggest of its kind worldwide).

The *mission*[249] expresses "what an organization aims at and why it considers [the organization's] existence as valuable."[250] It constitutes the mandate of the mandating stakeholders (donors, government) to the implementing NGO. Typically of the nonprofit sector, the objectives go beyond profit making, constituting an extended target horizon. As seen with the example of the case study project (Chapter 1.3.3.1), complex goal hierarchies are needed to break down a development target "to improve the living conditions of the most deprived people on our planet"[251] to the operational level. That these goals sometimes are accompanied by surprising non-explicit goals is illustrated by the following example:

Get the burn rate under control

The initial budgets were too high, and this became obvious as the project was running during its first couple of quarters.

At an informal project review with one of our three donors I was, however, quite surprised to see that the donor representative was totally unhappy with the under-spending even though that the agreed goals were mostly met. I was asked to 'get our burn-rate under control'. Was the objective to achieve the planned goals – and to achieve them with less money (surprise, surprise!)? Or was it to use the allocated funds?

While this may seem to be a singular example of a rather strange aspect of nonprofit goals, it none the less underlines how complex the findings of the project mission and its corresponding goal hierarchy can actually be.

---

[249] The author is aware that in practice the terms 'vision' and 'mission' are often used interchangeably. It is not the objective of this study to draw a clear separation between the two terms. Using only one of them, however, would deprive us of "the possibilities of revealing differentiation" (Müller-Stewens & Lechner 2005: 236, translation Renz).

[250] Waxenberger 2001: 105 (translation Renz). See also Ulrich H. 2001: 461.

[251] SDC 2004: 4.

The "*business principles* are the normative guidelines"[252] of an organization (see also Chapter 4.3 on integrity management). Going beyond legal requirements, business principles represent the "self-binding of the [organization] to principles and the resulting norms for the daily work."[253] They are of particular importance "where a quasi law-free zone exists and where legal regulations remain behind the requirements of legitimacy,"[254] which is often the case for the context of development projects.

Finally, with the *basic implementation strategy* a development approach needs to be chosen. For instance, in the context of SME development, strategic choices fall out between micro-credits schemes, market development approaches, cluster approaches etc. Here is an example:

Choice of fundamental implementation strategy

The donor consortium wanted a market development project – but was it following a fashion or was their conviction really based on a system understanding? One of the most renowned consultants for this market development approach once made an analogy which in fact illustrates the key issue our project was struggling with: You put an architect in charge to build a house for you, but as soon as the first brick is being laid you challenge him: "What are you doing?!"

It seemed that the funding donors had an idea of this market development approach, but they weren't really clear about the mission of the project: was it to build markets or to prove the approach? If they had clarified the four elements of vision, mission, business principles and strategy before mandating an implementation NGO, they could have avoided numerous interferences.

---

b) Stick to the strategy (in its wider understanding) for a while and support the project

It seems rather obvious that a governance board should stick to an agreed strategy and support the project in the implementation of such strategy: unlike tactics, the strategy is part of a longer-term constituting element. Strategies *are to be agreed upon and to be followed for a while.* They

---

[252] Waxenberger 2003: 239. Though 'project principles' would be the more appropriate term, it is hardly known. In building on the common terminology I maintain the term *business* principles. See also Ulrich H. 2001: 461.

[253] Waxenberger 2001: 85 translation Renz. See Ulrich P. 2001c: 45.

[254] Waxenberger 2001: 112 translation Renz.

should be changed or adapted when they prove wrong, but they should not be changed every day, for if they are then either they did not represent strategies in the first place, or they weren't agreed upon! This is illustrated by the following case study example:

Rewriting the project document

Why rewrite the project document (a document containing all the basics of the planned project)? When I was offered the job as project manager, a 300 page (!) project document already existed. What was the reason that I as project manager and my project team had to rewrite our own project document, as if justifying our own project all over again?

Looking back over the epic 17 months spent on negotiating and rewriting our project document makes it obvious: The project had not really been agreed upon when it started! And to make things worse, it had to deliver on the earlier promised deliverables while simultaneously undertaking the justification effort.

---

c) Define success criteria

The governance board needs to express its expectations in a way that "objectives and criteria […] are formulated in a non-ambiguous way."[255] Identifying whether success criteria in development follow any such rule as SMART[256] is a challenge, given the problematic of the extended or multidimensional target horizon typical of development projects. None the less, planning methodologies such as the LFA (Logical Framework Approach[257] in widespread use in development work), or balanced scorecards (BSCs),[258] allow multidimensional perspectives. A core question, in particular with the

---

[255] NZZ 8. Sep. 2005: 3 on the Volcker Report towards the UNO on the investigation of the "Oil for food" program in Iraq. See further Volcker, Goldstone & Pieth 2005.

[256] S = Specific, M = Measurable, A = Attainable, R = Realistic, T = Timely.

[257] See AusAID 2005, SECO 2005, Örtengren 2003. See also SDC 1999.

[258] See Kaplan & Norton 1992. For an overview of various scorecard methods, see Müller-Stewens & Lechner 2003: 706 ff. For usage of balanced scorecards in projects, see Fiedler 2001: 69ff. For a critical analysis of BSCs, see also Holmes, Gutiérrez de Piñeres & Kiel (2006). They point out that in government organizations of developing countries "implementation of the [scorecard] method by countries facing so many concurrent challenges would be difficult due to a lack of resources, politicization of public administration, and corruption" (2006: 1).

multi-hierarchy objectives of LFAs, is the question of accountability: The governance board needs to specify up to which level of the hierarchy of objectives the project is held accountable.

d) Set a financial framework and choose major milestones while pondering the risks of legacy-bound schedules

Jointly with establishing the mission and the strategy, a financial and time-wise framework needs to be set. Whoever has run a project knows that projects often arise out of specific opportunities, which may bind them to some type of legacy. For instance, administrative or budgetary reasons are often used to start a project at an otherwise inopportune time:

> **Immediate project start**
>
> "The project needs to be started within the next few weeks," wrote Brian, one of the donor representatives, to SwissNGO. For contractual and administrative reasons it needed to seamlessly follow a small pilot project which was about to end.

Another reason in development for starting a project is the "availability of excess funds," i.e. when a local donor office has not used all the funds budgeted and wants to spend them before the ending of a budgetary period. While it would be difficult to find public support for such behavior,[259] it is a reality within the bureaucratic complexities of some donor agencies. It goes beyond the scope of this book to discuss this further; none the less, project governance must consider such 'legacy-based' rationales and their associated risks when deciding to start a project. With Chandler's guideline in mind, the strategy should not follow the structure, because this may create additional legacy (see the example below called 'Let us work').

e) Challenge, agree to and support the phase plans

As an on-going strategic and support responsibility, the governance board needs to assure the strategic direction of phase plans (yearly business plans, plans of operations etc.). Here is an example illustrating a support issue in the case study project:

---

[259] As we will see later, public binding is a legitimacy criterion (see Chapter 4.3, integrity management). Such projects already leave with a shadow of doubt on their legitimacy. It is consequently no surprise if the respective beneficiaries or development partners may respond with a self-serving attitude.

Supportive head-office?

My whole project team had been working hard on the yearly plans. It had also created excellent momentum by achieving alignment on a number of points. Mack, my boss from the head-office, was coming for his quarterly visit, his main objective being to finalize the business plan so we could submit it to the governance board for comments and approval. Mack's visit went reasonably well; to our great surprise, however – after his departure – he sent us a list of around 100 questions and suggested changes. I tried to stay loyal looking at what we could incorporate within a limited amount of time and effort while feeling anger and frustration: What had Mack been here for in the first place? It seemed that there were diverging expectations about the support role!

f) Assure communication and operationalization

Deploying an indicated strategy needs more than communication. In the same way, a vision remains a dead letter if it is not *carried into the hearts* of the people concerned. To achieve this, possible adjustments as outlined with the process of sense-giving and sense-making may be needed. Only then can conformance of the project to the vision, and so forth, materialize. Project governance is responsible for controlling this deployment process and the final conformance, and if necessary taking appropriate action. Also, the project of the case study faced issues in operationalizing the indicated strategy:

Failed strategy for one project division

Parna's division was planned so as to emerge from a predecessor pilot project. Right after starting the project we conducted an external evaluation of the predecessor project. The good news was that it had certainly made interesting, though small scale achievements, but the bad news was that they did not constitute a sufficient base to build upon. The bottom line was that the division which was thought to have had the easiest start in fact had one of the toughest. The strategy (the development approach) had to be revisited and changed. The early detection of this strategy-mistake, communicated appropriately and substantiated with an external evaluation, allowed us to gather the right support and resources to give Parna's division a better second start.

g) Monitor and control achievements of success criteria[260]

This is the key control task of project governance, both in monitoring the project advances and comparing them to the established success criteria. For a committed governance board, this constitutes one of the difficult moments, because it needs to let go: The vision, mission etc. are established, the structure has been setup, and the project now needs to start and to learn how to run on its own. Micro-management at this stage can be counterproductive. This illustrates how the donor board of the case example had difficulties in 'letting go':

Let us work...!

"In this project, the sequence is upside down," a manager of mine used to say. It was true: The project was started with an acting project manager only, the contracts (with the implementing agency and between the donors) weren't signed, the project document needed rewriting, and the business plan for the first year needed first to be written. So, our first year was a tough one: all these constitutional issues had to be sorted out, while at the same time we were bringing the project up to size and speed in order to start delivering. From my business experience, I was used to performing under such circumstances – but the rudimentary project governance available, however, made the project into a football of missing agreements and structures. As a project team, we often expressed the view that we needed some space in which to perform, that "they should let us work..."[261]

To the monitoring function belongs the supervision of the mid-term reviews that are typical in development work, or any other evaluations of the project.

---

[260] See SDC 1997 for monitoring on the level of the development project. See also Hilb 1997, 2002 for success-evaluation.

[261] As mentioned in the introduction, exactly these extreme circumstances – in fact a pile of governance issues – finally made for the richness of examples in this research project, allowing me to propose a hopefully comprehensive project governance framework.

h) Define standards for impact assessment

Impact assessment is a special category in development work, where the contribution to the ultimate goals – such as helping to reduce poverty, or contributing to the GDP (gross domestic product) – is assessed. These ultimate goals usually lie outside the direct influence of a project, but none the less are the ultimate objective of a development effort. Assessing the impact is therefore a key task in development which needs to be commissioned by the responsible governance board.[262]

With this, we turn to the second structuring force, the structure itself.

4.2.2.2 The governance tasks within 'structure'

Structures enable one to "define suitable division of labor [...and to] coordinate intermediate outputs [...] so that they can be integrated effectively into the greater whole."[263] Two important structural categories need to be considered: "Organizational and process structures."[264] In the following, the key tasks of project governance relevant to structure will be discussed .

i) Set the basic organizational elements

The governance board is responsible for establishing the *fundamental* organizational elements. This comprises questions of local and/or international contracting, of in- and outsourcing, and of integrating the governance board into the line-structure of each stakeholder. For these tasks, the required core competencies need to be understood.

---

[262] In recent years, worldwide development objectives have been substantially influenced by the capability approach founded by Amartya Sen and Martha Nussbaum (see Sen 1999, Nussbaum & Sen 1993). Therefore, the impact assessment would target changes in capabilities. A case study conducted by Patry (2005) suggests the technical feasibility for assessing capability change.

[263] Rüegg-Stürm 2005: 36.

[264] Rüegg-Stürm 2005: 36. See also Gomez et al. who argue that considering today's high dynamics Chandler's rule needs to be extended to "structure follows process follows strategy" (2002: 75). The high process-orientation was also crucial in our project, for which we created a process model, with respect to which all our activities were oriented. See also the characteristics of systemic thinking as stipulated by Hans Ulrich (see Chapter 4.1.3).

In the chapter on Extended Stakeholder Management, we will see that the structures in development cooperation are of particular complexity, as strictly hierarchical dependencies are nearly absent. The following illustrates one basic organizational decision, the example of a subcontract.

The problem of the two implementation NGOs

The head-office of SwissNGO had subcontracted one of the project divisions to GerCon. Two expatriate staff, Paul and Narad, would report functionally to me while maintaining their administrative link with GerCon. The SwissNGO head-office was even proud of a gentleman's agreement with Paul and Narad's boss, which stipulated that acquisition of any further projects in Bangladesh would be done jointly.

It seemed to start well, but problems soon arose when Paul's confrontational style created numerous negative reactions and needed my intervention. The first discussions did not create the necessary improvement, so I had to get aligned with his administrative superior for more serious talks, perhaps even a written warning. Such a case of conferencing was not foreseen, however, in the contracts with GerCon: What would have been needed was an established process and assigned people for the evaluation of their staff. It was a costly mistake – for it required a long and tedious process to get his key superiors involved.[265]

Under the topic of basic organizational elements, the governance board may also consider questions regarding any temporal structure: Should a pre-project or a pilot be the first in line?[266] An alternative suggested by Matta and Ashkenas are the so-called 'rapid result teams'; these cut across normal project organization in a matrix form, with the objective of delivering early results and in that way catalyzing the greater part of the organization.[267]

---

[265] Maybe this mistake was not incidental: The fact that different interpretations of our inter-NGO collaboration coexisted finally came to light when GerCon tried to hire-off some of SwissNGO's employees in other projects.

[266] See SDC & Intercooperation 1995.

[267] In fact Matta & Ashkenas draw on the insights gained by a major World Bank agricultural project in Nicaragua (See Matta & Ashkenas 2003).

j) Establish the contractual framework

The joint collaboration of the various actors in the form of the planned project needs to be formally established in "a stable, but not stifling contractual framework."[268] While certain pragmatic reasons may suggest starting a project even before finalizing the contracts (using intermediary agreements) – see above – the beginning of the project with its initial phase of "euphoria and confidence builds a [more] favorable base,"[269] a factor which should be used to focus on finalizing the contractual framework. After the start, not only does the managerial workload increase, but also "conflicts between the partners either on task-related or interpersonal areas are more probable."[270] The following example illustrates a misjudgment of the importance of the contractual framework:

An unimportant contract?

The contract between the donors and the government, the so-called TAPP (Technical Assistance Project Proposal), took around 18 months to be finally approved. As this contract constituted the "license to operate" within the territory of Bangladesh, our work, particularly on facilitating a business-conducive environment, was obviously jeopardized by this delay. Had the donor consortium deemed it to be an unimportant contract, and if so, why then were their formulated project deliverables dependent on this TAPP?

In the ideal world, all contracts are signed in their definitive version at the beginning. The reality is quite different: It is the responsibility of the constituents of the governance board to include what-if scenarios and arbitration rules, but also to be prepared for compromises if the basis provided for a project proves not to be optimal.

k) Approve the proposed organizational structure

Based on the above directions, the implementing NGO draws up the detailed organizational chart and the respective process rules and responsibilities. This should also include a functional diagram or linear responsibil-

---

[268] Fuchs 1999: 145 (translation Renz).

[269] Idem.

[270] Fuchs 1999: 146 (translation Renz).

ity chart (LRC) specifying all major processes in the project, as well as who should take the lead and who else should be providing input, support or giving the final approval.[271] That the elaboration of a functional diagram is not a trivial task and may need monitoring by the project governance becomes clear in the following example:

The LRC workshop

Only for a few weeks after my arrival in Bangladesh Mack, my boss, had organized a workshop to nail down the LRC. Despite the good intentions and a good external moderator, it failed miserably. Instead of agreeing on a complete functional diagram, only a few sub-processes were analyzed and structured. On one side, a good template was lacking as a starting base; in addition, the setting of the workshop including the (to that point in time) entire team was not sensitive to hierarchical expectations (omnipresent in Bangladesh), nor to the need for 'safe spaces' where individual concerns and fears could be considered. Also, it was too early for the project to create and digest its own functional diagram. I started the LRC effort again later, using a template, first with the individual managers and then reconciling things in a group effort etc. Applied in that way, it turned out to be a valuable instrument for improving organizational effectiveness.

l) Appoint the project manager

Personnel decisions are *"the ultimate control of an organization* [...]. Therefore really experienced and competent leaders dedicate *by far the largest* part of their time to personnel questions."[272] The governance board in particular has the responsibility for selecting and appointing the project manager who fulfills the requirements stemming from the outlined strategy. The board confronts the following dilemma: What is wanted is usually the superwoman or superman right off the shelf, while on the other hand the time-wise limited character of a project does not particularly favor long-term personnel formation and planning. Therefore, instead of really taking personnel questions to heart (and spending a considerable

---

[271] See Ulrich P. & Fluri 1995: 217ff, Thommen 2002: 212f on functional diagrams.

[272] Malik 2002: 295 (translation Renz).

amount of time on them), a board typically delegates them to a contractor who himself is again under extreme pressure to minimize so-called 'management margins' that would allow for long-term personnel planning and capacity building. In my view, this downward spiral is what the public voices in the development sector are prompted by when they call for greater professionalism. And not only public voices:

An opinion from within

I was arguing with a good friend, himself the managing director of an implementation NGO for development projects, about what went wrong in the appointment of my successor (see also next paragraph). Though I know that I set high standards, his concluding statement left me speechless: "You too are expecting a superman as a successor, but the reality in this [development] sector is that you have to cope with fourth- and fifth-class professionals...".

Though I would not generalize from this quite extreme statement, what writing this book has shown, however, is that the current profile of a project manager needs to be *redrawn*. The development field needs qualified professionals with proven *general management* experience, ready to handle all the aspects of running a complete business or organization, with its personnel policy, risk management, audit management, stakeholder interactions, and so forth.

The governance board is responsible for selecting, appointing, and empowering a project manager; according to Kupper, this should be "a single person, not a team, not a triumvirate or a couple,"[273] i.e. co-leaders and the like. Ambiguities left unresolved at the top are unlikely to disappear as one goes down the organizational roster; indeed, on the contrary!

m) Succession planning

Succession planning is standard in business organizations, while quite understandably it is more difficult in projects, with their situational character. It is paramount, then, that succession planning be placed on the governance agenda.

---

[273] Kupper 2001: 28 (translation Renz).

Fatalism in succession planning?

The email from the head-office read: "*The day after tomorrow* Geoffrey, the head-office's preferred candidate for your succession will be coming to Bangladesh for an interview with the donors and to meet the project."

My team knew that I would be leaving in around three months, but were they prepared to face the change? Despite the less-than-ideal short notice, a complete agenda was set up, including a social programme and sight-seeing.

The days to follow became what some in the team called a nightmare: Geoffrey introduced himself as the confirmed successor (he had no contract), confronting people in the elevator about whether they knew who he was. My appeals for cooperation did not avail: He continued with his alienating style. People came crying into my office…

Obviously, I conveyed our experiences and my concern to Mack, my boss at the head office. The donors, too, had raised a number of questions. Nevertheless, Geoffrey was appointed. Mack commented on his decision as follows: "Sometimes you have to be a fatalist." Did he already present his faulty recruitment decision? One of the donors later commented that finding a successor for such a big project was "too big of a task for SwissNGO." (See also earlier examples: Geoffrey lasted only a few months in his assignment.)

This example illustrates a fatal result in succession planning, but it also indicates how all the responsibility was delegated to one person. As the people in a project are one of its most important influences, the succession planning for its leader, the project manager, needs to be a *joint* responsibility of the governance board (as it is in corporate governance).[274] Simply leaving it in the hands of the implementing NGO, which at the very same time is under high pressure from the same donors to reduce overheads (a factor which hinders long-term personnel planning, capacitating, and retaining high potentials) is just another face of fatalism. Succession planning, together with other personnel-related issues, not only needs *to be* on the agenda of project governance, it also needs to be *at the very top* of it.

---

[274] See for instance Hilb 2005.

n) Board self-organization, and processes and board building[275]

Another structural governance task is the self-organization of the governance board, referring to board structure / composition, board internal processes, and board building. These three aspects are briefly explained below:

Board structure / composition:[276] This refers to decisions or negotiations
about who should be part of the governance board, which stakeholders
should be represented, and by whom (see also Chapter 4.4 on stakeholder
management). A difficult question is how 'the poor' are to be represented,
namely the target group. If there is no formal representation, the board
members need to avail themselves of high normative maturity (see Chapter
4.3.4.1 on the differentiated responsibility concept): How is accountability
towards the target group to be anchored in the board composition? This
step also includes decisions on committees (such as an audit or risk committee) and the appointment of the chair of the board. The various roles
and expectations should be clarified.[277] The example below illustrates an
important task of the chair, whose role as a linking pin for the project requires, however, that he duly inform the other board members if anything
happens between board meetings.

Chair as a linking pin to the donor board?

Again Wednesday 4.30pm, time for the weekly beer with Frizz. Though
it was done frequently, I pursued this opportunity to link with Frizz, the
chair of the so-called donor board, in order to give him a 'warm and
fuzzy feeling' about our remarkable progress. What was not good, however, was that substantial information which I communicated to him did
not make it to the rest of the donors – for instance, I had briefed him
nearly daily during a number of so called law-and-order issues (abduction threat, car accident, harassment of employees by the police), but we
still had to organize a special debriefing session with the remaining
donors, even though Frizz had inquired in depth about the cases and
was satisfied with our actions.

---

[275] Hilb 2005 presents a comprehensive overview of board processes. This chapter
mainly draws on his contributions, complemented with insights from the case
study.

[276] For more on board composition, see Hilb 2005: 70ff and Brönnimann 2003:
286ff.

[277] See Hilb 2005: 107f for a list of the main tasks of the chair.

Board internal processes: These processes include:

- Meeting management (frequency of meetings, preparation etc.).

- Communication processes[278] among the board members, and with the project and stakeholders. Specifically, these processes need to include "agreed procedures for contact between [project] management and [governance] board outside board meetings."[279] In larger projects, it makes sense to appoint a liaison officer to channel communication.

- Board remuneration: The donor representatives are usually paid by their donor agencies, and it is part of their job to direct and control the project. So, too, are the representatives of the implementation NGO. Board remuneration may, however, be considered for outside members, for instance representatives of the target group.

- Board development:[280] Almost never do board members bring along all the needed qualifications. A targeted 'development' plan should be elaborated with the objective to "promote the integrated success intelligence"[281] based on three criteria: Analytical intelligence ("cool head"), emotional intelligence ("warm heart"), and practical intelligence ("working hands"). Concretely, this development process also includes the content of the project governance concept presented in this book, in terms of which the board members need to be trained in their roles, expectations, and tasks.

- Finally, feedback for board members, for instance in a 360° feedback assessment.

Board building: Structuring a board, and all the relevant tasks it needs to undertake, does not just fall into place. It is recommended that one conduct a board building exercise, ideally facilitated by an external coach familiar with development work, project management, and governance work. The following illustrates the experiences with board building that came up during the case study project:

---

[278] See Hilb 2005: 174ff.

[279] Carter & Lorsch 2004: 178.

[280] Hilb 2005: 140ff.

[281] Hilb 2004: 134 (translation Renz). See further 2005: 142.

Board building exercise

DRIVER was directed by a donor board, whose existence was a good idea and a first step towards creating holistic project governance. One day I heard that the chair had initiated a board building exercise, and had contracted Jane, a corporate governance consultant. Apparently, the three donor representatives spent several days on this board building exercise, and numerous documents were produced. These, however, were "difficult for the reader, creating reluctance to be used," even in the eyes and words of one of the participating donors.

What was the problem? It was a great idea, but it met with a less-than-great implementation: First of all, not all key members were involved (no target group or Bangladeshi representation; nobody from the project, or only for consultation – that is why it was a 'donor' board only). And secondly, Jane, an enthusiastic woman, who managed to 'tame' the three donors with her untiring patience, could not understand, however, the differing needs of corporate governance and the governance of a project. A lost opportunity!

Given the complex tasks and expectations for which board members are responsible, a board building exercise is indispensable. A comprehensive framework, such as project governance, can ease the task substantially.

o) Provide support on specific structural issues

In its supporting role, a governance board also plays the role of a sounding board,[282] helping with important structural issues such as performance issues with key positions (an example provided by the case study was the project deputy). In offering advice to the project management, a balance needs to be struck between conscious empowering and proper involvement, as illustrated by Figure 18.

p) Monitor the organizational effectiveness

Finally, the project governance has a controlling role to play in all the aforementioned tasks in giving strategic direction and support for the 'structuring force of structure.' The following points should be considered:

---

[282] I use the term 'sounding board' with reference to what Carter & Lorsch call "offering advice and counsel to management, especially the CEO" (which they name as one of the three key activities defining the board's role; the other two "monitoring the company and management's performance" and "making major decisions") (2004: 67f).

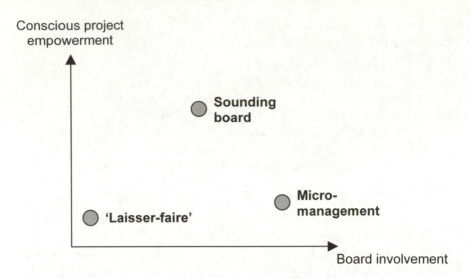

Figure 18. Differences in boards' support styles

- Basic organizational elements: Are they proving to be functional (for instance, are the outsourced elements contributing properly)?[283]

- Contractual framework: Are the contracts complete, or are amendments needed?

- Organizational structure: Does the approved organizational structure work, that is, does it deliver? Is the management level-appropriate or is there loose micro-management?

- Project manager: Assess the performance of the project manager. Hilb suggests a comprehensive form used for CEO evaluations as well as various possible processes.[284] This can be adopted easily in case a similar process and forms are not available from one of the involved organizations.

- Succession planning: Is it done in a timely manner and with the best contributions from within the governance board?

- Board self-organization and processes: This can be done through a self or external review. Hilb presents a comprehensive questionnaire

---

[283] See also Chapter 4.4 on extended stakeholder management, where a stakeholder controlling map is suggested.

[284] Hilb 2005: 124ff.

for board self-assessment;[285] this has been adapted and tested by Renz and Weichsler for the development sector.[286]

- Support on specific structural issues: Was enough support available, and did the provided support lead to useful solutions?

An additional possibility could also be to assess the project maturity using methodologies such as the Project Management Maturity Model developed by Crawford.[287]

Concluding this study's review of structure, the reader may wonder: "Are there optimal structures for organizations?"[288] With Schwaninger, it can be said that to date "there are no generally optimal structures."[289] It may sound paradoxical, but optimal structures need to be elaborated, as they emerge from process-intense work.

4.2.2.3 The governance tasks within 'culture'

In the St. Gallen Management Model, Rüegg-Stürm defines culture as "embrac[ing], in essence, all symbolic references and certainties around which we all naturally orient ourselves in our day-to-day words and deeds and upon which we can rely."[290] He further mentions possible cultural elements, among them "attitudes, norms and values, identity in general […], pattern of discourse […and] company language."[291] Those material or immaterial manifestations forming organizational culture create "a natural sense of purpose that provides a degree of orientation."[292]

Organizational cultures are not like a 'homogeneous monolith'; with respect to development projects, we could at least differentiate between the project and the board culture. The board is first responsible for its own board culture; secondarily, it has a role of strategic direction, support, and control to play towards the project team culture.

Of the three structuring forces, culture is certainly the most complex one. The famous iceberg analogy of French and Bell, further developed by

[285] Hilb 2005: 197ff. See also Hilb 1997, 2002 for success-evaluation.

[286] Renz & Weichsler 2005: 15f.

[287] See Crawford 2002.

[288] Schwaninger 2005: 71 (translation Renz).

[289] Idem.

[290] Rüegg-Stürm 2005: 43. See Ulrich P. & Fluri 1995: 36ff, Lattmann 1990.

[291] Idem.

[292] Rüegg-Stürm 2005: 42.

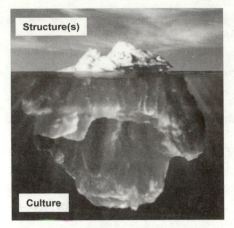

Explicit material dimension:
- Organizational regulations
- Rules, directives, manuals, handbooks
- Predefinitions of location and work space
- Information technology predefinitions

Implicit immaterial dimension:
- Observable behavior, myths, stories, typical argumentation patterns and wordings, 'company slang'
- Identity, collective expectations, basic assumptions, thought worlds ('local rationalities'), and inherent convictions
- Values, norms, and implicit rules
- Attitudes and 'taken-for-granteds' in practices of leadership, internal collaboration and external interactions with stakeholders

Figure 19. The organization as an 'iceberg': the explicit and the implicit dimension[293]

Rüegg-Stürm (see Figure 19) also highlights the fact that culture, unlike structures, is not visible, and, as such, may not be a conscious element.

Figure 19 also illustrates that culture cannot be regarded on its own, without the organizational context of at least structure and strategy. Culture has an integrated (and integrative!) nature: In fact, all six modules of project governance can be seen within a cultural perspective (see, for instance, the discussion of risk culture in Chapter 4.5.4, and see also the elaborations below).

The difficulty with culture is – using a practitioner's term – how to 'get our hands' around culture, a task which literally is impossible, but very well expresses the pragmatic and action-oriented desire of practitioners. The singular nature of projects, nearly 'coming to life out of nothing,' and particularly the intercultural context of development projects, additionally lend weight to the consideration that culture cannot be left to chance – that is, because "much greater effort is needed to steer the barely accessible cultural elements of an organization,"[294] culture needs at least the same top management, i.e. governance attention, as strategy!

Based on these introductory reflections, it is proposed here that the governance role of strategically directing, support, and controlling also be applied to the structuring force of 'culture,' and that this application take shape through the following four tasks:

---

[293] Rüegg-Stürm 2005: 47.

[294] Rüegg-Stürm 2005: 46.

q) Become conscious of the current organizational culture

The board members should ask themselves: "Do we know our culture? What are the current attitudes, norms and values, expectations, common experiences, the language used etc.?"[295] The following example illustrates how the project in the present case study became conscious of how important the language used was:

Introducing business language

Would our current development slang support us in building trust and credibility with our target beneficiaries, ultimately the SMEs? Several of them had expressed their frustration about how numerous development projects have come and gone without any noticeable improvements for the SME. This urged us – as one measure – to adapt our language: We were not a project anymore, but an organization. The donors became investors, the project manager became general manager, the components became divisions, the development specialists became consultants etc.

The suggested process of reflection may also reveal different cultures in the project; as mentioned earlier, for instance, the culture of the board may differ from the project culture.

r) Analyze the possible gap between the current and a more conducive culture

This step aims to answer the question of whether the current organizational culture is sufficiently conducive to the development project, that is, whether there are any gaps between the current culture and what is considered to be a culture-conducive factor. This can be structured along the lines of the six governance key responsibilities, as they all contain a cultural dimension (which stresses again the integrative character of project governance). Specifically, the following aspects should be considered:

1. Is the project's culture conducive to a *systemic* understanding? Are the managerial expectations towards a systemic thinking perceivable, and is there a corresponding attitude?

---

[295] Simple questionnaires, for instance the ten comprehensive questions on board behavior suggested by Carter & Lorsch (2004: 178), may be a good starting point for such reflection. A more sophisticated questionnaire is presented by Hilb (2005: 198f). It has been adapted for nonprofit boards by Renz & Weichsler (2005: 15f).

2. Does the project culture express the 'shared sense of purpose' for the *mission* of the project, i.e. is there a shared sense for the vision and the mission, and is this shared sense perceivable through the structures, and through the way how people describe and talk about their jobs? If a team structure has been set up, is there a team culture?

3. Does the project foster *a culture of reciprocal recognition*, and of *discursive conflict resolution*? Is there an "integrity culture"[296] that lays the groundwork for an "argumentation culture"? This should create what Hilb calls a "critical but constructive culture of trust,"[297] or in other words *a team culture of trust and open dissent* which is not only needed within the board, but also by the entire project. The following example displays openness and trust:

A culture of trust?

When Paul entered my office, something seemed to be bothering him: Two of our donor representatives had asked him (and the other three middle managers) for an after-work beer at one of the international clubs. He thought I should know about it (which I had not previously). I thanked him for his trust and loyalty. As the proponent of an open culture, I had nothing against meetings across hierarchical levels as long as the separate competencies and responsibilities were maintained. But something was wrong there: Not that I wasn't invited – I can understand that sometimes safe spaces are needed (additionally, the handover to my successor was close at hand) – but the fact that I wasn't *told by the two donors* something like "Patrick, we would like to talk with the remaining expatriates about…". Not only did this one-channel behavior create an awkward situation for me, but it also set up a loyalty conflict for my subordinates – which (I am proud) Paul resolved promptly.[298]

One of the curiosities of the development sector, which in the case study could be observed in numerous meetings (of all sizes and configurations), is that the interaction in meetings often looks rather like a political debate than a solution-oriented joint discussion. While this atmosphere is

---

[296] Ulrich H. 2001: 459 (translation Renz).

[297] Hilb 2005: 82ff.

[298] This is in fact a good example of the lack of argumentational integrity of the donor representatives, which will be discussed in Chapter 4.3.4.1.

understandable on the level of development policies, it none the less hinders a constructive team culture in an implementation project. The governance board has a role to play in assuring that a project-conducive culture prevails.

4. Is broad *stakeholder* understanding prevalent in the project's plans and activities? Is there a sense of responsibility and accountability which is expected and requested?

5. Is the project's attitude towards *risks* known, consciously treated, or left to chance?

6. Is the project's culture sensitive to *audit* requirements?

s) Conduct top 20% cultural change interventions

If the gap between current and conducive cultures is substantial, a number of "reinforcing or disturbing"[299] interventions should be undertaken. This book suggests selecting only the top 20% of possible intervention ideas. This focus and emphasis on the chosen ideas hopefully achieves close to 80% of the desired (and realistic) results. Following are several culture-related organizational elements, which will be discussed in Chapter 4.3 on integrity management. Setting up these elements or adjusting them could be part of one of the above interventions. These elements are: A code of conduct for the personnel and possibly also for subcontractors, creation of a whistleblower process (including the respective protection), and the appointment of an ombudsman or compliance officer.

t) Monitor the culture

This step represents the related controlling task, monitoring in an iterative circle the organizational culture as expressed through signals, symbols, language, attitudes, and so forth.

The proposed steps with respect to organizational culture as the third structuring force according to the St. Gallen Management Model round off the specific tasks of project governance within Mission Management.

4.2.3 Summary of tasks within mission management

Table 4 summarizes the tasks of the governance board within the key responsibility of Mission Management.

With this summary, we turn to the third module of project governance, the key responsibility called integrity management.

---

[299] See Rüegg-Stürm on routinisation through structuring forces 2005: 46ff.

Table 4. Governance tasks within mission management

	Strategic direction and support	Control
Strategy	a. Establish the vision, mission, business principals and basic strategy b. Stick to them for a while! c. Define success criteria d. Set financial framework and choose major milestones e. Challenge and support phase plans	f. Assure communication and operationalization g. Monitor and control achievements of success criteria h. Define standards for impact assessment
Structure	i. Set the basic organizational elements j. Establish the contractual framework k. Approve the proposed organizational structure l. Appoint the project manager m. Succession planning n. Board self-organization, internal processes, and board building o. Provide support on specific structural issues	p. Monitor the organizational effectiveness (focusing on the previously set elements, point i. to point o.)
Culture	q. Become conscious of the current culture r. Analyze gap between current and conducive culture s. Conduct top 20% interventions	t. Monitor the culture

4.3   Integrity management

> *Integrity is one of several paths. It distinguishes it-*
> *self from the others because it is the right path, and*
> *the only one upon which you never get lost.*
>
> M. H. McKee
>
> *There is no such thing as a minor lapse of integrity.*
>
> Tom Peters

In Chapter 3, the need for a normative foundation was established, and the corresponding key responsibility of integrity management was identified. This chapter first of all clarifies the objectives of integrity management. It then examines what the relevance and importance of integrity really are for development projects. Subsequently, it derives both a normative founda-tion and the respective moral point of view. In looking toward implement-ing such a normative foundation, one is faced with a variety of integrity challenges which require for their assessment a generic process model. Such process model is introduced. Then, a number of integrity challenges within respective tension zones are discussed in detail; numerous case examples illustrate the arguments. The chapter concludes with a few com-ments on how to get underway with integrity management.

4.3.1   Objective of integrity management

The objective of integrity management is to provide an *integrated platform to deal with integrity challenges*, on a fundamental level (what is our nor-mative foundation?) as well as on the level of specific integrity issues (how should our strategy, structure and project culture be shaped; and what is 'good' and what is 'bad' behavior in concrete situations?). In other words, it aims at illuminating and reflecting on values and their underlying norms, as well as on justifiability and bearableness (in German, *Verant-wortbarkeit and Zumutbarkeit*).

Integrity management as proposed here pursues this objective in a way that institutionalizes a platform for conscious and unavoidable reflection, a forum for exchange and *discourse*, without preempting either concrete outcomes or non-reflective prescriptions.

Placed within the management context of development projects, these objectives aim at the following effects:

- *awareness* is created for universal values and (relative) values which may be conflicting between cultures (i.e. which values are universal and which ones are relevant in the development context);

- respective expectations towards the project are made *explicit* (i.e. which universal values and which local values are relevant for the development project);

- the project leadership (i.e. governance bodies and project management) is *enabled for* as well as *bound to assume* their normative responsibility through a respective strategy and structure;

- managerial *guidance* is provided for concrete ethical challenges, such as mobbing, corruption, conflicts of interest, collusion, hidden agendas, accountability etc.;

- *higher decision makers* and top management (corporate governance) are brought into involvement in irresolvable integrity issues;

- a *climate of trust and respect* for differences is facilitated.

The term *integrity* is chosen because it is an open term, not having the possibly finger-pointing connotations of "ethics remind[ing] us of morals, authorities, religion"[300] – subjects which are particularly loaded in the context of intercultural development cooperation.

Etymologically, integrity derives from the Latin word 'integer' which means 'whole, complete or pure.' Today, integrity is used in a variety of areas, often with different connotations: Popular usage – in a blurred sort of way – refers to moral, virtue or even ethics; information technology talks of data integrity which is expected to be guaranteed by a well-functioning system (i.e. the comprised hardware and software); and finally, there are distinctions between personal and organizational integrity.

This text adopts a definition of organizational integrity by Paine, who defines integrity in the context of business ethics as "*the quality of moral self-governance*"(!).[301] Furthermore, integrity is "generally identified with one or more of the following related characteristics: moral conscientiousness [...], moral accountability [...], moral commitment [...] and moral coherence."[302]

4.3.2 Relevance and importance of integrity for development projects

What is the relevance and importance of integrity in the context of development projects, and what are examples of situations that pose threats to the integrity of a project?

---

[300] Waxenberger 2003: 235.

[301] Paine 1997: 335 (emphasis Renz).

[302] Idem.

With a view to the three fundamental objectives of development projects – "impact, sustainability and outreach"[303] – at least the following three answers to our question of relevance and importance can be derived from the above definition of integrity: (1) Liberty of action, (2) credibility and trustworthiness, and (3) self-commitment or persistence. They are explained below:

(1) Development projects, functioning in the midst of numerous interests, need to be "scrupulous in dealing with conflicts of interest or improper influences which might taint their judgment."[304] Such 'moral conscientiousness' finally results in *liberty of action* which allows the project to pursue *optimal ways towards achieving impact* – optimal in the sense that discursively derived compromises may be made, but no 'wrong' compromises.

Following are a few examples of categories that possibly restrict liberty of action for a development project (the additional questions which arise from each of the examples also point to the need for a clearer view of the normative issues behind the examples):

- Corruption: But what is corruption and what is it not – what is it for a Bangladeshi, and what is it for me?

- Hidden agendas: But what is the exact problem with a hidden agenda?

- Conflicts of interest: Yet are they not normal, a part of the 'conditio humana'?

- Collusion: But what is the normative problem of a "secret and illegitimate cooperation among organizational actors"?[305]

- Power struggles, or even class coalitions, already mentioned as downsides of an organizational theory: Why do they negatively impact liberty of action?

These category-examples point to cases in which reflections on integrity are relevant for development projects. It is precisely the objective of this chapter to support such reflections and thereby to illuminate the normative content of these challenges. With this objective in hand, we turn to the second reason why integrity is relevant for development projects.

(2) In the intercultural context, and in the midst of possibly divergent political considerations, 'moral accountability' fosters *credibility and trustworthiness* as being critical in the pursuit of nonprofit goals In particular:

---

[303] See Footnote 189 for a definition of these terms.

[304] Paine 1997: 335.

[305] See definition of collusion further down.

Credibility and trustworthiness are indispensable for a 'good' project mission in so far as they imply how the project is perceived by the target group as well as by donors and their taxpayers. Without credibility and trustworthiness, development impact, outreach and sustainability as well as future funding are doubtful.

The following points may represent a threat to credibility and trustworthiness, and thus to the integrity of a development project:

- Development paternalism: The target group may not 'accept' the development effort if it grounds itself in a paternalistic view of what the problems are.

- Accountability: Who is accountable for what within a development effort? Are the roles clear, accepted, and realistic?

- Involvement of the target group: How can the target group be involved so that a climate of joint cooperation and satisfaction is achieved?

- Local partnerships: How are 'good' partnerships achieved (and defined in the first place), and what might the reasons be for poor cooperation by partner NGOs?

- Involvement of funding countries: What is needed to foster trust and commitments for future funding?

With this, we turn to the third reason why integrity is relevant for development projects:

(3) Finally, 'moral commitment' creates a steadiness, *persistence or self-commitment* even "when confronted with adversity or temptation."[306] Development projects often face adverse and extremely difficult situations; in fact, contextual complexity is inherent to development. From the perspective of 'moral commitment,' integrity becomes a *driving force* for believing in and pursuing the project mission. A brief example illustrates a typical challenge to the moral commitment of a development project:

Who is on the ground if not the development project?

Bangladesh increasingly faces the rise of Islamic fundamentalism. For instance, this force frequently impinges in connection with the decline of law and order, particularly as the alleged source of the simultaneous explosion of around 500 bombs all over the country in the Fall of 2005.

---

[306] Paine 1997: 335.

> Should a development project withdraw under such circumstances, or should it not precisely be the one actor remaining at the forefront of a hopefully meaningful contribution to an intercultural discourse? This is where persistence or moral commitment comes into play.

To summarize briefly thus far, integrity with its various characteristics is of relevance and particular importance for a development project fostering (1) liberty of action, (2) credibility and trustworthiness, and (3) self-commitment or the persistence of the project.

4.3.3 How to approach managing integrity

What does the above mean for the operation of a development project, that is to say, what effects does integrity have upon what must concretely be done? The following case example illustrates a concrete integrity measure, and at the same time outlines a number of limitations of such a measure:

We have a code of conduct!

It was no surprise when Mack, my boss, announced that during his next visit to Bangladesh we would introduce a code of conduct: Following a case of fraud and sexual harassment in another project, SwissNGO created and introduced its own code.

In a meeting, he presented a code which defined and prohibited acts such as mobbing, fraud, sexual harassment etc. A few questions were raised and answered. Finally, he instructed me to organize a democratic election of a compliance officer within the project. My first thought had to do with context: Was this simple procedure possible in a culture with little democratic tradition, in an organization where the peons 'refused' to jointly use the elevator, jumping out of it with an embarrassed "Sorry, sir", when a manager waited to enter it? Who would be the person everyone would trust, not just the one who inspired hierarchical respect?

While Mack appeared to have accomplished his mission (he never mentioned the code of conduct anymore), I wanted to take the pulse of local staff members. I found that elections were definitely not preferred, and moreover it was suggested to me that I should select a person, an expatriate furthermore, rather than a local person.

I wondered why. Was it because the local staff did not trust each other and preferred to have an expatriate, or was it because local staff did not want anything to do with the position of a compliance officer, as they perceived it to be a 'non-functional' position?

This example illustrates how one might take a well-intended initiative to support the integrity of a project, but it also shows that the implementation of such measures requires sensitivity to cultural differences and follow-through.

It becomes obvious from such examples that intuitive ethical behavior is not enough for the integrity of a project, nor can challenges to integrity simply be 'resolved and tagged off.' A sounder understanding of the moral content of integrity is needed by managers (and ultimately their staff), one that leads them to ask what exactly the moral or normative content might be when it comes to the conscientiousness, accountability, and commitment that are important for good project implementation.

A development project should *be aware of the relevance of integrity* for its implementation. That is, it should *have the terminology and capability* for describing its own moral understanding (not in philosophical terms – that is an excessive demand, but in simple and concise terms). A project management group should be aware of how *integrity interrelates with the strategy, structures, and organizational culture* of the project. In other words, integrity is an active element of project management, whose exact leadership roles need to be clarified.

In the context of a "modern democratic society of free and equal citizens"[307] – with a relatively fair "economic and social order," where human rights are mostly respected – managing integrity within an organization means nothing more and nothing less than *operationalizing* the norms established for organizational and individual behavior. In an environment where the above conditions of a fair economic and social order cannot be assumed, managing organizational integrity calls for increased effort: Exactly because laws may be defective or absent, and the norms of justice may be unknown or remain unenforced, an organization is faced with the fact that *certain norms need to be defined or negotiated in the first place*. In doing so, certain meta-ethical standards should be taken into consideration.

The concepts of discourse ethics as established by the German philosophers Jürgen Habermas and Karl-Otto Apel[308] seem to offer a comprehensive approach *facilitating such definition or negotiation*, as they constitute "a far-reaching critical normative force of orientation"[309] in all respects, on the individual, organizational, and public levels.

---

[307] Ulrich P. 2001a: 286 (translation Renz).

[308] See Habermas 1981a, 1981b.

[309] Ulrich P. 2001a: 94 (translation Renz).

The guidelines representing the *normative foundation* of discourse ethics, and the extent to which these guidelines fulfill meta-ethical standards,
will be the subject of the next chapter. Before that, we shall briefly summarize the main meta-ethical standards for normative foundations. The
following standards draw on Peter Ulrich's critical review of philosophi-
cal-developmental lines for rational ethics, and are briefly tied to considerations typical of the development context:[310]

- *Universal validity* of the normative foundation. It should be valid for
  the context of the development country as well as for the country of
  the donor or other involved actors. Otherwise development efforts
  risk being confronted with the reproach of development paternalism.

- Existence of an (ultimate) *foundation* or *grounding independent of
  particular cultural or religious values.*[311] Development *cooperation*
  is characterized precisely by cross-border collaboration. More than
  ever today, the ultimate foundation for integrity needs to be independent of cultural and religious values, which may differ between
  the involved countries.

- *Capability* for differentiating between *strategic and normative* action orientation.[312]

- Consideration of teleological *bearableness and* deontological *justifiability.*[313] The bearableness factor, for instance, emerges repeatedly
  in discussions about the adoption of social standards (such as the
  elimination of child labor).

---

[310] See Ulrich P. 2001a: 57ff.

[311] The importance of an ultimate foundation is known to the author. For instance,
the lack of an ultimate rational foundation in Adam Smith's construct for the
standpoint of the impartial spectator is one of the criticisms directed at Smith's
theory of moral sentiment (see Ulrich P. 2001a: 63ff.). The ultimate foundation
of discourse ethics, however, is also challenged by Wellmer and Maak, in that
discourse ethics may "deprive itself of its moral-practical orientation power
[if...] it aims too rigorously at the completion of its procedural ideals" (Maak
2001: 136; translation Renz). What is relevant for this book, however, is that a
possible ultimate foundation be independent of cultural or religious rationality,
or in Wellmer's words, "not the completion of sense, but the elimination of
non-sense is the principle of moral progress" (1986: 127).

[312] See Ulrich P. 2001a: 57ff.

[313] Teleological, from the Greek *telos* = target, goal, and Deontological from the
Greek *deon* = obligation. See Ulrich P. 2001c: 45.

With this brief summary in view, we now turn to the ethical foundation provided by discourse ethics.

4.3.4 Ethical foundation – what is the moral point of view?

This chapter aims at deriving an ethical foundation to illustrate the moral point of view which will serve as grounds for developing the elements of integrity management.

Discourse ethics seems to "offer so far the most elaborated explication of the rational ethical point of view as the normative logic of interpersonal relations."[314] It not only has "superior power for reflective (universally pragmatic) justification,"[315] but also constitutes "a far-reaching critical normative force of orientation" on the levels of personal, institutional, and public responsibility.

The principles of discourse ethics seem to be applicable to the field of development *cooperation*, particularly to development understood not as a unilateral but rather as a joint cooperative development effort, characterized by a "broad-based deliberative participation in forging consensus [...], where] the 'right of rights' is citizen deliberation and agency."[316]

Based on the foundations of discourse ethics, Peter Ulrich has developed the St. Gallen approach called *integrative economic ethics*, widely considered to be a valuable and important contribution to the debate around business ethics.[317] Its point of departure is a comparative and critical reflection on the main philosophical explications of the principle of morals. The brief introduction to discourse ethics offered below draws largely on Ulrich's work.

4.3.4.1 Key elements of discourse ethics

What is the reason for placing discourse, "understood as that qualified form of talking which aims at rational communication between discussants,"[318] at the centre of ethics? Discourse is used as the grounding of a general ethics because any process of thinking, even the most solitary re-

---

[314] Ulrich P. 2001a: 94 (translation Renz).

[315] Idem.

[316] Crocker & Schenke 2005: 28.

[317] See Kirsch 2004, Leisinger 2004, Steinmann 2004, von Cranach 2004.

[318] Ulrich P. 2001a: 78 (translation Renz).

flecting, constitutes some type of *debate* with either real discussants or – in the case of quiet reflections – with oneself as a discussant. Furthermore, *reciprocal role-taking* is at the heart of understanding (though not yet accepting!) claims, rights, or expectations. Let there be no misunderstanding: Discourse ethics does not promote a moral principle for *consensus*; rather, it only aims at fostering ideal structures of rational argumentation. Discourse ethics as such is a "particular form of the explication of the general moral point of view, simply in the form of the *ideal discourse*."[319] On these grounds, ethics is at last able to relinquish its premodern authority as the "guardian of morals,"[320] while assuming a critical-regulative role as the "guardian of rationality" in a moral discourse.

With a view to the integrity issues outlined here, the practical value of discourse ethics lies in the "normative-*critical* orientational power of its *procedural ideal* [inherent] to the discourse-based clarification of moral questions."[321] The results are real attempts at resolving situations or tension zones arising from absent or incomplete norms.

Peter Ulrich describes four normative guidelines (D1 to D4) of discourse ethics:[322]

(1st guideline – D1) A *communicatively oriented attitude* of all parties involved, or *argumentational integrity*. The discussants are ready to assert only those claims they truly regard as right; they are willing to substantiate their claims without reservation and they display a genuine interest in nothing but arriving at a rational consensus. This guideline contains the Kantian condition of *good will*. It is the "normative foundation of communicative rationality"[323] – or simply "argumentational integrity."[324] The popular phrase 'let's agree to disagree' is usually an expression of the described reservation-free attitude.[325]

An orientation toward arriving communicatively at rational consensus strongly contrasts with a success-orientation that focuses (with Habermas)

[319] Ulrich P. 2001a: 81 (translation and emphasis Renz).

[320] Ulrich P. 2001a: 82 (translation Renz).

[321] Idem.

[322] See Ulrich P. 2001a: 82ff.

[323] Ulrich P. 2001a: 83 (translation Renz).

[324] See Blickle 1994: 10ff.; see further Groeben, Nüse & Gauler 1990: 3. In fact, discourse ethics is sometimes also called *argumentation* ethics!

[325] See Palazzo: "The search for consensus […] must be replaced by the search for the conditions of a reasonable disagreement" (2004: 52; translation Renz).

on the "technical rationality" that explains "instrumental acting" and "strategic acting."[326] The moral interest, for a communicative consensus-finding on conflicting claims, "acquires priority over the personal objectives" of the participants, constituting a paradigm shift from "the strategic to the communicative rationality type."[327]

With this, guideline D1 fulfills one of the meta-ethical standards, namely the capability of differentiating between strategic and normative action orientations.

(2nd guideline – D2) The *interest* without reservation in *legitimate action*. The previous guideline does not imply that personal objectives should not be pursued, but rather that their acceptance as legitimate should be tested by the other participants. Therefore, this guideline postulates a required genuine *interest* of those involved in a communicative coordination of their actions, with the objective being to *legitimize* them – precisely through this process of discourse with all participants. Discourse ethics then succeeds at the systematic development of the "teleological-ethical perspective within a deontological ethics"[328]; or as Habermas puts it, discourse ethics has "a built-in procedure that ensures awareness of consequences."[329] With this guideline, discourse ethics considers another meta-ethical standard, that of bearableness and justifiability. Following Chandler, this guideline could also be summarized as *success follows legitimacy*.

(3rd guideline – D3) A differentiated concept of *responsibility* ethics. The above-mentioned communicative attitude constitutes a regulative idea of "universal argumentative reciprocity between persons who recognize each other as responsible subjects."[330] A person acts *responsibly*[331] "who faces up to the demands for justification or solidarity and to the criticism of all

---

[326] Habermas 1981: 385 ff. (translation Renz).

[327] Ulrich P. 2001a: 84f (translation Renz).

[328] Ulrich P. 2001a: 86 (translation Renz).

[329] Habermas 1991: 23 (translation Renz).

[330] Ulrich P. 2001a: 87 (translation Renz). We will see later that for the context in which development projects take place a more differentiated concept of recognition is needed. For the moment, the principal guidelines of discourse ethics are outlined.

[331] Note also the linguistic relationship of responsibility and 'to respond to something,' both stemming from the Latin verb *respondere*, meaning 'respond, answer to, promise in return.'

who are affected by his intended actions."[332] This ethics of responsibility, however, faces problems in the case of incomplete reciprocity, i.e. in cases where reciprocal communication cannot easily be realized:

- "because the situation does not permit communication (as in the case of the unborn, minors or others not responsible for their actions)

- because of pragmatic difficulties (e.g. the inability to determine or delimit the potentially affected, when the numbers are too large or there are spatial, temporal, technical or financial obstacles)

- because other actors lack the motivation to seek agreement (strategic opponents!). In this case the bearer of responsibility cannot reckon naïvely with the goodwill of other, possibly influential actors."[333]

At this point, in order to clarify the central ethical question of responsibility, the following three-stage concept can be formulated along the lines of discourse ethics:

1. "When the preconditions for reciprocal communication are fulfilled to a fair extent, a person acts responsibly who makes an effort to engage in a *real* legitimation discourse with those concerned.

2. When the preconditions for reciprocal communication cannot in principle be fulfilled, a person acts responsibly who, to the best of his ability, engages in a proxy fictive discourse with those concerned in 'solitary' reflection, in order to weigh their legitimate 'claims' against his own interests.

3. When the preconditions for reciprocal communication cannot be fulfilled at the moment for purely pragmatic reasons, a person acts responsibly who first of all acts as proxy and takes on the responsibility unilaterally in his mind, but at the same time orients his actions to the regulative idea of the long-term best possible realization of the unrestricted communicative conditions and accordingly accepts his share of political responsibility."[334]

With this differentiated summary in place, we turn to the 4th guideline of discourse ethics.

---

[332] Ulrich P. 2001a: 87 (translation Renz).

[333] Ulrich P. 2001a: 88 (translation Renz).

[334] Ulrich P. 2001a: 90 (translation Renz).

(4th guideline – D4) A *political-ethical* notion of the *locus* of the morality in a modern society, or the notion of *public binding*. In practical terms, processes of communication always need an institutional context in which to take place. This institutional context should be characterized by an "adequate structural freedom from power and a normative openness,"[335] so that argumentational integrity and *good will* do not remain wishful thinking only. At the heart of this guideline is therefore the "matter of creating in each real communication community the best possible institutional basic conditions oriented on the regulative idea of the ideal communication community."[336] Project governance as such with its different key responsibilities, in particular the involvement of stakeholders such as beneficiaries and government (see extended stakeholder management, Chapter 4.4), offers exactly this kind of institutionalization. It constitutes an instance of "public self-binding."[337] It is important to add, however, that project governance *per se* is not a practical 'application' of discourse-ethical guidelines – such an application-specific interpretation of discourse ethics would instrumentalize the ideas outlined here with the consequence of losing their *normative* essence for an ideal communication community.[338]

The four guidelines as summarized here constitute a basis, a normative foundation, as illustrated by the four blocks in Figure 20:

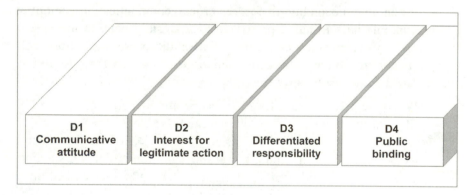

| D1 Communicative attitude | D2 Interest for legitimate action | D3 Differentiated responsibility | D4 Public binding |

Figure 20. The four guidelines of discourse ethics

---

[335] Ulrich P. 2001a: 91 (translation Renz).

[336] Ulrich P. 2001a: 91 (translation Renz).

[337] See Waxenberger 2001, 2003.

[338] See Ulrich P. 2001a: 92, 97ff, in particular 101: "Ethics provides critical-normative *orientation* knowledge and not 'implementable' *dispositional* knowledge – it is not a social technique for a good cause."

After this purposely very brief summary of discourse ethics, the next chapter critically discusses discourse ethics, in particular analyzing its validity for the context of development countries and the efforts of international development organizations.

4.3.4.2 Discussion of discourse ethics – introduction of recognition ethics

The normative foundation of discourse ethics as understood from the above four guidelines does fulfill the meta-ethical standards outlined earlier: Discourse provides the capability for differentiating between strategic and normative action orientation, and it considers the teleological bearableness and deontological justifiability, and its (ultimate) foundation is independent of religious values. But how universally applicable is it given social dependencies and cultural differences usually obtaining in the development context?

The above four guidelines are readily understandable in the context of a "modern democratic society of free and equal citizens."[339] The critical question, remains, however: To what extent can they be practiced in the context of a less developed country, where enormous social differences may exist, where caste systems – though legally abolished – still influence thinking, and where law and order are not enforced by government institutions but reinforce the force of the more powerful?[340]

Can we, in such an environment, assume, for instance, a 'communicative attitude' (D1) from everybody towards everybody?

It would be wrong to conclude that the ethical assumptions underlying discourse ethics are wrong. In fact, Habermas' four general conditions of argumentation (inclusiveness of all concerned, equal opportunity for contributions, honesty in what is expressed, and the absence of internal or external forces)[341] do not constitute factual premises, but provide regulatory ideas from a universally valid moral core.[342] But how do people living with different standards of autonomy, moral consciousness, or communication capabilities *act in a moral way* without themselves *arguing* about the normative basis of their actions and, hence, without being engaged in the kind of discourse as described by discourse ethics? What is needed is a complement to discourse ethical foundations in order to account for and

---

[339] Ulrich P. 2001a: 286 (translation Renz).

[340] See also Maak 1999: 146.

[341] Habermas 1996: 62 (translation Renz).

[342] See Benhabib 1995: 40

deal with possibly different development levels of autonomy and communication capabilities.

A solution for this complementary enhancement can be reached if one draws upon the concepts of *recognition ethics*, as developed first by Honneth[343] and later by Maak.[344] These are based on the fact that "we as human beings depend upon mutual recognition: We want our loved ones to love us, our friends and colleagues to recognize us for what we are and what we do, our employer to honor our achievements and our governments and fellow citizens to respect us and our rights as free and equal citizens."[345] Three terms of mutual recognition are distinguished: (R1) Emotional recognition, (R2) legal and political recognition, and (R3) solidarity:[346]

(R1) *Emotional recognition* is the most basic term. It takes place among colleagues, between partners, within a family etc. A non-observation of such recognition represents "moral injuries,"[347] causing "emotional damage through verbal, psychological and/or physical assault. [...] The absence of emotional recognition can hinder a person from developing self-esteem and ultimately from creating healthy and sustainable relationships with people."[348] In the organizational context, lack of emotional recognition prevents a person from performing well, not to mention from developing her or his potential to the fullest.

(R2) Positive emotional affirmation is the basis that human beings need to develop themselves as mutually recognized, free, and equal beings. This is the level of *legal and political recognition*. It is represented by "a set of basic rights as human beings and citizens."[349] Although their implementa-

---

[343] 1997. See also Honneth 2000, 2003.

[344] 1999.

[345] Pless & Maak: 2004: 131.

[346] The roots of the term 'solidarity' stem from the Latin phrase 'obligatio in solidum', meaning a reciprocal financial liability of the individual towards the community and vice versa. The term 'solidarity' is widely used in ways that lie beyond the scope of this paper (see, for instance, Bayertz 1998: 11). Rather, this paper draws on the usage of solidarity from recognition ethics as described by Honneth and Maak.

[347] Maak 1999. For a detailed description of the term, see Maak 1999: 78ff.

[348] Pless & Maak 2004: 131.

[349] Maak 1999: 99 (translation Renz).

tion varies, the Universal(!) Declaration of Human Rights by the United Nations[350] in 1948 proves to be – in principle – of universal validity.

(R3) Finally, the 'recognition of the other as a social person' is the social recognition of the individual person. Through *solidarity* the individual is recognized as a person "whose capabilities are of constitutive value for a concrete community."[351] Practiced solidarity could be described as "a face-to-face recognition among equal but different people providing affirmation and motivation."[352]

The concept of recognition ethics provides an "excellent platform for a simultaneously universal but nevertheless sufficiently particular moral point of view."[353] Recognition ethics is culture- or development-independent insofar as the *need* for recognition *does* exist independently of how far the "battles for recognition [are already] fought in a certain society at a certain time"[354] – battles, for instance, for rights and democracy. In a word, recognition is universal as it is part of the human condition. With this, the concepts of recognition ethics can be instrumental in *understanding and and explicating* certain cultural particularities: For instance, in cultures where 'saving face' is crucial, social, and emotional forms of recognition are often of fundamental importance for human dignity, to the point where legal and political recognition may be ignored (see blood revenge).

The following example illustrates an issue from the case study of legal and political recognition (R2):

---

[350] See UNO 1948.

[351] Honneth 1997: 37 (translation Renz).

[352] Pless & Maak 2004: 132.

[353] Pless & Maak 2004: 131. As an aside, Pless & Maak refer to recognition ethics in the context of "building an inclusive diversity culture." They argue that 'diversity culture,' which is currently playing a prominent role in management theory and practice, can only be successful if "built on solid moral grounds." Current practices of 'assimilation' or the focus on strategic diversity policies and processes have led many organizations to be "disappointed in their efforts" to build a diversity culture. International development projects face (not by choice, but by nature) the same challenges of diversity cultures, and hence the inclusion of recognition ethics into the context of this text seems to make a lot of sense.

[354] Pless & Maak 2004: 131.

Recognition ethics in development environments[355]

One day I was asked why our drivers had longer working hours than the other staff. I wasn't aware of it, but asked the administration officer to investigate the issue. It was true, their contracts stated longer working hours without substantiating the difference or adding an additional salary component. Immediately we arranged to have their working hours reduced to the common level. It was notable how the drivers felt more recognized after this (as politically equal beings) and how their identification with the project (the trust granted in return) was strengthened.

4.3.4.3 Summary – a combined approach: Recognition ethics and discourse ethical guidelines

The previous chapter suggests supplementing the discourse ethical understanding with the three elements of recognition – emotional recognition, legal and political recognition, and solidarity. With this, recognition ethics supports discourse ethics in contexts where argumentative reciprocity is precluded by social dependencies or cultural differences, and where argumentative reciprocity cannot be achieved for the time being. Hence, discourse ethics, with its universally valid moral core, attains *universal applicability* – through the above recognition-ethical supplements. This enriched understanding constitutes a combined approach to the moral point of view. Figure 21 summarizes this combined approach.

This combined approach constitutes a normative foundation of universal validity, with an ultimate foundation independent of particular cultural or religious values, and applicability particularly well-suited to the context of development.

Going back to the relevance of integrity for development projects, and the need for a better grounded understanding of integrity, the logical questions are: What does this combined approach now signify for the integrity of a development project, and for the management of such projects? The next chapter will elaborate on the concrete implications of these questions.

---

[355] SDC, the Swiss Agency for Development and cooperation, refers in a simplified version to "mutual recognition as the foundation of the value orientation" (w/o year: 16).

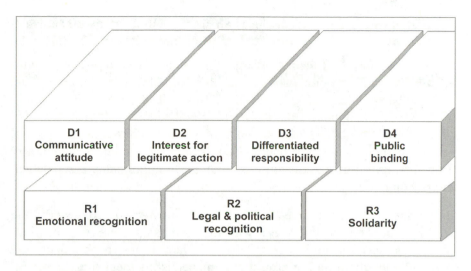

Figure 21. The combined approach – recognition ethics and discourse ethics

4.3.4.4 Implications of the combined approach – a definition of integrity in development projects

A project of integrity is not only built on personal integrity of individuals. It is also true – following Paine – that through "organizational strategies, structures and systems"[356] such 'organizational integrity' is supported.

From this, we can establish that the integrity of a development project arises if its strategy, its structure, and its organizational culture resort for normative grounding to the combined approach of discourse and recognition ethics outlined here. In other words (and referring to the terminology and elements introduced under mission management, see Chapter 4.2), a development project is also a project of integrity if its *strategy*, mainly its mission, business principles, and involvement of stakeholders, resort to the combined approach for normative grounding; if its *structure*, i.e. its contracts, its management- and team-structure and the responsibilities, normatively resort to the combined approach; and if its *(organizational) culture* fosters recognition and discourse-oriented problem resolution. Finally, such a development project is a project of integrity if the organizational elements elaborated in this way (structure, strategy, culture) underlie a controlling process and shortcomings are corrected.

---

[356] Paine 1997: 336.

Integrity of development projects

A development project is a project of integrity if its strategy, its structure, and its organizational culture resort to the combined approach of recognition and discourse ethics for normative grounding, and if the elements established in that way are subject to a continuous process of controlling and improvement.

This implies a number of consequences and requirements for practical implementation:

1. Being of a normative nature, this is a *leadership task*, where the primary responsibility lies with the leadership of development actors, such as the leaders of donor organizations, government, and NGOs. The forum of project governance is the ideal vehicle to safeguard the integrity of the specific development effort.

2. The existence of a *process model* concretizing the normative foundation from the combined approach towards those (normatively relevant) organizational elements seems necessary to facilitate this leadership task, while also contributing to bridging the gap between ethical theories and daily practice.

3. 'Good' integrity has both a constitutional and a situational aspect. The constitutional aspect refers, for instance, to how a strategy is set up in the first place, and what normative elements need to be considered for an integrity-filled strategy. The situational aspect refers to the need for handling daily issues of normative relevance, or integrity challenges. The combination of both accommodates the fact that in practice not everything is set up perfectly from the beginning. A strategy may need to be fine-tuned to incorporate lessons learned from situational challenges, allowing for continuous improvement.[357] The above process model needs to consider both aspects integratively, the constitutional and the situational aspect.

4. Other key responsibilities of project governance may also comprise elements of normative relevance (which is the reason why they may face integrity challenges). They need to be 'integratively' included.

---

[357] In the terminology of knowledge management, the process model needs to foster single-loop learning, i.e. resolving the situational challenge at hand, as well as double-loop learning, i.e. reviewing the underlying constitutional strategies, structure, and organizational culture (see Argyris & Schön 1978).

With this discussion, the relevance of a normative foundation for development projects has been clarified, and implications for its practical implementation have been derived.

That the implementation of such integrity management is of utmost importance for a development project can be substantiated from the fundamental understanding of development cooperation: In the implementation of a development project, the sense of such integrity management is also to teach and develop an understanding of what the implications of certain principles may be for others. Although such a *way* for how a development project is implemented is in fact not *the* objective of development, it is at least *one implicit* objective of development *cooperation*. Or in other words: For true development *cooperation,* the way is part of the objective! Integrity management offers such a way, additionally bridging the gap between ethical theory and practical reality.

The next chapter looks at the concrete implementations of these findings.

4.3.5   Implementing integrity management

4.3.5.1   Organizational elements and related integrity challenges – tension zones

As seen above, the striving for integrity in a development project means shaping the organizational elements by resorting to the normative foundation of the combined approach (built on discourse and recognition ethics). Exactly which of these organizational elements are of normative relevance, and what are the possible integrity challenges they may face, *challenging the integrity of the project*?

The research for this case study has identified 130 cases of normative ethical relevance out of a total of nearly 400. Through the analysis and categorization of these cases, integrity challenges and corresponding organizational elements have been identified. They are shown in Table 5, which lists on the left the organizational elements of normative relevance, grouped along the three structuring forces of strategy, structures and (organizational) culture, and correspondingly the integrity-wise conflicting challenges on the right.[358] These conflicts are typically experienced as

---

[358] While the table does not claim completeness, it should be noted that it is exactly through the qualitative depth of the participant observation that such an extensive list could be derived. The consistency of the table has also been crosschecked with the other organizational elements discussed throughout this book, mainly stemming from the chapters on mission management (4.2) and extended stakeholder management (4.4).

Table 5. Integrity challenges in strategy, structures and organizational culture

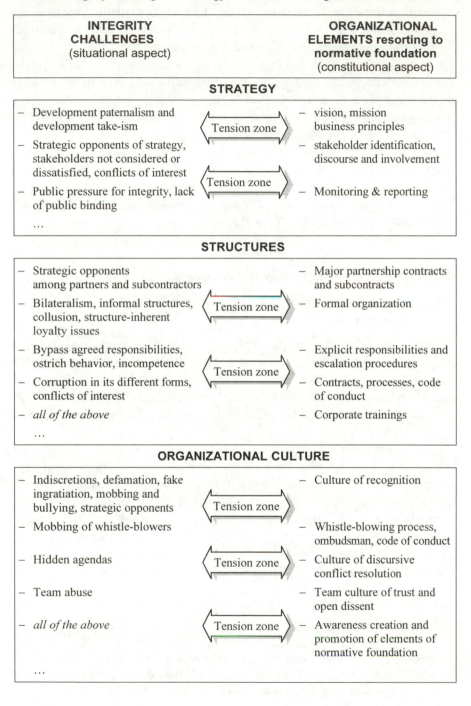

INTEGRITY CHALLENGES (situational aspect)		ORGANIZATIONAL ELEMENTS resorting to normative foundation (constitutional aspect)

STRATEGY

- Development paternalism and development take-ism
- Strategic opponents of strategy, stakeholders not considered or dissatisfied, conflicts of interest
- Public pressure for integrity, lack of public binding
...

Tension zone

- vision, mission business principles
- stakeholder identification, discourse and involvement

Tension zone

- Monitoring & reporting

STRUCTURES

- Strategic opponents among partners and subcontractors
- Bilateralism, informal structures, collusion, structure-inherent loyalty issues
- Bypass agreed responsibilities, ostrich behavior, incompetence
- Corruption in its different forms, conflicts of interest
- *all of the above*
...

Tension zone

- Major partnership contracts and subcontracts
- Formal organization
- Explicit responsibilities and escalation procedures
- Contracts, processes, code of conduct
- Corporate trainings

ORGANIZATIONAL CULTURE

- Indiscretions, defamation, fake ingratiation, mobbing and bullying, strategic opponents
- Mobbing of whistle-blowers
- Hidden agendas
- Team abuse
- *all of the above*
...

Tension zone

- Culture of recognition
- Whistle-blowing process, ombudsman, code of conduct
- Culture of discursive conflict resolution
- Team culture of trust and open dissent
- Awareness creation and promotion of elements of normative foundation

ethical dilemmas or *tension zones* as illustrated in the table. Integrity requires that the organization "deal with such conflicts and overcome the tensions inherent in them."[359]

The majority of the organizational elements (the column on the right) are known from mission management (Chapter 4.2), or will be discussed under extended stakeholder management (Chapter 4.4).

From this discussion so far, two questions arise: What exactly are these tension zones and what is the relevant integrity aspect in them, and how should a project react when facing such tension zones?

To address these questions, the next chapter introduces a generic process model, initially answering the second question about how a project should react when facing such tension zones and related challenges. The explanation of the various tension zones will be set forth in Chapter 4.3.5, illustrated with numerous concrete case examples, by way of identifying the *integrity specific* aspect of the challenge and – resorting to the generic process model – also identifying possible ways of overcoming the resulting tensions.

4.3.5.2 Generic process model for integrity management

A generic process model helps to resolve concrete (situational) integrity issues at hand while simultaneously considering and improving constitutional organizational elements. It supports the development project, its management and governance, in a process of *bridging the often found disparities* between 'theory and practice.' Through a conscious and discursive confrontation with and within the tension zones, the process aims at *converging* general rules and obligations with solutions for imminent singular challenges (where such rules could not yet be directly applied). It is this process which furthers 'moral self-governance,' leading to 'wholeness,' i.e. integrity within a development project.

The process model comprises five steps, built on the normative foundation of the combined approach of recognition ethics and discourse ethics, as outlined in Figure 22. The different elements of the model are explained hereafter.[360]

---

[359] Paine 1997: 336.

[360] The model draws upon, and incorporates, several elements of Waxenberger's organizational model for principle based management (see 2001, 2003).

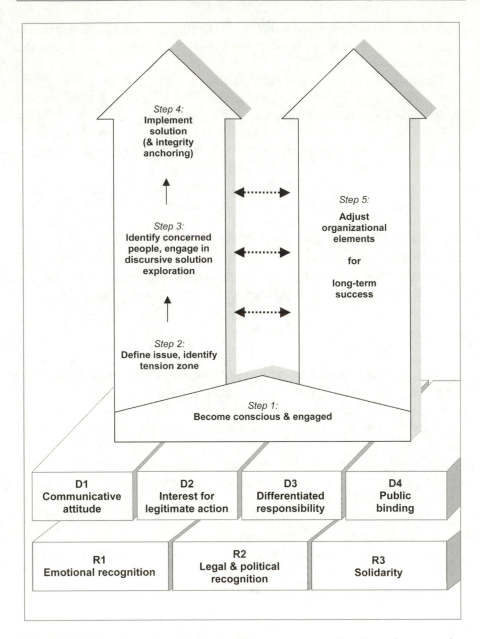

Figure 22. The process model for integrity management based on the normative foundation of the combined approach

Though the steps are displayed and described in a consecutive way, it is clear that some of them may be repeated in an iterative approach.

Step 1: *Become conscious and engaged.* Often issues arise in a blurred way – sometimes they are not recognized as such at early stages, and sometimes an integrity challenge is the hidden, but *real* root cause behind some apparently mundane problem. This first step is an expression of 'good will' and one's *own* interest for legitimate actions (D2) marking "the crucial difference between ethical and only strategic action."[361] From a leadership perspective, this is the key point requiring constant top management commitment, without which integrity is left to chance. For the governance board a proactive approach would be to go through a generic list of possible integrity challenges during each board meeting, asking whether and where there might be a possible integrity issue or tension zone.

Step 2: *Define the issue and identify the tension zone.* This step supplies a first definition of the problem at hand. What is it, and what is the tension constituted of? What is the existing, incomplete, or missing organizational element standing in tension with the current issue? How exactly does the issue at hand pose an integrity threat to the project? This step should also identify whether the issue is a threat to the integrity of the project, the donors, the development country, or anybody else.

Step 3: *Identify the people concerned and engage in discursive solution exploration.* The identification of the persons or groups concerned, and an assessment of the *preconditions for reciprocal* communication with them, serve as preparation for the discourse. In case of doubt about the reciprocal communication conditions, the existence of recognition on any of the required levels should be assessed. Potentially at this point, higher-level management may also need to be involved.

The discourse with those concerned can be conducted according to the described concept of differentiated responsibility (D3). The discursive solution exploration represents a debate within the tension zone between existing organizational elements (the strategy, structures, or organizational culture) and the concrete case at hand. Precisely because some of these organizational elements may not exist or may lack important details, ambiguous, or conflicting interpretation is possible. For some of these organizational elements, it makes sense that they be enhanced or adapted (see Step 5).

---

[361] Waxenberger 2003: 237.

Step 4: *Implement a solution*, with particular emphasis on an *integrity-* focused anchoring. Integrity focus means appropriate communication and public binding (i.e. the simultaneous engagement in political responsibility) as well as appropriate formal or informal training.

Step 5: *Adjust organizational elements for long-term perspective of integrity*. The issue at hand possibly reveals a weakness in some of the organizational elements, for instance the business principles may be incomplete. This is where integrity management links back to the elements of other key responsibilities, mainly mission management and extended stakeholder management. Step 5 assures that lessons learned from specific issues are captured, and that the respective organizational elements are updated and revisited periodically, or are created in the first place if they have been absent.

We are now ready to look at the specific integrity challenges and tension zones in detail.

4.3.6   The tension zones in detail

Thus far, a normative foundation – the combined approach of discourse and recognition ethics – has been presented. An overview of integrity challenges within specific tension zones has been given and a generic process model helping the project to resolve concrete challenges was developed. Now we will look at the integrity challenges and tension zones in detail. Each tension zone will be analyzed with a view to answering the following questions:

- What is it, and what is meant by the specific challenge?

- Why is it a challenge to the integrity of the project, where does the conflicting tension zone lie, and what is its effect on the project? This line of questioning draws on the combined normative approach.

- What to do about it, and what are the steps and ideas facilitating the resolution of such challenges? This draws on the process model.

Numerous case examples are introduced for illustration.[362]

---

[362] As mentioned earlier, the best illustrational learning effect is gained through examples in which something went wrong; the objective is not to show how few errors were committed.

For pedagogical reasons, the order of the subsequent chapters has been adjusted in a way that initially allows for a discussion of integrity challenges with respect to structure, followed by those challenges associated with culture and finally strategy. This adjusted order is also an acknowledgment that integrity issues on the strategy level are influenced by the project only to a limited degree, as several of them are linked with the overall development policy of a country or a donor, i.e. not only resulting from the project's own strategy. Nevertheless, for the sake of completeness some of those issues (like development paternalism) are briefly discussed here, too.

A final remark: At times in this text, the elements of the combined normative approach are referred to, for instance with (D1), referring to the 1st discourse ethical guideline as illustrated earlier in this chapter.

4.3.6.1 Integrity challenges on the level of structure

Strategic opponents among partners and subcontractors vs. major partnership contracts and subcontracts

The development project may face strategic opponents within its closest allies, i.e. the partners or subcontractors, who jeopardize a 'good' evolution of the partnership or subcontract-relationship as intended in the formal contracts.

How can the concept of a strategic opponent be understood? Earlier a strategic opponent has been defined as an actor "lack[ing] the motivation to seek agreement."[363] They usually differ from a notorious complainer in that the latter raises complaints loudly and is easily identified. A strategic opponent may be hard to recognize – for who would expect one among one's closest allies? Sometimes only a series of indications may supply the evidence, as illustrated in the next example:

Do I have a strategic opponent?

Something was wrong within the leadership team of the project. I had tried numerous things, from team building to responsibility clarification, but it was as if we were not all pulling in the same direction. Could it be that there was an issue with my deputy, Narad?

---

[363] See 3rd guideline of the normative foundation, Chapter 4.3.4.1, or Ulrich P. 2001a: 88.

Why wasn't he here to help in recent law and order issues, as a responsible deputy? Why his resistance to engage a monitoring and evaluation officer? Why did he hardly disclose his network? Why did he initiate discussions on internal reorganization during my absence? What if the rumor was true that he was bad-mouthing me in the international community?

What if there were a conscious and consistent strategy behind all that? Was my own deputy such a strategic opponent? When I started thinking along those lines, I could suddenly spot around 30 examples like those above. Now it was clear – even if only half of the details were true, my deputy was a strategic opponent!

Why are strategic opponents among partners and subcontractors a challenge or a threat to the integrity of the project? A strategic opponent is then problematic if he lacks the 'argumentational integrity' (D1) to raise concerns. Instead, such a strategic opponent pursues his strategy within the partnership without clarifying whether his strategy is within the expectations arising from the structural element of the partnership contract. His strategic success is more important than its legitimacy (note the saying 'he or she goes over dead bodies'). A partnership contract maybe incomplete or ambiguous, but the lack of an 'interest in legitimate action' (D2) prevents the strategic opponent from surfacing to engage in a process of discursive solution exploration. From this, it becomes clear that a strategic opponent does not constitute a strategic challenge – which could be resolved in case there were existing argumentational integrity through 'let's agree that we disagree' – but instead constitutes an ethical challenge to the integrity of the organizational structures.

How can a conflict arising from strategic opponent be resolved? Let us put ourselves in the context of a concrete example:

Discrediting the LRC (linear responsibility chart)

Setting up the responsibilities and competencies in a new team is always a sensitive subject: In a major effort – numerous offsite and 1-to-1 discussions – the needs and claims of the management members had been aligned and outlined in the so-called LRC. We also were in agreement that the key element had been the process for arriving at the conclusion, having itself clarified a lot of fears and doubts.

Why was Narad, then, a couple of months later, addressing the whole management team and discrediting the LRC in a by-sentence as 'unusable'? When asked for clarification he was evasive, murmuring something about 'rigid' and 'no real system'.

It was shocking: Why in the first place did Narad, after all this processing, generally discredit the jointly elaborated LRC? He could instead have raised the need for modifications, particularly in his deputy responsibility!

This example not only illustrates the violation of the LRC finding process. It also indicates that possibilities for resolving the issue of a strategic opponent are limited: It lies exactly in the nature of a strategic opponent that he does not allow binding measures for cooperation to be enforced – independently of whether they were derived in a discursive way or not. In such a case, the only solution is to issue a reprimand, and if that does not help to eliminate the strategic opponent from the partnership or subcontract.

Bilateralism, informal structures, collusion, structure-inherent loyalty issues vs. formal organization

The next few integrity challenges – bilateralism, informal structures, collusion and structure-inherent loyalty issues – have in common that they bypass the formal organization. As always, let us first try to explain what is meant in depth by these expressions, then identify the integrity challenge inherent in them, and finally look for possible ways of resolution.

Bilateralism, informal structures

This book refers to *bilateralism* as the existence of bilateral relations in *substantial disproportion* to an existing formal organizational structure. Bilateral relations are often at the root of an informal organization. Figure 7 in Chapter 1.3.3.3 illustrates the informal organization and underlying bilateral relations.

Informal lines outside formal organization

Figure 7 illustrates a chaotic picture of bilateral relations prevalent in DRIVER. One donor representative, for instance, regularly maintained up to eleven bilateral relations outside the established lines of authority or information exchange.

When do bilateral relations or informal structures constitute an integrity challenge to a project? They challenge the integrity of the project where a formal organization exists but where there is no effort to integrate or bring the bilateral relations or informal structures in line with the formal organization. In other words, there is a formal organization in force, but business follows to a considerable amount a different informal structure, and there is *no recognizable will* to resolve the disparity between formal and informal structures. This absence of will corresponds to an absent interest in legitimizing actions (D2) in the way of a discursive solution exploration (D1) to align the differences in organizational structures. The effect is that such relations undermine, and weaken, the established organization in the first place but also the credibility of formal agreements in principle.

How can integrity issues of bilateralism or informal structures be resolved? The process model serves as a comprehensive guide here and can be followed easily. Bilateralism and informal structures can be identified relatively easily if one has become conscious and engaged (Step 1). Defining the issue and identifying the organizational element with which the issue stands in conflict, thereby creating a tension zone, will lead to an organizational chart and a possible visualization as illustrated in Figure 7 (Step 2). Following are the discursive solution exploration with the involved actors (Step 3), and the solution implementation (Step 4), which in this case probably also means undertaking something with respect to the formal organization (Step 5). Another step may also be to undertake reinforcing measures for a culture of open dissent, encouraging the organizational members to propose organizational adjustments themselves. The governance board has a directing and controlling role, but it also needs to be directly engaged in discovering and removing bilateralisms which involve the governance board itself.

Collusion

A worse sort of integrity challenge to a project and its formal organization arises when such bilateral relations or informal structures are kept *intentionally secret*. This can be called a form of *collusion*.[364] Following the definition by the *Concise Oxford English Dictionary* 2004, of collusion being a "secret or illegal cooperation in order to cheat or deceive others," this book defines collusion in the organizational context more generally as

---

[364] Collusion comes from the Latin words 'col-' (=together) + 'ludere' (=to play). In business, price arrangements, often at the cost of the consumer, are also a form of collusion, and as such are prohibited by the laws of market economies.

a *secret and illegitimate cooperation of organizational actors*. Let us look at a case example of collusion:

> ## Collusion between a donor and a subordinate
>
> Who was calling me on this holy Friday morning?[365] Brian, one of the donors called to say that it had come to his ears that I was upset about his suggested meeting agenda.
>
> True, the day before I had shared my surprise with my division managers about Brian's proposed agenda for the upcoming donor meeting: In my eyes it was excessively detailed and unrealistic. They agreed with my perspective, they even sympathized with my anger, pointing out that Brian was known for his micro-management.
>
> How come Brian had learned about it, how come our internal exchange had leaked-out? Who had told him about our reaction – seemingly about my reaction only – before we could get back to Brian with an official answer? This was a small but obvious indication of what later became clear: There was collusion between Brian and one of my subordinates which bypassed the official lines of authority.

Just as with strategic opponents, collusion may be difficult to prove. For instance, the case example points to the fact that possible collusion may exist.

Why is collusion illegitimate, or why does it constitute a challenge to the integrity of the project? In addition to the forsaking of any interest in legitimate actions (D2), the problem of collusion lies in its *secrecy,* in the way that the involved parties display a well-thought-out intention to sabotage a communication-oriented attitude (D1). The actors intentionally accept that their behavior may be of an undermining nature. The effects on the organizational structure are that such collusive action may undermine and weaken the established organization in the first place, and also that the credibility of formal agreements in principle is diminished.

How can the above issues be resolved? Collusion is difficult to identify; confronted with it, one learns that the step of becoming conscious is particularly important (Step 1). This may last for weeks or months. For the resolution of collusion, the governance board may need to be involved directly (Steps 2 and 3).

---

[365] Friday is the day of prayer and rest in a Muslim country like Bangladesh. Working days are usually Sunday to Thursday.

Structure-inherent loyalty issues

A final integrity challenge in the tension zone for the formal organization arises from *structure-inherent loyalty issues*. In this case, an organizational member is assigned to a position where his or her loyalty may differ from the structural authority, causing a specific case of a conflict of interest.[366] A brief example illustrates such a loyalty issue:

A solution or a Trojan horse?

Jefferson might solve our problems! At one point one of our divisions needed content-wise backing. Kenneth, one of our donor representatives, strongly suggested that we bring in Jefferson, a young and smart colleague of his, currently based at his European head office. In fact, Jefferson was looking for a field assignment. Kenneth suggested having him assigned 80% on our project and 20% working with him.

Project-internally we were concerned that this arrangement would create a loyalty issue. In case of conflicts, we would have to assume that Jefferson would be loyal to Kenneth and not to the project.

Why is this arrangement a challenge to the integrity of the project? Such a loyalty issue may prevent the affected person from seeking a solution in the best interest of the organization, because his interest in legitimate action (D2) and with this his liberty of action may be compromised by his loyalty to another organization, and therefore by diverging interests. The effect of this situation is that he may only make second-best decisions from the perspective of the project. It is also important to understand the difference between slavish obedience and loyalty as outlined here: Within the normative foundation outlined in this book loyalty is understood as "follow[ing] the rules – or, at least, to challenge them openly and fairly,"[367] displaying argumentational integrity (D1) and interest for legitimate action (D2). It is this open and fair challenge which may be compromised by structure-inherent loyalty issues.

How can the above issues be resolved? If one is conscious of this possibility of integrity challenge (Step 1), structure-inherent loyalty issues normally can be identified easily (Step 2), because per code of conduct (see

---

[366] See Page 145 below on conflicts of interest.

[367] Paine 1997: 335.

below) conflicts of interests need to be disclosed and discussed. Structure-
inherent loyalty issues are one specific type of conflict of interest. They
can be resolved through a change in assignment, or they may also be tolerated if the related assumed risk is low. But there are also cases which cannot be resolved, as illustrated by the below example:

A solution or a Trojan horse? – Part II

We wondered how the possible loyalty conflict could be brought up and
resolved: By bringing it to the attention of the donor consortium? Mack,
my boss in Switzerland, avoided getting involved, though he saw the
problem.

When the other donor colleagues were not informed in a timely way
of his plan, it became obvious that Kenneth was well aware of the loyalty issue: He had an apparent intention of using it in his favor. How to
react? From the project side, we were lacking a forum and an agenda
point to bring this to the attention of the donor consortium. Fortunately,
it was Kenneth's own boss who stopped it – apparently, he was himself
sensitized to Kenneth's personnel politics.

A well-functioning project governance could have helped to put this
possible issue onto the table – if not by my boss, then other donor representatives would probably have intervened.

The example illustrates several things: First, there may be no solution for a
structure-inherent loyalty issue other than to dissolve that piece of the structure; second, in such sensitive cases, a well-functioning project governance,
having integrity management on the agenda and being sensitized to the integrity challenges of such issues, brings them automatically to the table for a
discourse-oriented solution exploration. As mentioned earlier, this would
happen for instance if the governance board would cross-check at each board
meeting for possible integrity challenges (Step 1, to become conscious)
based on a list such as the above list of integrity challenges and tension zones.

Bypass agreed responsibilities, ostrich behavior, incompetence
vs. explicit responsibilities, escalation procedures

Bypassing agreed responsibilities and related 'ostrich-like' behavior (i.e.
hiding or avoiding the assumption of agreed responsibilities) constitute
not only a breach of agreement but also an integrity problem. This can
happen on all levels, within the project, within the governance board

(bypassing its self organization), and in collaboration with partners. Let us look at a simple example:

Issues requiring management attention

Ashique was one of our most capable local professionals, smart, fast, thinking beyond his barriers, always willing to help.

In two separate instances Ashique had brought a number of what he deemed important concerns to the attention of Dennis his direct manager: Not only was he worried about delays in the results of a partner, but he also had questions whether this partner would be the right choice in the long term.

Dennis had received both reports – both marked confidential and urgent as deemed by Ashique. Dennis however did not react; it seemed as if he had not recognized the expression of seriousness in Ashique's act of drawing his attention to certain points.

After going without response for a while, Ashique went to ask his boss whether he had received the reports and what he thought about them; casually Dennis acknowledged the receipt of the reports, but seemed however to avoid the discussion; Ashique had always to get back to his points.

The example shows a case where a manager (Dennis) avoids assuming leadership responsibility towards his subordinate (to *respond*!) – independently of whether he was in agreement with the concerns raised or not, which would be perfectly legitimate. Where is the integrity challenge of the project?

The key lies in a tension between the words *bypassing* and *agreed*: The fact that responsibilities were *agreed* means that some type of discourse has taken place which had arrived communicatively at a rational consensus (D1). This can be an explicit discourse, or an implicit discourse, for instance, through accepting a position of leadership implying certain managerial responsibilities.

Furthermore, the act of *bypassing* or avoiding a previously agreed responsibility can be intentional or negligent behavior. Such intentional behavior, however, expresses a lack of will (D2) to correct such an agreement (if it were wrong, not practical, ambiguous etc.) or to address the point (D1) with whomever might be the counterpart of the agreement, or, if both are not possible, to assume the political responsibility for resolving the tension with a long-term perspective (D3).

Negligent behavior may happen, but if it happens repeatedly this may be an indication that the person is not in a position to respond, or to assume the consciously agreed responsibility, and is therefore incompetent. From an organizational perspective, such incompetence poses an integrity threat if it is not tackled and resolved.

How to resolve such issues? Let us look again at how Dennis in the example could have reacted:

> **Issues requiring management attention – Part II**
>
> Dennis theoretically had two ways of legitimate action. The first was by engaging in a discourse with Ashique (i.e. not ignoring his managerial responsibility), which does not necessarily mean to agree, but to acknowledge and discuss the concerns brought forward. Dennis' second option would have been to challenge the agreement, i.e. to come to see me (as his manager) and lay out why he did not want (D2) to respond to Ashique's reports or to manage Ashique in the first place. In the concrete case example Dennis did not pursue either of these ways.

The example also gives rise to the question of what happens if such responsibility is not assumed long-term? And that is where the most important integrity issue for the project lies: The responsibility structure becomes porous, energies are lost, inefficiencies arise. From an organizational perspective, there is therefore a need to intercept such bypassing of responsibilities. Some ways of doing this are to establish escalation procedures ('a red telephone') as well as an institutional forum such as project governance for the issues on a managerial level. From a discourse ethical perspective, the person escalating such an issue assumes a 'differentiated responsibility' with the goal of achieving a long-term solution (D3); project governance represents a forum for the discursive communication of such issues (D4).

Corruption in its different forms, conflicts of interest vs. contracts, processes, code of conduct

Conflicts of interest and corruption, a particular form of a conflict of interest, constitute a serious integrity challenge to a project. The seriousness arises because the project's integrity is challenged on several levels, as we will see below. As usual the terms are clarified, then different forms of corruption are shown. Later the normative content will be analyzed, discussing why and where conflicts of interest or corruption constitute a challenge to the project's integrity. Finally, examples will illustrate these issues.

Conflicts of interest in the organizational context usually refer to situations in which organizational interests conflict with the personal interests of employees or managers of an organization. They pose an integrity issue – for reasons which will be elaborated below – if that conflict remains *unresolved*, that is to say, if it is not brought to the attention of the employer or an (empowered) superior for resolution. The general usage of the term usually refers to *unresolved* conflicts of interest. From the normative foundation of this book, we would expect an employee to act on the honest intent to *communicate* such conflict (argumentational integrity) and to be genuinely interested in *legitimating* his action.[368] Often these expectations are also laid out in a code of conduct.

Corruption is a special and prominent instance of conflicts of interest.[369] Transparency International (TI) defines corruption "as the misuse of entrusted power for private gain." Leisinger differentiates the notion further by identifying four criteria: "misuse of an existing power-position, gain of an advantage of those which commit (in the active as passive sense) such action, undesirable effects (externalities) on third parties, secrecy of the transaction."[370] Here is a simple example from the case study:

Paying for your electricity consumption

In Bangladesh, people having a regular electricity connection are usually visited by an official in charge of reading their consumption from the electricity meter, as in many other countries.

It is apparently not uncommon, however, that in this transaction of reading the meter, the official asks for money, and not just to manipulate the meter in one's favor: In fact one has to pay him money so that he reads the meter correctly!

This may explain some of the high double-digit 'system losses' of the electricity providers.

---

[368] In some companies, this uncovering of possible conflicts of interest is an institutionalized process. Procter & Gamble, for instance, requires each employee yearly to sign a declaration that there are no conflicting personal and business interests, or if so to state them and certify that they were cleared with the superior.

[369] See www.transparency.org. On the ethical problem of corruption, see also Ulrich H. 2001: 322f, Leisinger 1997: 62 – 83, Stückelberger 2001, Eigen 2003.

[370] Leisinger 1997: 96 (translation Renz).

Corruption manifests itself in a variety of forms:

1.   "Active corruption or bribery (giving)
2.   Passive corruption (receiving), including extortion
3.   Misappropriation and fraud"[371]

The list of possible forms of corruption can be endless, as seen in Figure 23, from a TI publication of 2000:[372]

The most commonly recognized forms of corruption are:
- Treason; subversion; illegal foreign transactions; smuggling
- Kleptocracy; privatization of public funds; larceny and stealing
- Misappropriation; forgery and embezzlement; padding of accounts; skimming; misuse of funds
- Abuse of power; intimidation; torture; undeserved pardons and remissions
- Deceit and fraud; misrepresentation; cheating and swindling; blackmail
- Perversion of justice; criminal behavior; false evidence; unlawful detention; frame-ups
- Non-performance of duties; desertion; parasitism
- Bribery and graft; extortion; illegal levies; kickbacks
- Election tampering; vote-rigging; gerrymandering
- Misuse of inside knowledge and confidential information; falsification of records
- Unauthorized sale of public offices, public property, and public licenses
- Manipulation of regulations, purchases and supplies, contracts, and loans
- Tax evasion, excessive profiteering
- Influence peddling; favor brokering; conflicts of interest
- Acceptance of improper gifts, fees, speed money, and entertainments, junkets
- Links with organized crime; black-market operations
- Cronyism; cover-ups
- Illegal surveillance; misuse of telecommunications and mails
- Misuse of official seals, stationery, residence, and perquisites

---

Figure 23. List of possible forms of corruption

Exactly where does the *integrity challenge* lie in unresolved conflicts of interest or in corruption? For the sake of simplicity, the following argumentation focuses on corruption, although it can be generalized to conflicts of interest. In either case, primarily resources are not being used the way they were *intended* to be used. This means corruption constitutes a violation of the expectations towards the executing *agent*, which could be an employee as agent, a project as agent, or also a donor as agent. From the organizational perspective the expectations as outlined in the work contract, in the project implementation mandate, or the donor mandate as agent of public funds are not being fulfilled. This – as a first ethical problem – constitutes a structural issue, i.e. the integrity of the agency contract

---

[371]   Arvis & Berenbeim 2003: 9.
[372]   TI 2000: xviii, adapted from Caiden 1988.

is challenged. Corruption committed by the contracted agent is a challenge to the integrity of the contract.

Now, often contracts foresee a possible risk of corruption and include an anti-corruption clause, as in this case example:

Anti-corruption clause

The work of SwissNGO in the project DRIVER was based on a project implementation mandate, a contract between SwissNGO and the donors. That contract included an anti-corruption clause where SwissNGO would "commit itself neither to offer to any third party, nor seek, accept or have promised directly or indirectly [...] any gift which would amount to an illegal or corrupt practice."

Similarly, all employees we hired for DRIVER had to sign a code of conduct as an integral part of the contract, defining corruption and the expectation towards the employee.

Usually, such contracts also specify rights of examination, external audit requirements, or references to a code of conduct. In other words, the problem of corruption is dealt with preventively, through processes such as control processes and the promotion of respective cultural elements ('how to conduct oneself'). Corruption in such a case is even more aggravating – and leads to the second normative problem: It compromises such established processes, i.e. showing a *structural incapability* of the organization to establish effective control procedures. And it finally compromises the organizational culture: The *organizational identity* as projected in a code of conduct or in business principles does not correspond to the reality. Also, corrupt employees are extortionable. From an ethical perspective, this ultimately causes a loss of trust or – building on the combined approach of our normative foundation – a de-'recognition,' possibly on all levels, including emotional de-recognition of the involved agents, legal and political de-recognition (the person or entity may be sued), and eroding solidarity.

Because of these double issues, the *seriousness* in the integrity challenge of corruption is considerable: Corruption constitutes a challenge to the integrity of the *agent contract* (individual work contract, project mandate etc.) as the expectations outlined therein are not fulfilled as intended and therefore challenge the integrity of the agent's *process capability and cultural identity*.

An integrity challenge not directly to the project, but to the whole development sector, occurs when such cases of corruption are not resolved properly and become public: The overall trust in, and public opinion of, the sector decreases; corruption undermines the "common welfare through particular interests"[373] similar to a "cancer."[374]

How to 'resolve' corruption and conflicts of interest? The above process model serves as a comprehensive guide.[375] Step 1 is of paramount importance: Become conscious and engaged. Here is an example of deficient engagement:

Support in anti-corruption expertise

What were the elements which the 'agent' SwissNGO, which specialized in implementing development projects (in complex environments), provided to their projects? DRIVER had received a code of conduct enforced by the head office in a way as described earlier (see example 'we have a code of conduct,' earlier in this chapter). Did I as a project manager receive additional training or instructions, such as what to do if asked for bribes, or whether we should pay in case of physical danger, torture etc., or how to document, report to, and account for?

Nothing unfortunately, apart from the code of conduct! Only when I asked for help or guidelines and insisted that an internal awareness-creation workshop should be set up which could be used by each project manager in the different projects, did I receive a comprehensive publication of the donor SDC.[376] This still, however, was not directly applicable for training local staff in awareness creation around issues of corruption. Must every project create its own training material?

---

[373] Ulrich P. & Maak 2000a: 28. See Michelman: "Corruption is the subversion, within the political motivation of any participant, of the general good by particular interest" (1986: 40). See also Ulrich P. 1999b: 60 and Ulrich P. 2001a.

[374] Idem.

[375] The 'Business principles for countering bribery' (an initiative of Transparency International and Social Accountability International) mention two steps: (1) "Prohibit bribery in any form" and (2) "Commit to implement a programme to counter bribery" (TI 2002). The approach here is adapted to projects in particular, and therefore it is less isolated and more holistic, as it makes corruption part of an integrated integrity management through the leadership endorsed project governance. Otherwise, it is left to the discretion of single project managers as it was the case in the project observed in the case study.

[376] SDC 1998

This example illustrates the need for institutionalized support of a project in questions of corruption, emphasizing that corruption is a topic *belonging on the agenda* of any development project and any steering body, as assured by Step 1.

In Step 2, the issue needs to be further defined, and associated with a tension zone with which the issue stands in conflict. The following example illustrates such a process of definition of the issue:

Is speed money corruption?

Jibon came to me worried that for the five external phone lines needed for our 50-staff office we might have to pay speed money (or facilitation payments speeding up official administrative processes). Otherwise we may not even get them, or at the earliest get them within 6 months.

The problem was two-fold: (a) How to get the phone lines and (b) were we willing to pay any speed money? Our code of conduct prohibited corruption, but wasn't clear about speed money. Is speed money corruption? If not, where to book it in the accounts? Probably we would not get an official receipt.

Subsequently (Step 3), a discursive solution exploration should be initiated. To what extent direct actors can be involved in discursive interaction, such as a person asking for a bribe or someone allegedly misappropriating funds, depends on the situation, as per the differentiated responsibility concept (D3). In that case, resorting to the recognition level may help one to understand and possibly resolve a corruptive issue or more generally a conflict of interest: Are people emotionally recognized (is their work appreciated), and are they legally and politically recognized (in the organizational context, for instance, by fair working conditions and fair worker's rights)?

Implementing (Step 4) and adjusting organizational elements (Step 5) obviously also depends on the type of corruption issue. Sometimes, tough actions must be taken as illustrated by the next example:

Living a zero tolerance policy

We were principally living a zero tolerance policy (as per code of conduct). While it was also clear that a development project in Bangladesh (according to the corruption perception index[377] one of the most corrupt countries) can be a white island only with difficulty, we made it understood that any indication about corruptive practice would be investigated.

In one case, we found out that one of our employees had been asking for (and receiving) kick-backs from four providers; her contract had to be terminated immediately.

A tough action, such as the one in this example (removing the 'cancer'), may be needed, helping staff to maintain integrity in the project and to live up to the requirements established by the contract as an 'agent' while helping management maintain the relevant processes.

In cases where a project is forced into corruptive practices (for instance speed money), as a part of the political responsibility (D3) and the perspective of public binding (D4), the project could keep a record as to what function and for what reason corruptive money had to be paid, and publish or distribute a summary among key stakeholders.

The extensive elaborations on conflicts of interest and corruption have shown that in particular corruption constitutes a serious challenge to organizational integrity. Project governance[378] can help assure that integrity management *is a topic dealt with* and that all involved actors and 'agents' understand and live up to the agreed expectations.

Various integrity challenges vs. corporate trainings

For the sake of completeness, it is important to mention the role of corporate training. Corporate training material may be incomplete or ambiguous with respect to ethical concerns. Integrity challenges may arise from that ambiguity. When analyzing integrity challenges, an organization should always also consider whether there is a need for new corporate training or whether an existing manual needs to be adapted to avoid a case of integrity issue in other instances.

---

[377] The corruption perception index CPI is calculated yearly by Transparency International (TI).

[378] See also Wallace & Zinkin, who emphasize the need for good corporate governance to resolve the typical conflicts of interest in the principal – agent relationship (2005: 2).

4.3.6.2 Integrity challenges on the level of organizational culture

Indiscretions, defamation, fake ingratiation, mobbing and bullying, strategic opponent vs. culture of recognition

The first tension zone discussed on the cultural level looks at indiscretions, defamation, fake ingratiation, mobbing and bullying, and strategic opponents.[379] They are in conflict – hence create a zone of tension – with an organizational culture of basic recognition. First, the different issues are defined and illustrated, and then the project specific integrity challenge is discussed.

Indiscretions, i.e. acts of being indiscreet, refer to the purposeful sharing of *confidential* or sensitive information with interested parties (in politics often the media). The following is an example of a quite audacious indiscretion:

Black carbon copy (BCC) of confidential report

A sister project of ours had just undergone a big external evaluation, apparently outlining a number of sensitive points. I was quite surprised to receive a BCC (= black carbon copy, email copy invisible to the addressee) of an email at the address of that sister project: One of our donors had black-copied me on his loaded comments on the evaluation report. The email also included an attachment with the original and confidential report.

In contrast to indiscretions, *defamation* refers to purposefully placing *wrong and untrue* information so as to calumniate somebody. Furthermore, *ingratiation*[380] refers to "bring[ing] oneself into favor with someone by flattering or trying to please them."[381] As we will see later, acts of *fake* ingratiation may constitute an integrity challenge for the project. Here is an example:

---

[379] Strategic opponents may appear on all levels, i.e. threatening the integrity of structures, culture, or strategy.

[380] From Latin 'in' (=into) + 'gratia' (=favor).

[381] Concise Oxford English Dictionary 2004.

> **'I would have loved...'**
>
> At her farewell the middle manager Chanchal said to Anawara, one of our best professionals who had resigned after a few months: "I didn't know that you would be going, I would have loved to have you in my division, but higher level order did not allow...".
>
> While we had made alternate offers to Anawara, it was only later that we understood the true reason for Anawara's resignation: Her work was systematically being hindered by Chanchal's division.

This example illustrates fake ingratiation, but moreover it indicates that such ingratiation may be only one more side of another challenge, in this example of both defamation (of Chancal's superior) and mobbing (of Anawara).

Furthermore, *mobbing and bullying* are classified by ILO, the International Labor Organization, as "violence at work,"[382] mentioned jointly with homicide, rape, sexual harassment, and so forth. Mobbing and bullying consist "of repeated actions which, by themselves may be relatively minor, but which can cumulatively come to constitute serious forms of violence."[383]

Workplace bullying constitutes "offensive behavior through vindictive, cruel, malicious or humiliating attempts to undermine an individual or groups of employees. Such persistently negative attacks on their personal and professional performance are typically unpredictable, irrational and unfair."[384]

Mobbing or ganging-up is "another form of systematic collective violence [...] subjecting [an employee] to psychological harassment, for example by means of continuous negative remarks or criticism, isolation, spreading gossip or ridiculing the person concerned."[385] Mobbing is typically associated with wrongdoing against a 'simple' employee. There is, however, also mobbing against management, as illustrated by the following example:

---

[382] ILO 2002.

[383] Idem.

[384] Idem.

[385] ILO 2002. It is further stated that "although such practices might on the surface appear to be minor single actions, they can have a very serious effect. It has been estimated, for example, that about 10-15 per cent of suicides in Sweden each year have this type of background."

Mobbing against a manager?

Our policy of promoting gender-sensitivity among our beneficiaries didn't seem to take off – the division headed by Michael had elaborated a policy helping our staff to integrate gender-related topics into their work for SME promotion. At the time, everybody had accepted the policy.

Instead, Michael himself began having credibility issues among his peer division managers. He and his staff seemed more and more isolated, to the point that one of the donor representative demanded that he be replaced. "Sacrificing pawns," the head of SwissNGO commented.

Things improved only when – through a detailed email exchange between Michael and Pavanjit (a peer division manager) – a fundamental undermining of the initially agreed gender policy (and with this of the staff representing it) came to light: "Our division will affect women indirectly when their husbands earn better income," was Pavanjit's excuse. I wondered why any serious concern with the agreed policy had not come onto the table? And why now this unveiled hidden resistance?

Following that disclosure, I insisted on physically 'implanting' some of Michael's staff in the office space and work plans of the other divisions. All of a sudden people started realizing the possibilities and opportunities. Michael's final rehabilitation happened half a year later when the donor consortium members applauded the achievements of Michael's division.

The above example not only illustrates mobbing on the managerial level, but also the difficulty inherent in discovering it.

Finally, the integrity challenge of *strategic opponents,* referring to an actor "lack[ing] the motivation to seek agreement,"[386] has already been analyzed above in the context of acting against the intentions of a major partnership contract or subcontract. A strategic opponent also poses a challenge for the integrity of the organizational culture.

Why do all these points constitute an integrity challenge to the project? For this, we will look first at the normative conflict behind them. All of them have something to do with recognition, or lack of recognition, towards an individual or a group of people. They express tension on the recognition level, with respect to emotional recognition (R1), social recognition (R3), or sometimes even legal and political recognition (R2).

---

[386] See the 3rd guideline of the normative foundation, Chapter 4.3.4.1, respectively Ulrich P. 2001a: 88.

For instance, defamation and usually indiscreet behavior aim to harm somebody's reputation and with this their social recognition (solidarity),[387] which is a particularly strong act in cultures where saving face is of fundamental importance (as was the case for the culture where the case study took place). Fake ingratiation is the act of searching for emotional (or social) recognition. Mobbing expresses a lack of emotional recognition in the mobbed person or of the position she/he represents. Mobbing may also be grounded in a lack of social recognition (in a minority group, for instance) or even from inadequate legal and political recognition (not recognizing somebody's legal and political rights as a human being, as a woman, as a child). The same holds true for strategic opponents, who in fact often use mobbing as a strategy. In the extreme case, someone's sheer existence or presence represents – in psychological terms – an apparent 'false consciousness' towards someone else, motivating his act of defamation, fake ingratiation, and so forth.

What is the effect on the integrity of the project? First, all such conduct undermines the culture of a project. In discrediting an organizational member or a group, they erode the mutual recognition necessary for a culture's trust and recognition. They constitute a threat or challenge to the integrity of the project culture. Secondly, all these acts of defamation, mobbing etc. are an expression of defective or missing 'good will', or argumentational integrity (D1), for resolving any real or perceived problem. Reciprocal communication does not happen, as there is no *emotional handshake* between the parties. With this, the project is drained of its capacity for efficient problem resolution and impacted in its culture of open dissent. Finally, the project may even be the object of or involved in law suits in cases of mobbing, gender discrimination etc. committed by some of its members.

How can such issues be resolved? What to do about them? The first step of the process model is of particular importance here, that is, the need to become conscious and engaged. This is because the given existence of such issues is mostly half-conscious or blurred (sometimes even for the wrong-doer) because the issue comprises distorted compensatory transactions on a very fundamental level, the level of recognition. As the next example illustrates, such early consciousness or awareness can even sometimes solve a possible mobbing problem in time:

---

[387] An exception to an indiscretion not intended to harm somebody on the emotional or social recognition levels is the whistle-blowing discussed above. It is exactly the existence of emotional and social recognition that creates the difference.

Do you know what is wrong?

Kumar's performance had raised question marks in the past. His boss Paul had spoken several times to him, he explained to me when he suggested that his contract be terminated. Later that day, I had a talk with Kumar. Belonging to the Hindu minority in Bangladesh, he felt mobbed – nearly by default. What made me raise my eyebrows, however, was that while he had, in desperation, apparently called all his friends asking them what they thought he could do to improve his behavior (!), he was unable to describe concretely what was being criticized in his performance and thus how to move on from there.

I asked him to do the following: To put down in writing what he understood was wrong, adding a column about what he would do differently, and another column about what he needed as support from his boss for each of the points to be changed. Then he should discuss that with Paul (whom I debriefed on my talk with Kumar.)

Within three months Kumar's performance, his self-esteem, and his acceptance in the group improved visibly.

This example illustrates how a combination of factors (lack of people management skills, minority feelings) led to perceived mobbing and how alertness prevented a bigger problem, i.e. the undue termination of an employee (not to mention the psychological damage in the employee concerned).

The second step, i.e. to define the issue and identify the tension zone, also requires particular focus. A purely discursive thinking is not sufficient; in fact, the bearers of responsibility 'cannot reckon naïvely with goodwill' from the people involved. What is required is intuition, creative imagination, and fantasy (see also risk management): Fantasy to grasp what is going on, and fantasy to perceive what lies outside our normative foundation, such as illegitimate behavior. Psychologists, from the context provided by fairy-tales, would advocate for the need of "a fantasy for evil."[388] In other words, the process of defining the issue should not naïvely exclude the idea that "evil is a possibility of the human being."[389]

---

[388] Kast 1987: 39 (translation Renz).

[389] Fest 2005. Further: "We need to accept the evil in our accounts of the human being stronger than it happened since the Enlightenment. The Enlightenment pretended that the human being is good and it is only because of external influences that he falls into the evil. That is wrong. There is the possibility for good and evil in the human being. We think of this too little in the western industrialized nations." Questions of good and evil in human beings are core phi-

The solution exploration (Step 3) and implementation (Step 4) also require a differentiated rather than a naïve approach to responsibility, as offered by the differentiated responsibility concept (D3). Solutions for problems on the recognition level usually require *drastic measures*, as seen above: A strategic opponent may need to be terminated from the organization or the subcontracts, because it is exactly the strategic aspect of the opposition that inhibits a peaceful establishment of consensus.

The review of the steps for resolving such integrity issues stemming from particularly mobbing and strategic opponents has underlined the importance of sensitivity for such issues, a kind of ethical alertness – which the normative foundation of the combined approach we have outlined may help to sharpen. However, it also becomes obvious that such sensitivity and alertness cannot be simply delegated to a compliance officer. It is the task of project governance and management to assure a very high level of sensitivity towards any such issues that might possibly pose an integrity challenge to the project.

Mobbing of whistle-blowers vs. whistle-blowing process, ombudsman

What are whistle-blowers, and what is the mobbing of whistle-blowers? The concept of whistle-blowing has become important in the context of the need of corporate governance to find help in detecting misconduct. The revised OECD principles of corporate governance specify that "[i]n fulfilling its control oversight responsibilities it is important for the board to encourage the reporting of unethical/unlawful behavior without fear of retribution. The existence of a company code of ethics should aid this process which should be underpinned by legal protection for the individuals concerned."[390]

To fully understand the background of this principle, we should look at what differentiates 'honest' whistleblowing, for instance, from defamation or from an employee taking revenge. The differentiating factor is – in short – 'integrity'; more precisely, honest and sincere whistle-blowers have a genuine interest in legitimate action (D2), their own as well as their organization's.

The reality, however, is that affected organizations, or society at large, often persecute whistle-blowers, probably because in practice it is difficult to identify their genuine interest (D2). That is where governance has a role to play as specified in the OECD principles.

---

dustrialized nations." Questions of good and evil in human beings are core philosophical debates. While they go beyond the scope of this book, the *possibility* of their existence is acknowledged. (See also Neiman 2002, Tibi 1991).

[390] OECD 2004: 62.

This helps explain why the mobbing of whistle-blowers constitutes an organizational integrity issue: 'Honest' whistle-blowers in the first place try to reveal misconduct, but if the organization tolerates their persecution (mobbing) the organization loses even more credibility: It may even seem that the organization is not interested in discovering any unethical or unlawful behavior – a seemingly strange but principally correct alternative would be to "celebrate [a whistle-blower's] act of responsibility."[391]

It is therefore a task of integrity management to encourage the report of unethical or unlawful behavior and to assure protection for the whistle-blower. This needs to be incorporated into a code of conduct, and an ombudsman or compliance officer needs to be assigned. With these steps taken, the outlined process model should allow management to identify possible mobbing issues of whistle-blowers in time.

Hidden agendas vs. culture of discursive conflict resolution

The project may face hidden agendas within its team, or with the donors, partners, or the wider environment. Hidden agendas are often at the root of other integrity challenges, for example in bilateralism or with strategic opponents.

What exactly are 'hidden agendas'? 'Hidden agenda' has become a commonly used term, to the point that it is even contained in the latest draft version of the *Oxford English Dictionary*, where it is defined as "a concealed or unexpressed intent behind the ostensible purpose of an action, statement, etc.; an ulterior aim or motive."[392] In a related way, a hidden agenda could be defined as "a set of unstated *individual* goals that may conflict with the goals of the *group* as a whole."[393] Even then, however, the definition is not complete: Hidden agendas may not only stem from individuals but also from groups (for instance from a government). The dichotomy 'individual goal / group goal', however, facilitates a practical understanding, and is therefore used in the subsequent elaborations.

What is the issue with a hidden agenda, or in what respect does a hidden agenda pose a challenge to the integrity of the project? Does not every person have his or her own personal objectives? The issue of a hidden agenda lies primarily in the word *hidden* and in the *rationale* behind hiding. It reveals the lack of a communicatively oriented *attitude* (D1) and a lack of interest in legitimate action (D2). From the project perspective, this

---

[391] Gandossy & Sonnenfeld 2004: 147. See also Leisinger 2003 and 1997: 130-141.

[392] *Oxford English Dictionary* 1989 & 2003.

[393] Lucas 2004 (emphasis Renz).

prevents an effective culture of discursive conflict resolution from forming, and thereby undermines trust and mutual recognition (R1). In other
words: Not only may the (individual) goal conflict with group goals, but
the rationale or motivation behind "conceal[ing something] *intentionally*
from the view or notice of others"[394] is in conflict with the values and culture of the group. Consequently, hidden agendas pose a threat primarily to
the *integrity of the project culture*.

As expected from a project culture of trust and discursive conflict resolution, the rational alternative (to hiding) would be to resolve the possible
issue with sincere intentions through *communicative* action. The pure existence of personal objectives is quite normal. Only through discourse enabled
by a communicative attitude, however, can anyone determine whether these
personal objectives represent *interfering* problems or not. A lack of communication grounded in fear, which is shown by someone *while holding on* to
these goals, however, reveals a corresponding lack of interest in legitimate
actions. "The attempt to pursue or enforce pre-decided personal success"[395]
is carried out while *strategically* hiding an existing (*per se* not necessarily
illegitimate) agenda or objective.

Beyond the integrity challenge to the project culture, the *impact* of
hidden agendas is aggravating, especially because it may compromise
project culture: Hidden agendas probably interfere negatively with the
ostensible purpose or group goal, i.e. they can impede progress towards
the declared goal (see above, where integrity issues undermine the project mission or any contracts). And the longer a hidden agenda is maintained, the greater and more sustained the possible interference becomes,
and the more compromises the project culture suffers, and with it the
credibility of the project.

What to do about hidden agendas? It is clear that the resolution of hidden agendas is not necessarily easy. For development work, whose success
depends on its credibility more than in a private business (see Chapter
4.3.2), it is indispensable to clear out at least the major hidden or ambiguous agendas. Looking at our process model, Step 1 is again the most important way of becoming conscious and getting engaged. From the perspective of management and the governance board, this also means showing visible commitment towards a culture of discursive conflict resolution.
As mentioned earlier, this is best done – as with all other integrity challenges – through the placement, for instance, of a generic topic 'resolution

---

[394] *Oxford English Dictionary* (emphasis Renz).
[395] Ulrich P. 2001: 84 (translation Renz).

of hidden agendas' on the *governance board agenda*. The board in its meetings should ask itself, have we had any hidden agendas which need to be resolved? In the sense of a communicatively oriented attitude (D1), this should be enough to start the discussion. If that does not happen, the project culture is in fact compromised, specifically in its ability to promote trust and discursive problem resolution.

Team abuse vs. team culture of trust and open dissent

When an organization decides to foster team work structures, that effort is based on the assumption that joint collaboration yields better results. Team abuse is the *intended instrumentalization* or manipulation of a team, i.e. using the team platform differently from its original intention. In other words, team abuse occurs whenever somebody implicitly agrees to work on a team (through accepting a work contract, or accepting – and not challenging (D1) – the collaborative idea), but instead uses the team for their own agenda or does not contribute their best effort, again without explicitly clarifying their different position or agenda.

The integrity challenge for the project lies in the fact that team abuse poses a threat to the team *idea per se*, and to a project-specific *team culture* of trust and open dissent. The project is deprived of such efficient joint collaboration as originally intended by the team set-up. A team forum to explore solutions in a discursive way, based on argumentational integrity (D1) and mutual recognition (R1-3) of the team members, becomes impossible.

The analysis of the case study has provided several examples of team abuse, for instance by strategic opponents instrumentalizing and undermining teamwork, or even torpedoing various team-building measures.

What to do about it? Team abuse is very difficult to recognize, and nearly impossible to spot from the outside (because the team has also allowed itself to be manipulated). From the inside, possible indicators could be the lack of openness (i.e. "candor, fostering a culture of open dissent"[396]) despite team-building measures, poor interest in team-building measures or social / off-work events, persons adorning themselves with the plums of team merits, or a soaring team atmosphere of tension despite the effort to improve it. Again the first step acquires primary importance; that is, becoming conscious that there is such thing as team abuse and getting engaged the moment that there is any doubt.

---

[396] Sonnenfeld 2002: 16. See also Hilb, who underlines the importance of a culture of trust enabled through ying-yang team cooperation rules (2005: 82-85).

Various integrity challenges vs. awareness creation and promotion of elements of normative foundation

Similar to corporate training, the cultural element for creating awareness and promoting elements of the normative foundation is of ubiquitous importance. Whenever dealing with an integrity challenge, it should be asked whether there the organization is knowledgeable enough and aware of the principles worked into its normative foundation. That does not necessarily mean understanding the ethical background and foundation, but rather understanding the notion of guidelines, for instance as follows: 'If there is an issue, it needs to be put on the table,' thereby corresponding to the first discourse-ethical guideline (D1).

4.3.6.3 Integrity challenges on the strategy level

A project also faces possible integrity challenges on the highest strategic level, challenges which may impact the fundamental vision or mission, or the way in which stakeholders are being considered. These obviously are some of the most difficult challenges for the integrity of the project, in part because they can only partially be influenced by a 'rational,' i.e. ethically reflective solution.

The focus of this book rests explicitly not on the level of development policies but on the responsible implementation of such through appropriate project governance. Our universal normative foundation, the combined approach of discourse ethics and recognition ethics and the process model, however, help us to understand such issues and possibly make a contribution towards a broader understanding of the challenges.

In this sense, this chapter takes up only a few issues for discussion and illustration.

Development paternalism and development take-ism vs. vision, mission, business principles

Paternalism is an attitude and/or the real expression of "power and authority one person or institution exercises over another to confer benefits or prevent harm for the latter regardless of the latter's informed consent."[397] Paternalism in matters of development topics can therefore be called development paternalism.

Paternalism in development is hardly compatible with the idea of development *cooperation*. The problem of paternalism lies in that it is "a threat

---

[397] Honderich 1995: 647.

to autonomy"[398] in a way that prevents those who are affected from taking responsibility on their own. From the perspective of our normative foundation, a development paternalist probably displays emotional recognition, but lacks a true feeling of solidarity, "a face-to-face recognition among equal but different people."[399]

What is the challenge of this phenomenon to the integrity of project? A project grounded in development paternalism will have difficulty in engaging in true discourses with stakeholders, particularly the target group. It possibly faces exaggerated claims and expectations stemming from a mentality of 'free assistance,' *taking* help for granted (which is, of course, again fed by development paternalism). This book refers to such a mentality of expecting free assistance as *"development take-ism."*[400] The following is an example illustrating such 'take-ism':

How big is your donation?

One of the key interventions of the project was an awareness-creation campaign for local SMEs that would show them that by using simple accounting services they could understand their business better.

The partner of the awareness creation campaign was excited. But had he really engaged with us on our own principles of always finding true business partners, in this case for instance SME associations, who were interested in cooperating and sharing costs? The answer to this doubt came quickly – unfortunately negative, when he asked us 'how big our donation' would be for this campaign.

This difficult kind of stakeholder dialogue with development partners, free of neither paternalism nor take-ism, is grounded in a lack of argumentational integrity, i.e. the discussants are probably not ready to "assert only those claims they truly regard as right" (D1).

---

[398] Idem.

[399] Pless & Maak 2004: 132.

[400] The author is aware of the philosophical debate about whether the wealthy *by default* are required to assist the poor. The dichotomy examined here - development paternalism and development take-ism - is not to preemptively qualify that well-justified philosophical debate. The only objective here is to name challenges which a development project may face, and be challenged by, in the implementation of its mission.

What can a project do about development paternalism and development take-ism? Only a limited degree of influence can come from a project. The above example, however, also illustrates the importance of assuring that the project be conscious and engaged (Step 1 of the process model) towards this issue. It further shows how important it is that the messages communicated by the business principles and the project mission take these possible challenges into account, as well as that continuous 'political responsibility' be exercised in spreading such messages.

The following example shows, however, that because development paternalism is far-reaching, a project by itself can make only a limited contribution, not a major change:

How credible are development projects in Bangladesh?

We were discussing how much we were being taken seriously by our partners and target group. Anawara, an experienced and reflective development professional in Bangladesh, made the following comment, which – though an individual opinion – was thought-provoking:

"Development projects in Bangladesh would get a low score from the target group. Although local partners, with whom development projects implement interventions, present a convincing picture to the project that they have high credibility and trustworthiness with their target group, in reality, even the local partners are often not convinced of the project's credibility – let alone the ultimate target group. None the less, they still form partnerships with development projects as they need these 'big brothers' as a source of their own survival."

The far-reaching and often historical roots of development paternalism are beyond the scope of this book. From a normative perspective (based on our universal normative foundation), however, development paternalism and take-ism could possibly be overcome through *reciprocal solidarity*, i.e. the reciprocal recognition of each other on a social level, within the community. This would mean that "development policy has to obey the ethical primacy of solidarity."[401]

---

[401] Peter & Kraut 2000: 19 (translation Renz).

Strategic opponents of strategy, stakeholders not considered or dissatisfied, conflicts of interest vs. stakeholder identification, discourse and involvement

The concept of the *strategic opponent* has been outlined, but it remains to observe that not uncommonly one finds a strategic opponent at work on the strategy level. The particularity of the strategic opponent is, paradoxically, not that he constitutes a strategic challenge but that through his behavior (of withholding open dissent) he makes discursive exploration impossible. If this withholding occurs on the level of project strategy and mission, the impact can variously be that possibly *stakeholders are not identified* correctly, that claims and expectations are not identified properly, or that wrong claims are being considered. The integrity of the project is impacted in a fundamental way: Challenges arise from a sub-optimal stakeholder dialogue, with the results that the project mission is not designed accordingly (and not properly legitimized) and promotes stakeholder dissatisfaction.

Another normative issue challenging the project on this level can be conflicts of strategic interest. In the following example, it is doubtful whether the impressive project idea with its noble objectives is not simply rooted in personal motivation:

Building the personal Eiffel tower?

Was Frizz trying to construct his personal monument? Full of ideas – some called him 'Crazy Frizz' – he was the driving force behind our huge project: 5% growth in the Bangladeshi SME sector, with a project volume of around 30 Mio US$. In comparison, other projects with the same approach were running at a volume of only a couple of hundred thousand to a few million dollars.

Why all this extreme commitment and push behind our project, while the other 20 projects he was coaching (all of smaller size) hardly got any attention? Was such a mega project his 'journeyman's piece' or was it actually justified by the needs of the Bangladeshi context? How consistent was it with the overall economic growth strategy of Bangladesh?

What to do about such challenges on such a strategic level? Some of them obviously go beyond the influence of a development project, related as they are to donor and government *internal* processes.

The following example outlines the limits of a discursive solution exploration, but also shows possible ways of still assuming an ethical responsibility as described under the discourse-ethical guidelines (D3):

Alignments for a new project?

That looked like a gigamanic project: 50 million pounds! A number of resident development practitioners were listening intently to Brian as he presented his latest idea: A multi-donor project targeted at improving the efficiency of the Bangladeshi bureaucracy. It was clear that this project was taking direct aim at the government's wide spread corruptive practices. The project architecture looked interesting, and there were many excellent ideas!

What could not be recognized, however, was an overall mission, or a clear political alignment or will behind the project – there were a lot of tactics and some strategies, but exactly what for?

With corruption being such a touchy subject, this lack of clearly-stated mission was somehow understandable. Still, such a huge project reared upon such an unclear base was, in my eyes, doomed to failure. I conveyed my thoughts to him and suggested that, should an open alignment for a common political will not be reachable (for instance because of support withheld by ministry representatives), an alignment in a subgroup of key stakeholders was needed. Otherwise, the project would produce pretty actions but have no strategic impact.

While such issues go beyond the scope of project governance, both the tools (the process model) and the normative foundation based on discourse ethics and recognition ethics remain valid.

Public pressure for integrity, lack of public binding vs. monitoring and reporting

As we have seen earlier, a project faces to a certain extent justified high public pressure and expectations merely by virtue of the fact that its funding stems from public sources and that a broad set of stakeholders is involved. The role of communication is critical here: A project needs to display its commitment to dealing with any integrity challenges it faces. Likewise, monitoring and reporting requirements need to mirror themselves in the integrity perspective, to forestall those public reproaches that depend on unfocused charges and indistinct claims.

With this, we have concluded the review of integrity challenges along the structures, organizational culture and strategy. The final section of this chapter looks at how a project, in particular its governance board, can get started on integrity management.

4.3.7   Integrity management – how to get started

Integrity challenges are inevitably on the agenda of a governance board of development projects, either through the back door when certain issues take the project by surprise, or as normal business handled in a proactive way, as strengths and not as issues. Either way, integrity management is an integral part of the governance of projects. It needs to be a continuous agenda topic, treated in every meeting, as much as project advances are treated by mission management.

The graphic in Figure 22 (with the process model and the normative foundation) and Table 5 (of integrity challenges and tension zones) are proposed as a roadmap. They constitute a comprehensive overview for starting integrity management or for following and monitoring it on an on-going basis.

In as much as integrity is a long-range quality, just so is the responsibility for integrity long-range as well. Along the lines of Tom Peters' saying that "there is no such thing as a minor lapse of integrity," it can also be said that there is *no partial management for integrity*. Integrity management offers a concrete solution, with the final benefit of enabling a true cooperation in development efforts.

4.4   Extended stakeholder management

4.4.1   Objective of extended stakeholder management

The objective of extended stakeholder management is to identify, manage and monitor the broad variety of stakeholders confronting a development project. This chapter outlines a systematic approach to such stakeholder management; it introduces several tools and highlights a series of related particularities of the development sector.

The brief review of the organizational theories (see Chapter 3) has assigned the governance *roles of linking, coordinating, and negotiating* to extended stakeholder management. The research of the case study has allowed for identifying related governance tasks which substantiate the requirement for strategic attention to stakeholders through the means of project governance.

In this chapter, the first task is to refine the term 'stakeholder' in consideration of its particular importance and complexity in the development context. Subsequently, a model of stakeholder management is presented in outline, adapted to the particularities of the development context, and illustrated with numerous case examples.

Extended stakeholder management is interlinked with most other key governance responsibilities, as follows: The stakeholders are identified through system understanding gained from system management, and extended stakeholder management assures that the identification is complete, assesses what function a stakeholder should play in the project, and initiates the involvement. The structural tasks within mission management may establish formalized contracts (particularly with key stakeholders such as implementation NGOs and Government). The normative foundation from integrity management delivers the basis for stakeholder recognition, assessment, and discourse. Finally, risk management accounts for particular risks in the context of stakeholders.

4.4.2   Particularity: What stakeholders are in development cooperation

In Chapter 4.1, stakeholders were defined as "individuals, organized or not-organized groups of people, organizations and institutions, which are affected by or do affect the development project's value-creating activities and sometimes also its value-destroying activities."[402]

Why are stakeholders of paramount *importance* in the development sector? "The purpose of aid is to enhance the economic and social development and well-being of recipients. This means fully taking into account recipients' views on objectives […] concerning themselves and the society in which they live in."[403] It is therefore not surprising that terms such as "stakeholder participation, partnerships, participatory approaches," and so forth are widely used in the sector.[404] Participation by stakeholders is not only a question of principle, but also of practice: "effectiveness and sustainability depend practically, in part, on the commitment [and involvement] of interested parties."[405] In other words, there is no development *cooperation* without some type of partners. Similarly to integrity management, it can be said that for real development *cooperation* stakeholder involvement is *not only part of the way, but also part of the objective.*

---

[402] In modification of Rüegg-Stürm's definition 2005: 12.

[403] DFID 1995: 3. DFID is the British Department of International Development. See Wood, who points at the dependencies with the following paradox: "the interdependence of many charitable nonprofits and government units is incompatible with the assumption that the sector is 'independent'" (1996: 5).

[404] See Hickey & Mohan 2005: 239ff for a comprehensive overview of approaches to participation in development.

[405] Idem.

Considering the great importance of this role, it is called *extended* stake-holder management.

Stakeholder management in development projects is also of particular *complexity*, compared to its similar function in a traditional business organization:

- Who are the customers of a development project? Are they the target audience (recipients or beneficiaries) or the fund providing donor?

- How can the beneficiaries be defined, that is, is the project working directly with beneficiaries or are they unknown because the project works rather on structural (i.e. systemic) elements? How is one to measure impact in such cases (see also examples '… and who are the beneficiaries?' in Chapter 4.1.5.2)? What if projects aim at impersonal 'beneficiaries' like animals, nature, etc.?

- What about the equivalent of investors and shareholders: Do they exist, and what is their role?

Not only is the identification of stakeholders more difficult, but also the interactions with the stakeholders are often more complex, justifying the term "pluralistic value chain arrangement"[406] as Peter Ulrich describes the manifold interaction of a business with its environment. Indeed, such usage is even truer in the development context. Development projects acquire the character of a joint venture, of "cooperation"[407] in the narrow sense. The next example illustrates how complex the growth of real development partnerships can be:

Is it now a dream partner or not?

As a development project we 'have money to spend.' This is obviously known to local development organizations ('development businesses' as I sometimes called them). Is it now a partnership with "equal powers of

---

[406] Ulrich P. 2001a: 438 (translation Renz). See also Post, Preston & Sachs (2002: 198ff) who stress the learning processes involving stakeholders, another facet of the pluralistic value chain arrangement.

[407] See Fuchs analyzing the project management of (business) cooperation. He defines cooperation as "the voluntary collaboration of two or more legally independent enterprises with the aim to pursue common and individual objectives" (1999: 25; translation Renz).

decision-making"[408] (or a simple subcontract) if we pay them to organize a trade fair for agro tools? We thought that in IDO we had found an ideal partner – complete with local knowledge, local staff and good references. But what was their contribution to the partnership: Was it in money as ours was, or in kind? And if in kind, how were we to compare it to our financial contribution?

Through a complex partner incentive scheme and a type of deficit warranty (and mainly by not taking a shortcut to simply engage in subsidization), the partner organization became highly motivated, spreading the idea among the exhibitors so that at the end our contribution was only 10% of the total cost!

One can imagine the effort it takes to establish, and coach, such complex partnerships as the one described in the example; once more, however, this is a normal aspect of effective development *cooperation*.

In summary, the paramount importance of stakeholder management, and its associated complexity, calls for a ranking on the level of strategic management, so that it becomes essential for project governance to include a key responsibility called 'extended stakeholder management.' It can already be noted here that because the success of a project depends to a certain extent, but also critically, on stakeholder contributions and ownership, governance has a strategic role to play not only in linking, coordinating and negotiating, but also in monitoring stakeholder performance. This will be further elaborated within the subsequent model for stakeholder management.

4.4.3   A model for stakeholder management

This chapter introduces a model for stakeholder management adapted to the needs of a development project. Accordingly, then, the four steps of stakeholder identification, stakeholder classification and assessment, stakeholder actions and stakeholder monitoring are described, illustrated along the way with case examples.

---

[408] DFID 1995: 9.

4.4.3.1 Overview

In principle two different schools of thoughts can be identified:[409]

1. The strategic stakeholder value approach as formulated by Freeman,[410] which is based on a concept of strategic power and the potential for "influences and interfering forces"[411] of stakeholders.

2. The normatively critical stakeholder value approach, as defined by Peter Ulrich, which considers stakeholders as "all groups having legitimate claims on the [organization]."[412] The criterion is not the possible "impact of stakeholder concerns, but solely the ethically justifiable legitimacy"[413] emerging from "discourse ethical categories of rational communication."[414]

The first approach is problematic when applied either in an unreflective way or in the misguided belief that it is a business ethical concept.[415] The second approach builds on the same discourse-ethical understanding dealt with in Chapter 4.3 on integrity management.

Following Wilbers, in practice one encounters a mix of both schools of thought. With respect to development cooperation, in fact both are relevant: On one hand, the normatively critical stakeholder value approach helps one to consider, recognize, and assess the legitimacy of all possible concerned parties, and to differentiate between strategic and normative reflective behavior. The recognition level of the combined approach of discourse ethics and recognition ethics introduced earlier may add further explicatory force in assessing the legitimacy of stakeholders' involve-

---

[409] See Ulrich P. 2001a: 441ff. See also Wilbers (2004) and Rüegg-Stürm (2002, 2005) building on P. Ulrich's distinction.

[410] Freeman 1984.

[411] See Gomez et al. 2002: 88.

[412] Ulrich P. 2001a: 442 (translation Renz).

[413] Rüegg-Stürm 2005: 20. See Ulrich P. 2001a: 442ff.

[414] Ulrich P. 2001a: 450 (translation Renz). See also Post, Preston & Sachs who talk of "organizational morality" forming the "normative core of the stakeholder model: legitimate stakeholder interests require managerial recognition [!] and attention as a matter of moral right" (2002: 29; emphasis Renz).

[415] See Ulrich P. 2001a: 443. See also Kirsch 1997, in particular the comment under Footnote 137.

ment.[416] On the other hand, however, we should also resort to the strategic stakeholder value approach, obviously not as an ethically justified framework *per se*, but simply as a data triangulation method assuring that all possible stakeholders are identified and assessed correctly. The combination of both approaches may in particular help to sharpen one's attention in detecting possible strategic opponents, "surprise stakeholders" or free riders, i.e. parties with illegitimate claims, the identification of which may be catalyzed through an inner attitude of *recognition* or a certain "fantasy for evil."[417] The following example illustrates the impact of possible surprise stakeholders:

Surprise stakeholders

The closer the deadline came for moving our offices, the more that certain strange issues turned up: The landlord who all of a sudden produced additional invoices for certain types of services, or a real estate agent who claimed a house-hunting provision etc. – some of them reinforced with criminal threats (see the example 'abduction threat' in the risk management chapter), or with simple harassments: The landlord turned the elevator off on the day we were moving…

This brief example illustrates how in a development environment of weak conditions of law and order, neglected surprise stakeholders can possibly take a substantial toll by interfering with the normal course of a project. Their identification, supported by the *combination* of stakeholder approaches and careful monitoring, is essential.

The following model as illustrated in Figure 24 is a further development of Wilbers' model of how to deal with stakeholders.[418] The different steps will be explained in the following chapters.

---

[416] See chapter 4.3 on recognition ethics

[417] See the 'surprise stakeholders' in Chapter 4.5.2.3 on risk management. For the 'fantasy for evil,' see Chapter 4.3.6.2 on strategic opponents.

[418] Wilbers 2004: 331ff. In contrast to Wilber, the proposed model merges the two steps of classifying and assessing stakeholders: Particularly from the perspective of the normative critical stakeholder concept, the distinction remains ambiguous. A second enhancement is that a monitoring step is added, as suggested in a similar model by Gomez et al. (2002: 86ff). Thirdly, the normatively critical concept is complemented by elements of recognition ethics.

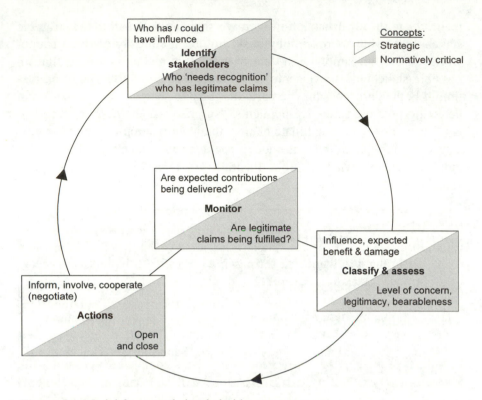

Figure 24. Model for extended stakeholder management

The particularities of the model are its consideration of both stakeholder concepts, the strategic and the normatively critical one, as these are enhanced by elements of recognition ethics and the central significance of a monitoring step (also explicating the reciprocity in interactions). This last dimension serves as an additional reason for calling it *extended* stakeholder management.

The next few chapters will elaborate on the four steps of extended stakeholder management, with particular emphasis on the governance role within these steps, illustrated again by numerous case examples.

4.4.3.2 Stakeholder identification

Particular attention should be given to the fact that the relationship to a given stakeholder may have either the character of a passive voice (is affected) and/or an active voice (does affect). Stakeholder identification should not be a one-time exercise but a periodically repeated one which adjusts earlier phases of identification. The main difficulty lies in achieving as *complete* an identification of as many stakeholders as possible. Therefore, this book proposes a number of guiding questions and a matrix for working with them which is explained below.

From the perspective of the strategic stakeholder concept, the following questions should be asked:

- Who has an influence or impact on the development project (an active voice), as distinct from
- who can be influenced or impacted by the project (a passive voice)?

From a normatively critical perspective, it should be asked:

- Who – based on an attitude either of emotional, legal and political, or social recognition – may be concerned with the project's mission, from which legitimate claims arise, independently of whether they are brought forward or not? (passive voice)
- Which contributors are those who, through their involvement (or recognition), finally legitimize the project's mission, and therefore who may also come to exert legitimate claims upon the project? (active voice)

In order to achieve an identification which is as complete as possible, the following matrix built on two (of the most relevant ones in this context) categories of the St. Gallen Management Model, supports the process:

Table 6. Systematic stakeholder identification[419]

Process levels / Environment	Management, strategy	Business processes	Support processes and infrastructure
Society (political, cultural, social etc.)			
Nature			
Technology			
Economy and development sector			

[419] The matrix is inspired by Gomez et al. (see 2002: 89), and enhanced so as to be consistent with the categories of the St. Gallen Management Model.

The last column of Table 6 reveals another particularity of development projects: Running their course, as they usually do, in an environment with 'sub-optimal' infrastructure, projects may depend in an existential way on providers of basic infrastructure. This can be a factor of substantial complexity if a development project starts from zero (in relief operations this is handled by specialized logistics units of the relief NGOs, often supported by military logistics). It is not unusual, however, for either a previous project to have existed there or for donor representatives or other key stakeholders to be already on site. Their support in infrastructure establishment is crucial, as the next example illustrates:

Facilitating infrastructure needs

We were lucky to be provided with vehicles from the car park of one of the bigger donors. Other topics, such as expatriate visas or links to local banks, were facilitated by a smaller donor office. The visas, however, got delayed, creating a serious issue. To make things worse, the bigger donor reproached the smaller donor for unprofessional behavior, (he did not want to offer better alternatives (although he himself ran a professional logistics and procurement operation on site). This sandwich position for a start-up project for us proved to be a lost opportunity: Numerous contacts and contracts on infrastructure questions had to be established from zero, with us learning our lessons the hard way and spending our project time and money on various resources, such as the IT infrastructure, the selection of a trustworthy corporate lawyer, the selection of the office building, security support etc.

The example shows the manifold areas of support processes and infrastructure provision. If infrastructure providers can be seen as part of extended stakeholder management, and as such receive the management attention of project governance, then a development project can avoid a number of redundant experiences and improve its efficiency, particularly in its start-up phases.[420]

One can now look at the particular governance responsibilities within stakeholder identification. The initial stakeholder identification, involvement, and negotiation are most probably done in the first place when the

---

[420] See Paris declaration on aid effectiveness (2005) in its call for more efficiency in project implementation units.

project is planned by the governance board (probably at that point not yet formalized). The further responsibilities are to properly hand over that initial work to the project unit as well as to provide on-going support to the development project where needed so as to identify other stakeholders.

4.4.3.3 Stakeholder classification and assessment

The classification of stakeholders and the assessment of claims and contributions aim at building the basis for taking decisions on possible actions. From a strategic perspective, the factors of influence and expected benefits or possible damages need to be assessed. From a normatively critical perspective, the levels of concern, legitimacy, and bearableness should be assessed. This requires an "absolute openness towards all [possibly] legitimate claims"[421] (which, described in terms of the combined normative foundation, refers to an attitude of recognition resorting to real or quasi-discourses with the stakeholders, based on argumentation integrity and the differentiated responsibility concept[422]).

The literature is extensive on providing classification schemes for priority, level of concern, level of influence, persuasability etc., for which there is no need for further elaboration in this book.[423]

The responsibilities of the governance board with respect to this step are to discuss and challenge stakeholder classification and assessment.

4.4.3.4 Stakeholder actions

The possibilities for stakeholder actions are nearly infinite: Partnering, consulting, informing, avoiding or manipulating (for instance in the case of illegitimate stakeholders), being consulted, being informed, being manipulated, and so forth.[424] The two stakeholder approaches create certain lines of orientation: Depending on the foregoing assessment, the *strategic* concept helps to decide whether "informing, involving or cooperating respectively negotiating"[425] is the right action. The *normatively critical* approach helps to decide on stakeholder actions, differentiating between actions of

---

[421] Wilbers 2004: 354 (translation Renz) .

[422] See Chapter 4.3.4.1.

[423] See, for instance, Müller-Stewens & Lechner 2005, Gomez et al. 2002, Wilbers 2004.

[424] See DFID 1995.

[425] Wilbers 2004: 355 (translation Renz).

"opening"[426] toward a discourse-and-recognition oriented relation, and actions of "closing" from irresponsible relations based, for instance, on illegitimate claims (see example 'lawyer on call' in Chapter 4.6). Also, one particular action is to decide which stakeholders should be included in the makeup of the formal governance board. The project DRIVER of the case study also pursued an additional option for including important stake-holders in creating a consultative advisory board.

As seen in Chapter 1, legitimacy is of particular importance for the man-agement of a project, and finally for the development project itself. It is pre-cisely through responsible stakeholder identification, stakeholder assess-ment, and stakeholder actions that such legitimacy arises. The combined normative approach helps to understand what it means to act 'responsibly.'

The communication of a project with its outside world is also of special interest within stakeholder actions: How does it communicate, and in what way does it assume its political-ethical role and carry out the notion of public-binding? The 'public' of a development project has a variety of faces, as illustrated by the next example.

Forward branding – backward branding

Bangladesh has a tradition of development work that extends over 30 years. Therefore, a key challenge for us was finding a way to differenti-ate ourselves from numerous NGOs which, though they have become part of the society, are none the less doing non-sustainable development work, that is, subsidizing good ideas which collapse the moment the donor-funded input is gone. A second challenge was that our donors were – understandably – demanding to receive information, reports, updates etc. For this, we created a communication strategy in two are-nas which we called 'two-way branding': Backward branding with a communication strategy and a face turned towards the funding sources (i.e. the back end of the 'value chain'), and a forward branding with its face and the messages we wanted to disseminate turned toward the beneficiaries and our partners.

This example illustrates a solution to disparate communication needs through the usage of "communication arenas."[427]

---

[426] See Ulrich P. 2001a: 438ff, 459.

[427] Wilbers 2004: 335 (translation Renz). See Dyllick & Meyer 2004: 120ff.

The possible actions in a development situation are only as manifold as the contributions of the governance board can be. The main responsibilities, however, relate to the two roles of linking and negotiating as those are identified by the organizational theories in Chapter 3.

The *linking* role is borne out by the members of the governance board whenever they can facilitate access to important resources or organizations, not lastly because the board members may be established on site while the development project is new and starting up.[428] The next example illustrates a missed opportunity for linking the newly starting project and, through this 'accreditation' jump-start, the project-sided stakeholder management

---

The networking party

Early after my arrival Brian, a resident representative of one of the donors offered to organize a welcome event at which he would officially introduce me to the local development community and kick-start my networking needs. His great idea – which under the linkage role of governance is not just a favor but an explicit responsibility –never materialized, however (ironically Brian wanted to include the government representatives once they would have officially approved the project – which only happened a year later…). I had to organize my own networking, in some cases working door by door.

This linking role, or from the example even an 'accrediting' role, is one level of involvement for the governance board.

An additional level is that of *negotiations*. In development countries where hierarchical thinking is strongly rooted in the culture, it would also be a lost opportunity not to use the leverage the governance board members could have to involve themselves or their respective superiors in difficult stakeholder relations. Developing a negotiation strategy involving all needed and available levels is a paramount role for the board, therefore. The following example illustrates the effect that arises in negotiations with (particularly complex) stakeholders whenever the available hierarchy is not optimally included in negotiations:

---

[428] See also Figure 11: Project Governance in a multi organization environment, illustrating the potential a multi-organization governance board has to contribute to the project's mission.

Establish a relationship with the government

The government was a very important stakeholder in our project, in a variety of roles: On one side, it would (hopefully) partner up for suggested regulatory improvements, and furthermore it was officially required to approve the project, and finally governmental offices were involved in visa questions. Further complexity arises because of the fact that government is obviously constituted by numerous actors and ministries, most of them wanting to be stakeholders in such a big project, with indistinct boundaries between official and unofficial interests.

Brian, the donor representative responsible for negotiating the official project approval, tried to succeed in a solo attempt, obviously underestimating the complexity. Official approval was received only when we were already 15 months into the project. What might have helped in this situation, then, was establishing a strategic plan (based on the analysis of who the legitimate persons were and who would raise illegitimate claims) that involved all possible hierarchical levels in a coordinated way.

With this, we turn to the final step of extended stakeholder management, which is the monitoring of stakeholders.

4.4.3.5 Stakeholder monitoring

A systematic monitoring of stakeholders is often forgotten or neglected. Some of the literature does mention it, but without further elaboration.[429] Yet this function is a powerful one, for the effectiveness of all the preceding work of identification, assessment and action can be substantially improved through controlling or monitoring, which is a matter of course in management. Assuring an effective and continuous stakeholder monitoring therefore becomes one of the key tasks of the governance board within extended stakeholder management, particularly in development cooperation.[430] Through its authority (and access to higher authority), it can also help resolve possible stakeholder issues, not by performing stakeholder management on its own – that would be micro-management – but in a coordinated and supportive way.

---

[429] See, for instance, Gomez et al. 2002: 85ff.

[430] See Fuchs 1999: 176ff on the need for an effective controlling of business partnerships and co-operations.

This monitoring must assess for each stakeholder whether the relation or interaction that is involved is *within or outside the expected* (and possibly agreed) *range*. This means specifically whether

- stakeholders contribute to the project within the expected range (no intervention needed) or

- stakeholders claims are being fulfilled within the expected range (no intervention needed) or

- (negative) interferences, for instance of opposition stakeholders or illegitimate claimants, fall within the expected range (no intervention needed)

This book proposes a simple monitoring map showing current status and progress over time, which constitutes a basis for *discursive evaluations* (see Figure 25):

Principal stakeholders	Previous 4 quarters				This quarter (Q0) assessed by				Rationale, comments
	Q-4	Q-3	Q-2	Q-1	Board	Project	Self	Avg.	
Donor 1 head office				1.3	2	2	1	1.7	
Donor 1 field representative				1	1	1	1	1.0	
Donor 2 head office				2	2	3		2.5	
Donor 2 field representative				2	2	2	3	2.3	
Implementation NGO head office				1	2	2	1	1.7	
Implementation NGO program director				2.6	3	2	1	2.0	
Bangladesh ministry of commerce				1.5	1	1	1	1.0	
Representatives of beneficiary group 1				1	1	1	1	1.0	
Representatives of beneficiary group 2				2	2	3	1	2.0	
....									
Subcontractor head office									
Subcontractor project backstopper									
...									
Others									
Key infrastructure providers				1	1	1	1	1.0	
Corporate lawyer									
Landlord						3		3.0	

1 = white (in range), 2 = grey (watch-out), 3 = black (action needed)

Figure 25. Quarterly Stakeholder Monitoring Map[431]

To the degree that board members are also stakeholders, this figure also represents a self-assessment by the board members.[432] The importance that such a monitoring map could have in providing a platform for discursive conflict resolution is illustrated by the next example:

---

[431] A similar chart has been applied by the author in various business settings.

[432] See also Chapter 4.2.2.2 on the monitoring of organizational effectiveness, which includes the board's effectiveness.

"I don't think you are getting the support you need"

From the beginning, Frizz, a donor representative, had made no secret of his opinion that he thought I would not get the appropriate support from the head office to carry out this project. These usually informal remarks put me in a difficult position, so I invited him to talk directly to my boss or the director of SwissNGO. I myself gave the head office the benefit of the doubt, particularly at the beginning. The longer the project went on, however, the more the lack of support became obvious.

But not only were we lacking input and backing from SwissNGO, there was also no legitimate way in which this issue could have been brought up. Or better, where it would pop-up in the normal process of stakeholder evaluation.

Had such a way of proceeding been in place, then the fact that the project was inadequately supported by its head-office would have become a topic on the project governance agenda; actions would have been investigated, and monitoring would have allowed for appropriate follow-through.

Project governance, with one of its tasks being the regular monitoring of key stakeholders, provides an institutionalized platform on which such contribution issues of stakeholders would pop up as part of a normal monitoring process, laying the groundwork for discursive explorations toward a solution.

4.4.4 Summary

Stakeholder Management is not new, particularly not in development cooperation. This book, however, proposes an approach adapted to the context of development from management and business-ethics theory. This approach draws on two different schools of thought, the *strategic* stakeholder approach and the *normatively critical* stakeholder approach. The extended foundation of the normatively critical approach worked out in this book has already been illustrated in Chapter 4.3 on integrity management. Its adaptation to stakeholder management in development contexts further provides development actors with a more rooted foundation, in terms of critically reflection and rational understanding. Modestly, but also actually, the book hopes to make a contribution to meaningful stakeholder interactions.

Within the process model for stakeholder management further developed here, two steps are of particular importance: *Stakeholder identification,* which faces the challenge of how to identify stakeholders as *completely* as possible, and *stakeholder monitoring,* which allows one to assess anticipated contributions and provides a basis for discourse-oriented solutions of problems. Tools and control questions for both steps have been provided.

The notion of *extended* stakeholder management can be understood in the context of development *cooperation* only when one recognizes that appropriate stakeholder interactions are not only a way but *also a part of the objective.* Jointly with the complexity of stakeholder management in the development context, this fruitful duality of role explains why extended stakeholder management needs leadership attention and is therefore a part of the project governance agenda.

4.5   Risk management

4.5.1   Objective of risk management

Our brief overview of organizational theories has identified risk management as one of the key responsibilities of project governance (see Chapter 3). Therefore, this chapter focuses on "the task of the [governance] board and the top management to define an integrated, future-oriented risk management concept,"[433] adapted here to the context of development projects.

This book defines the objective of good risk management as the proactive recognition and preparation for possible (positive or negative) events and situations in such a way that *initiative of action is retained* within the project, so that project success is maximized and losses or casualties are minimized.

Development projects have a particular need for the kind of risk management system outlined here, for most development projects are probably high-risk matters. External risks are larger due to the very nature of the development-project environment, and by the same token internal risks are larger, too, as development approaches are often based on fairly young (and often disputed) approaches. It is consequently not surprising that development actors possess a natural risk inclination, which is further leveraged through the continuous flow of new development funds (in contrast to business practice, whose closed finance cycle allows for the funding of new endeavors only from previous financial successes). These development characteristics therefore call all the more for conscious and committed risk management as outlined below. Of course, the wish to foresee and plan for all cases and contingencies is illusory; but good risk management

---

[433] Hilb 2005: 165.

none the less provides pragmatic tools and enables one to take an ongoing inventory, continuously assessing a project's risk situation and determining whether sufficient 'coverage' or 'insurance' is available.

Despite the fact that risk management is not a new topic, "the understanding and implementation of formal risk management is extremely inconsistent,"[434] a finding which is confirmed by our case study. This finding is also supported from a business perspective: Hamel and Prahalad have found that management spends less than 3% of its available time on risk management.[435]

This chapter develops a risk management system for the project governance level. In doing so, it draws on existing risk management approaches from both the project management[436] and corporate governance levels.[437] Numerous case examples serve to unveil specific gaps and weaknesses in current approaches. The intended result is a risk management system on project governance level with the following characteristics:

1. (close to) *Complete risk inventory* (as opposed to preparing for the worst, often low-probability risks, and omitting the higher-probability, but unspectacular risks);

2. Continuous and broad-based *risk identification based on a participatory culture* of *creativity* (as opposed to opportunistic assessments on the eve of management presentations);

3. Complete *risk-treatment processes*, i.e. mitigation, down-side[438] planning, monitoring and communication (as opposed to mitigation planning which lacks any follow-through)

4. *Strategically anchoring* and integrative management providing *up-front support* (ideally eliminating justification and mis-communication issues in the event of down-side hits).

---

[434] Thomsett 2004: 1. This inconsistency is also mirrored in the corporate governance literature in particular: Monks & Minow (2004), Steger (2004), Carter & Lorsch (2004) merely mention risk management, while Schwarz fails to mention it (2005) in his discussion of nonprofit organizations.

[435] See Hamel & Prahalad 1997.

[436] "Risk Management as per Project Management Institute" (PMI) is one of the nine knowledge areas of project management. Numerous books follow the same or a similar categorization usage.

[437] See, for instance, Hilb 2005, Boutellier & Kalia 2004, 2005.

[438] The 'down-side' of risks is referred to as the event, catastrophe, or scenario which risk management tries to foresee and possibly prevent.

This chapter looks first at the particularities of risks in development projects, using the system-oriented categories of the St. Gallen Management Model. Then, a cyclic risk management model is presented, and finally risk management specific needs with respect to the organizational and cultural elements are outlined.

4.5.2   Particularity: Understanding risks in development projects

4.5.2.1 Definition of risks

At this point, the reader is invited to imagine that his organization entrusts him with the task of leading the implementation of a huge project – huge not only in being the biggest project within the organization, but also in being the largest *worldwide* of its kind. What would risk assessment look like? Would the risks as described in the following example have been included in the assessment plan?

Stakeholder internal conflicts as a risk factor?

I had met Tom, one of our donor representatives, at a social event. I ended up asking why we as the contractor, one year into the project, still had not received the final donor sign-off of the revised project document. "My counterpart in the head office was absent, on maternity leave, when the basic green light was given. Trying to catch up now, she seems to have a difficult time accepting what has happened in the meantime," Tom explained. Why then would he not push this unsatisfactory issue to the next higher level, I wondered out loud.

I received no real answer. Instead Tom asked: "Instead of me, couldn't you as an outside contractor push this matter to a higher level at my head office?"

Apparently, we had walked onto the scene of internal power struggles with this donor and were served as their political football.

Risks can be manifold; as is obvious from this example, some of them turn up where least expected. Let us, therefore, first look more precisely at definitions of risk. Thereafter, we can introduce different categories of a risk and a number of examples in order to broaden the reader's understanding of possible risks.

Risk can be defined as "the probability that the actual development / form of a future event deviates from the anticipated one (positively or negatively)."[439] In a more formal way, it can be said that

"risk = probability of occurrence   x   effect."[440]

Boutellier and Kalia supply an interesting enhancement of this basic definition, introducing a surprise factor which formalizes a proportional factor, that the higher the surprise about possible 'disruptive factors,' the higher the risk:

"risk = probability of occurrence   x   effect   x   surprise factor."[441]

Often, risks are also brought into close connection with *opportunities* (a factor that is inherent in the ubiquitous SWOT analysis). Also, all opportunities carry risks and all risk entail opportunities. Dealing with opportunities, however, requires a different skill set than dealing with risks. Identifying and pursuing opportunities is inherent to entrepreneurial thinking (see Chapter 4.2 on mission management), whereas risks are not – or at least not to the same extent. This book does not deny that it is useful to have a dual understanding of risk management (as a controlling and enabling function, see Figure 26), but it acknowledges that there is also a separate governance function with a *main focus* on opportunities, which is mission management. The integrative element between risk management and mission management is that they both build upon a system understanding as facilitated by the St. Gallen Management Model (see the next few chapters for a risk-specific application of the St. Gallen Management Model).

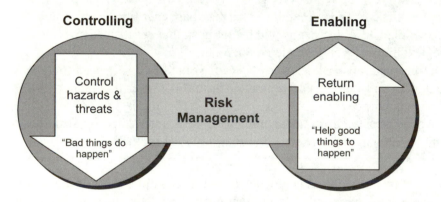

Figure 26. Dual nature of risk management[442]

---

[439] Thommen 2000: 472 (translation Renz).
[440] Boutellier & Kalia 2005: 6.
[441] Boutellier & Kalia 2005: 8.

Another important characteristic of risks is their *categorization*. Numerous ways of categorization can be set forth:

- Business risks, project risks, production-system risks, benefits-realization risks and personal risks,[443] or simply
- Internal and external project risks[444] just to name two examples.

These categorizations may lead one to infer that risk identification is nothing more than running through a check list of categorized risks. Identifying risks, however, is a highly creative task; checklists of possible risks and upfront risk categories may actually obscure the creative horizon, because no matter how comprehensive, they cannot replace a highly creative 'what-if' search. A more appropriate means than checklists is needed, a model which guides the risk manager in "steering his attention"[445] without limiting his focus by the constraints of the rationale behind a few predetermined categories.

This book therefore proposes to resort to the new St. Gallen Management Model adopted for the development sector (see Figure 16). It allows one to analyze and understand a project and its surroundings in a systemic and systematic way. It also represents a good framework for the systematic identification of risks.[446] The six basic categories in the model serve as reference categories when conducting risk assessment. The rest of this chapter presents several practical case examples within these basic categories. The intent is not to lay out an overview of all possible risks – only a process-oriented and creative approach can supply the insights for each project – but rather the objective is to sensitize the reader to the broadness of possible risks, using a concrete model to steer attention.

---

[442] Adapted from Bodenmann 2005: 113 and IFAC (International Federation of Accountants) 1999: 7.

[443] Thomsett 2004: 4. See PMI 2003: 82, Keiser 2005: 160, IFAC 1999: 15.

[444] DRIVER 2002.

[445] Rüegg-Stürm 2003: 14.

[446] Haller further elaborates on the risk management function within the St. Gallen Management Model. He modifies the St. Gallen Management Model by introducing into it a new risk-process model (see 2004: 168). This more sophisticated model overall is certainly justified for use by developed enterprises of a certain size. For development projects, however, where risk management is often not yet done systematically, a simpler approach is chosen here which uses the basic St. Gallen Management Model.

4.5.2.2 Risks from environmental spheres

The environmental sphere covers firstly the society and secondly society related perception of nature, technology application, and forms of value creation. Understanding these environmental spheres in their integrity allows one to preempt risks stemming from the wider environment of development projects. Here is one example of how situational conditions posed a risk to the timely roll-out of the case-study project:

Time as risk factor – delays in establishing a legal base for project operation

In Bangladesh, there are several options for the legal form of a development project:

- Registration and establishment as a local NGO (implying government-controlled fund transfers and possibly taxability[447]).

- Negotiating a project-specific agreement (so called TAPP[448]) involving several ministries.

- Basing operations on existing bilateral agreements between Bangladesh and (for instance) Switzerland. This option would require funding flows and agreements between donor head offices in the case of donor consortia.

It was certainly right not to set up shop as a local NGO under existing circumstances. For instance Proshika, a major NGO involved with international funding, had its fund blocked and the general manager arrested apparently because of links with the opposition party. Donor interventions were without effect.

The donors chose the TAPP option, assuming project completion within 3 months. It finally took around 18 months, with changes of government officials and ministers included. Later inquiries into similar experiences (within the same donors) revealed other projects with delays of 30 months and more. The third option, in fact, would have caused less effort; a number of important activities, particularly in collaboration with the government, also could have started on time.

---

[447] Despite the fact that according to international agreements international development funds are not supposed to be taxed.

[448] Technical Assistance Project Proposal.

Other possible risks for development projects stemming from the environmental spheres might be:

- Social problems, religious conflicts

- The social position of women

- World events impacting locally, for instance the Iraq war possibly creating social unrest against foreign projects and representatives

- Political power struggles and their potentials for political conflict (for instance, the tolerated emergence of radical forces in Bangladesh, climaxing with the explosion of over 500 simultaneous bombs in August 2005)

- Natural disasters (Bangladesh experiences heavy flooding nearly every year, and there is also the possibility of earthquakes)

- The availability of public infrastructure.

4.5.2.3 Risks from stakeholders

As seen in Chapter 4.4, stakeholders have particular importance for, and bring a special complexity to, development projects: There are no shareholders; the funding donors are the key stakeholders (sometimes with diverging agendas) and the influence of beneficiaries on the project's value creation probably differs from the influence that customers can have on markets, and so forth.

We have already seen how, from the practice of extended stakeholder management, a number of risks were identified. Similarly, risk management may come up with new stakeholders by looping back into the extended stakeholder management. For stakeholder risks, the following points should be considered:

1. Is the stakeholder's internal structure transparent, i.e. negligible, or is the stakeholder composed of various actors whose intra-organizational tensions and power struggles need to be considered and treated separately (see the example at the beginning of this chapter)?

2. Are there surprise stakeholders or stakeholders who bring unaccounted-for opposition? With respect to surprise stakeholders, international projects wear – to certain extent through their own fault – something like a label pasted on their forehead which says, 'We have money to spend.' The more visible a project, the more exposed it is to any type of approach with inappropriate claims.

3. The assessment of stakeholder claims introduced earlier[449] should be reviewed critically: Have expected benefits and possible damages been assessed correctly, and what would worst-case scenarios look like? What if our rationale for legitimacy and reasonable expectations is not understood or is challenged?

The following example shows how a certain visibility (in this case simply through moving offices) can foster undue opportunism leading to unexpected dynamics of events:

Abduction threat – surprise stakeholders and free-riders

"Jibon, our Chief Administrator, is in danger" the employee shouted as he ran into my office on this pre-monsoon morning. Apparently, seven to eight armed men had come to our office building the evening before with the intention of abducting our Chief of Administration.

What could lie behind that? After a moment of deep breathing I started to collect the facts. It was said that the men were sent from a real estate agent called Mayeesha. (A woman called Mayeesha had in fact presented unjustified commissions for office-hunting). Jibon couldn't add any perspective because he was scared to death, having locked himself up in his apartment. I talked to our drivers, who might have been around the scene.

After three hours of detective work I could surmise that the abduction was probably wishful thinking on the part of our current landlord. He was having serious issues with Jibon who had rejected a number of undue claims which the landlord had presented from the moment he had heard that we were moving out of his building. I could give the all-clear, helped my staff to calm down, but I also worked out an agreement with the police to intensify patrols in our area for the time being.

This example also shows – as always in crisis situations – that an issue never comes up alone: The landlord (himself a source of issues) had been free-riding along with undue claims from another surprise stakeholder. Preventing these kinds of issues from arising through appropriate stakeholder management, risk management and down-side strategies[450] is an essential practice for allowing a project to sustain a reasonable focus on its core mandate.

---

[449] See Step 2 of the Four-Step-Model for Stakeholder Management, Chapter 4.4.3.1.

[450] Down-side strategies refer to strategies on how to proceed when the down-side triggers in, that is when the risk becomes reality, see Chapter 4.5.3.2.

4.5.2.4 Risks from issues of interaction

As we have seen in Chapter 4.1, issues of interaction refer to the numerous exchanges and interactions between the project and its stakeholders on various, sometimes controversial subjects. These *issues of interaction* can be grouped into (1) *concerns and interests*, (2) *norms and values,* and (3) *resources*. Risks stemming from one of these three groups are ultimately also risks emanating from issues of interaction. They will be examined in due order below.

As we have also seen, *concerns and interests*, along with *norms and values,* are particularly important in development projects, as the very nature of development contains normative discourses and interactions. In order to cope with this fact, *integrity management* was introduced as one of the key responsibilities of project governance.[451] What, then, are the risks stemming from concerns and interests, and norms and values? In principle, all the integrity challenges and their tension zones (see Table 5) constitute risks for the project. Just to name a few:

- Risks of corruption, or related unclear processes
- Risks of mobbing, related loss of efficiency, resignations or law suits
- Strategic opponents in key positions, who pose a risk to the fulfillment of the expected results or contracts etc.

Finally, risks stemming from *resources* may have to do with the availability of resources and their conditions of utilization. The following example shows how a not unusual combination of factors can make the availability of human resources a critical and underestimated risk:

Are the desired profiles of human resources available in Bangladesh?

The project plan foresaw a project headcount of 50+ people and numerous partnerships with local NGOs and businesses. Usual team training, the input of international experts and team building-measures were included in the plan. Would we be able to find these resources short term? Were these measures enough in the event of a possible (worst-case) combination of the following factors?

---

[451] See Chapter 4.3. on integrity management.

- High number of resources to be recruited instantaneously;

- Newness of the chosen development approach, with few skills available on site;

- A development approach highly dependent on the human resources;

- Absorbability / Trainability: Would senior development workers or partners absorb the various paradigm shifts and cultural changes of the new approach?

- What were the educational levels available on the labor market in Bangladesh?

On the ground, we quickly discovered a serious bottleneck in finding the planned resources: instead we ourselves needed to substantially invest in building capacity: Internally by hiring young professionals or graduates from the best business schools, and building them up through extended training and coaching, and then externally by continuous training and close supervision of partner organizations. The promised deliverables for the first year had to be postponed.

Lack of available human resources is a project risk, leading – as in the example – to possible delays. Sometimes, there are also surprises with hired staff. The following example shows how a love affair involving an originally very reliable person seriously hindered the project over a period of several weeks:

Risks from employees' behavior

Barkat, the new accountant, had impressed us through his decisiveness about prompt deliverables, which eliminated the backlog from his predecessor. We were all happy. All of a sudden, however, he grew quite distracted – he lost control in a love affair with a married woman. Swift aggression by the jealous husband resulted in a police raid of our offices and the arrest of several employees (see respective example in Chapter 2.2.3.2) and defamation in the press. The consequences for us involved 9 months of complicated law suits, and various extortion schemes aimed at the project, some of these even from his own family. Terminating and replacing a formerly indispensable employee proved to be the least of our headaches even though he himself was quite a package to handle.

Again, a 'rare coincidence of events' – which involved highly improbable risks – led to very serious project issues.

The next basic category from the St. Gallen Management Model is that of structuring forces.

4.5.2.5 Risks from structuring forces

Structuring forces consist of the strategy, the structures, and the organizational culture. All of them can become sources of risk.

Strategic risks are usually anticipated and not forgotten; their identification and the appropriate mitigation strategies are mostly laid out in the respective strategy documents.

Much less frequently considered, however, are structural risks. As the following example shows, they might be known to management and even be considered when deciding on strategy and structure, but are they really thought through to the end?

Structures and their ability to handle structural issues

As we have seen earlier, SwissNGO had subcontracted a substantial portion of the project DRIVER to a German NGO, GerCon. What looked good on paper, with seamless integration and functional reporting lines, worked out only partially in practice – which again is not necessarily unusual. But where was the mitigation strategy in the event of performance problems with the staff provided by GerCon? What was the procedure to use in case the functional subordination was bypassed? If need be, how was the process we used going to reprimand an underperforming employee from the subcontractor? While the joint structure allowed for us to complement the capabilities of SwissNGO, our risks in entering into the joint structure were not anticipated, and the corresponding down-side strategies were not developed.

Project success depends not only on the right strategy, but also on a high level of coherence and fine-tuning of all activities which we would expect of a certain structure. The more complex the structure, the more numerous are the structural risks.

Risks from cultural aspects also relate to the *integrity challenges* identified earlier, particularly those posing threats to the integrity of the organizational culture (see Table 5). That table can serve to suggest the range of possibilities.

4.5.2.6 Risks from processes

The fifth category of the St. Gallen Management Model, the category of processes, allows one to identify and assess further risks. These occur:

- on the level of management processes (for instance, what if the development approach is highly process-oriented, while donors want to see short term deliverables?)
- on the level of business processes (what if project beneficiaries are tired of development projects and their 'theories of change,' when after numerous questionnaires they have not seen visible results?)
- on the level of support processes (what if processes are not up to best standards, for instance on purchasing procedures?

4.5.2.7 Risks from modes of organizational development

Project start-up and project closure may pose particular risks. What are they? What are both the risks and opportunities for achieving results within the first year of existence? What if the initial infrastructure (office building, visas, IT infrastructure) cannot be made readily available?

While the case study has obviously not provided any examples of the close-out phase of operations, such periods in the management of development projects also have their particular risks. What if essential employees quit early because they have found other jobs? What if there are resentments towards the closing of the project due to lost job security? What if the project needs to be abandoned due to a critical security situation?

Thus far, the risk-specific review of the St. Gallen Management Model has introduced a framework allowing one to systemically and systematically understand and identify risks; the numerous case examples have sensitized the reader to the broadness of possible risks. Thus equipped, we can now turn to the cyclic model of risk management.

4.5.3 A model for risk management

This book suggests a cyclic and continuous approach to risk management, constituted by risk identification and assessment, risk mitigation, risk down-side planning, and a central monitoring and controlling of risk, as illustrated in Figure 27. The four processes will be introduced subsequently.

4.5.3.1 Risk identification and assessment

Risk is a relative term. What one person perceives as a risk is a 'no-brainer' negligible case for another person.[452] The result for planners is that often only the undisputed, big risks actually are identified.

Figure 27. A cyclic risk management process

Riots against the project due to the imminent Iraq war?

Our project had just started when the Iraq war was about to break out. During the war in Afghanistan in which American-led forces went after the Taliban regime, Bangladesh was experiencing riots against Western installations and representatives. It was possible that this would happen again with the outbreak of the Iraq war. The risk was identified, security measures were taken, foreigners were advised not to travel outside the diplomatic areas and some evacuation plans were prepared for worst-case scenarios. Fortunately, however, nothing really happened.

---

[452] Though the apparent 'no-brainers' in particular are the ones that ought to raise the red flags!

Often, the substantial and sensational risks are also low-probability risks as well, whereas the less sensational risks with a higher probability are regarded as 'not worth mentioning.' In the end, however, they may be a lot more dangerous. In order to identify as many risks as possible, a *broad-based identification process* is proposed here, involving representatives of all functions and levels in the organization and creating risk awareness and commitment at the same time. Boutellier and Kalia adapt an engineering risk process, called FMEA,[453] originally an enterprise risk process, for the purposes of corporate governance.[454] The main contribution and key result is a *team-based* risk management approach, which also satisfies the project governance requirements for strategic orientation and organizational integration.

The following are the recommendations for an effective risk-identification and -assessment process:[455]

- Team-based (participatory) approach for risk identification and assessment, involving as big a team as possible (including key stakeholders!)

- Moderated sessions with particular focus on an open risk culture, in which "not exactness, but completeness is asked."[456]

- Identification of possible (and impossible!) events by applying brainstorming or any other creativity methodology. The St. Gallen Management Model, as illustrated in Chapter 4.5.2, serves either as an upfront attention guide or as a cross-check for completeness.

- Identification of the proper risk inclination, for instance through positioning on the 'risk continuum' as illustrated in Figure 28; this will help one to maintain "the balance between the extremes of risk avoidance and risk abdication"[457] when further assessing events and deciding on mitigation and down-side strategies.

---

[453] FMEA = Failure-Mode-and-Effect-Analysis. See McDermott, Mikulak & Beauregard 1996 or Dailey 2004.

[454] Boutellier & Kalia 2004, 2005.

[455] There is abundant literature on risk assessment, mainly on the level of project management (see, for instance, PMI 2003, 2004, Gassmann, Kobe & Voit 2001, Schott & Campana 2005, Fiedler 2001, Buchta, Eul & Schulte-Croonenberg 2004, Führer & Züger 2005). The process summarized here draws on elements common to these approaches, supplemented by insights from the case study and by contributions of specifically mentioned authors.

[456] Boutellier & Kalia 2004: 10.

[457] Lambert 2003: 2.

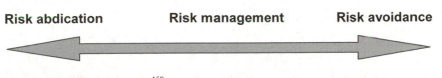

Figure 28. Risk continuum[458]

- Assessment of probability and the 'surprise factor' of events.[459]

- Assessment of impact in case of an event's occurrence, in correlation to possible counter measures (prevention or avoidance).

- Priorization of risks, in case of limited allocation of risk management resources.

The result of this highly creative process are lists of risks, prioritized, categorized, or grouped according to various criteria such as source of occurrence, probability, level of impact, and so forth. They are usually visualized in a portfolio presentation (see, for instance, Figure 30) showing the three dimensions of probability, impact, and surprise.

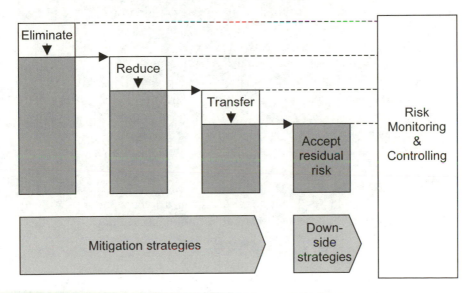

Figure 29. Dealing with risks[460]

---

[458] Lambert 2003: 3.

[459] See Boutellier & Kalia 2005: 8 and Chapter 4.5.2.1.

4.5.3.2 Risk mitigation processes

How should the identified and assessed risks be dealt with? Figure 29 illustrates the different possibilities.

As a first step, risks can be eliminated, reduced, or transferred, all of which are the focus of risk mitigation strategies. The residual risk needs to be accepted (i.e. assumed or consciously incurred), and corresponding down-side strategies need to be developed, which will be discussed in Chapter 4.5.3.3.

Risks can be *eliminated,* for instance, either by renouncing a project entirely or by using a "proven technology instead of a new technology."[461] The following is an example of reducing the risks of wrong recruitment decisions (see also earlier example):

Recruiting process

Karim, 36 years old, seemed to be a very strong candidate when applying for the vacancy of marketing specialist. He had gone through several interviews already. All our interviewers liked him, until Parna, one of our division managers, called: "The guy is 46 and not 36; he omitted 10 years in his resume and his certificates!" He had learned this from informal small-talk in a follow-up interview.

Earlier we had established a formal recruiting process that involved a screening interview, a written test, follow-up interviews (where the diversity of interviewers was a selection criteria) reference checks and possibly field tests. The explicit objective was to gather as broad a picture as possible and to give every interviewer a veto right, allowing us to identify and take seriously any doubts or hints that might appear at any time during the process.

Karim wasn't hired. Though we liked him, we were not sure what he might be omitting in his professional life when 10 years had just slipped through his resume. The detailed (and continuously optimized) recruiting process thereby prevented us from running bigger risks.

How risks can be *reduced* is shown by the following example, which shows the preventive creation of a support structure, particularly for coping with the high degree of vulnerability typical of development projects.

---

[460] Enhanced from Swisscom 2001, cited in Haller 2004 and Boutellier & Kalia 2005.

[461] Boutellier & Kalia 2004: 9.

Risks can also be *transferred,* for instance, to other organizations or subcontractors. Once transferred, however, can we forget about them? The following example illustrates once again a recruitment risk (i.e. of recruiting unqualified drivers) that had been transferred to a donor:

Risk example: Using drivers certified by a donor

To recruit our drivers we could rely on a drivers' pool managed by one of our donors. This was a comfortable arrangement, as technical abilities were basically assured.

Hannan had been a reserve driver of ours for a few weeks and was the candidate for an upcoming opening for a new driver. Coming back from a business trip, I was confronted with formal and informal complaints that Hannan was 'violent and did not integrate into the drivers team, that he had been in jail for a year, that he had threatened the other drivers if they should complain...'.

Information from various sources seemed to corroborate these allegations. But, what to do now, since we also had to try to avoid any violence in the resolution of this problem?

Transferred risks, then, may still impact the project after they have left the scene. They need to be monitored closely. In the above example, the project was hit by the down-side of an outsourced risk which looked like a dead-end street, although it could though be resolved through the following actions:

We resolved the case as follows: Our vacancy was filled with a senior and more qualified candidate; we made certain that everybody understood this difference in qualification; at the same time, we were able to find a temporary (three-months) position within a sister project that we could offer to Hannan,[462] hoping with this palliative measure to prevent any undue action against us. (The sister project was made aware of the risk; they accepted the risk of helping us out, as their project was set to close within the same three months).

When dealing with possible risks, good risk management always needs to make educated choices. Particular attention should be given to high probability, high impact, and high-surprise risks. Figure 30 illustrates, via portfolio visualization, how 'high' risks can be chosen for mitigation:

---

[462] As an aside, it is worth mentioning the time and effort involved in searching, finding, and elaborating solutions for a case like the one here described.

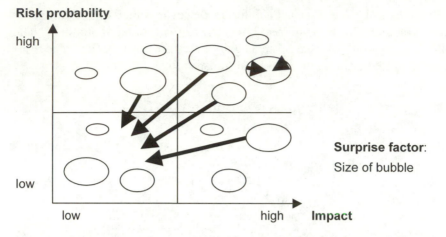

Figure 30. Selecting high probability, high impact, and high-surprise risks for mitigation

The risk categories that remain after risk elimination, reduction, or transferals need to be actually taken on, that is, accepted or incurred. This different step of risk management is examined in the next chapter.

4.5.3.3 Risk down-side planning

Down-side planning means accepting the risk and planning for the worst to happen: What-if *really*?

> **What-if really?**
>
> What if Bangladesh is really flooded (which unfortunately happens nearly every year, not infrequently affecting major parts of the country)? What if there are 'hartals' (general strikes, a currently popular political process played out between the governing and opposition parties) posing security risks for personnel, halting or restricting project activities?

Down-side planning is required for residual risk, i.e. the kind of risk that cannot be (completely) eliminated, reduced or transferred. Down-side plans need to contain at a minimum the following two key elements:

1. Reaction plan: How should the project, or its involved employees, immediately react to the crisis when it hits, and what mediating measures are required to keep operations running so as to stabilize the situation.

2. Support structure: What support structure is needed to minimize the impact of the crisis or the incident? Does this support structure need to be prepared in advance?

3. Communication plan: Who needs to be informed, of what, and how?

The following example shows a risk which was accepted, but where unclear communication plans led to subsequent risks.

Road accident (part 1)

'Driving in Bangladesh is dangerous. Drivers involved in a traffic accident are often lynched by an infuriated mob, and so drivers usually flee from the scene', read the travel guide which I had consulted previously to my move to Bangladesh.

How should our project face this risk? A first risk-reduction strategy was to hire professional and qualified drivers. My Chief of Administration confirmed the lynching risk; he also reassured me that he would take care to duly instruct the drivers. The risk seemed under control, even when we cross-checked directly with the drivers: "I would keep you, the vehicle and myself safe," was their answer.

Or so it seemed until that early morning when Ahmed, a local professional, came into my office looking like a nervous wreck. Apparently the day before his driver had hit a young boy running onto the street from behind a bus and might have killed him. I let him explain the details. Finally, I asked why they did not report things the day before, both having mobile phones for any emergencies. Apparently, the driver had implored him not to tell us anything about it, but then Ahmed himself couldn't sleep and decided to clear his conscience.

In trying to locate the driver, we found out that he had left that very morning with a consultant for another mission to the same area. So he was driving the same car and was passing through the same location where the accident had taken place the day before. Intending to cover up by doing this, the driver none the less was exposing himself and his passenger to the risk that somebody might recognize the vehicle and possibly attack them. While the casualties caused in such incidents represent one aspect of risk, the driver – through his behavior – had just incurred another risk (of consciously exposing himself and his new passenger to further danger).

As noted above, problems come in crowds rather than alone. This example shows that apart from any immediate casualties caused (Risk 1), the driver risks both his own life and possibly those of his passenger (Risk 2). Obviously, our driver was afraid to report the incident because he feared the consequences. The example therefore demonstrates just how complex down-side strategies need to be, and how a variety of factors, some of them follow-ons from others, need to be considered.

Road accident (part 2)

In fact the driver was terminated the same day, not because of the accident, but because of covering up and incurring increased risks.

But what to do about the boy who had been hit? We did not know anything: Whether he was alive or not, injured seriously or not. How were we to find out more? As a development project, we knew that it was obviously important to assume our responsibility and try to compensate for the pain and the damage caused. But on the other hand how could we avoid the risk of being milked for excessive compensation, especially since we were apparently a rich development project? How were we to find the right line?

I was strongly discouraged from following the official procedures involving the police since these "only increase the transaction cost without helping the case per se."

We were lucky to have a reliable 'exceptional situation manager,' an external person of integrity available for just such crisis cases, who could be assigned immediately to get involved, investigate the facts and negotiate a solution.

This example shows the value of having in place an existing support structure, in this case an independent 'exceptional situation manager,' a measure that is particularly important for development projects operating in a field of increased complexity.

When establishing down-side plans, it should be considered that the reaction plan must often ignore normal procedures and hierarchical structures in order to be both efficient and effective (which is a lesson learned from crisis management in so-called 'high-reliability organizations' like aircraft carriers or electricity suppliers[463]).

---

[463] For instance, resolving or identifying a technical issue during the landing of an airplane on a carrier: This kind of fluidly adaptive and immediate reaction draws on the characteristics of high reliability organizations when handling a crisis. See Schulman et. al. 2004.

In summary, it can be said that down-side planning is unfortunately often neglected. When adequately taken into consideration, it needs to cover three elements: Reaction, support structure, and communication. Project governance has to make certain that these elements are in place. That certainty is best assured through effective risk-monitoring, such as the kind outlined in the next chapter.

4.5.3.4 Risk monitoring and controlling

Risk monitoring and controlling are tasks which lie at the heart of project governance. Risks need to be monitored continuously and communicated adequately. This process needs to include *all* categories of risks: Eliminated, reduced, transferred, and in particular the assumed residual risks. Such monitoring also obviously needs to cover the mitigation and down-side strategies, revealing whether they are up-to-date and are proving to be efficient or not.

One aspect of risk monitoring and controlling is how, and to whom, risks are communicated. There are many ways of considering the variety of communication media which should be chosen, depending on the complexity of risks or the level of crisis from a risk in case it has triggered in. This variety of ways and media is illustrated in Figure 31.

The particularity of the risk approach proposed in this book lies in (1) its cyclic approach, which is capable of targeting continuity, with monitoring

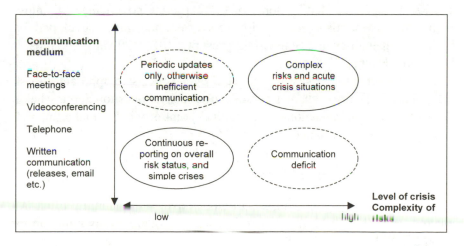

Figure 31. Communication media appropriate to type of risks or crisis level[464]

---

[464] Adapted from Boutellier & Gassmann 2001: 39.

in the center of the risk management steps, and (2) its anchoring at the strategic level, through making it a project governance topic in the first place. The following example illustrates how risk management is often practiced with a lack of continuity and managerial attention:

No risk management at all in the project?

Risks were assessed on several occasions, but in isolated ways. The initial project appraisal reads that "considerable efforts have been made in developing strategies to mitigate such risks, both through project design and through technical assistance in key areas." However, only a summarized risk list was available. Also, before accepting the job I had made my own assessment of the project's risk, and later some SWOT analyses were conducted. None of those, however, made reference to earlier assessments. Apart from systemic risk identification, the short-coming of the project's risk management lies (1) in its absence of conti-nuity, which ideally would build on and enhance previous assessments, and (2) in the lack of strategic positioning for risk management (it was not integrated into the newly established project assessment done for the foundation council of SwissNGO).

Risk monitoring can also include overall basic risk management fitness checks, as recommended by some of the corporate governance literature: Hilb refers to a quick check with 15 yes/no questions, developed by KPMG.[465] Gandossy and Sonnenfeld present a list of 50 warning signs of impending trouble.[466]

This chapter thus far has introduced a cyclic four-step approach to risk management. The next chapter pursues the practical question about what is needed from an organizational and cultural point of view to make this risk management actually happen.

4.5.4   Risk organization and risk culture

Why is risk management, and in particular down-side planning, often ne-glected, even though Murphy's law is widely known: 'If anything can go wrong, it will'?

---

[465]   Hilb 2005: 171ff based on KPMG 2003.
[466]   2004: 103ff.

Conscious risk management requires an appropriate risk culture, in which the identification of risks, the act of planning for disaster, and a certain '*fantasy* for the evil' are seen as positive, business-supportive activities rather than pessimistic and uncomfortable ones. Employees who raise the prospect of risks should consequently be commended for *assuring business continuity*. The need for a risk culture has two implications: First, risk management needs to have the *sponsorship* and active participation *of top management*. Risk management is not only a task of the governance board; it also needs integration in the risk management of the stakeholders, head offices, donor headquarters etc.

Second, *risk culture* is *per se* a topic to be dealt with on both the project- and the project-governance level – as seen from the team-based (participatory) approach for risk identification and assessment. Analyzing and critically reflecting on a project's risk culture needs to be a conscious effort undertaken by personnel at all levels of the organization. Still, possibilities for influencing a risk culture are limited: Repeated usage of the proposed risk management measures, and awareness creation through training and a corresponding management style, are probably the most important measures that can be taken in this respect by project governance.

Figure 32 describes the organizational integration of project risk management into the risk management on the top-management and board levels.

Risk management responsibility consequently needs to be thoroughly worked into the job descriptions of the people involved in the broad-based risk identification and assessment process. Whether the assignment of a 'chief risk officer' as known from the insurance industry is necessary depends largely on the size of the project: The high-risk nature of development projects very likely makes this a reasonable request for big projects. In any case, specific risk responsibility needs to be assigned to both the management and the governance levels of the project. As we have seen earlier, this responsibility is not limited to a supervisory function, but requires an active 'hands-on' involvement (be it through involvement in the risk-identification process or through providing part of the risk-support structure, such as access to local donor security officers, governance liaison points etc.).

4.5.5 Conclusions

From the perspective of organizational theory, we have seen the manifest need for risk management on the governance level. This chapter has developed a risk management model and risk understanding adapted specifically to the needs of development projects as follows (returning to the four characteristics introduced at the beginning of this chapter).

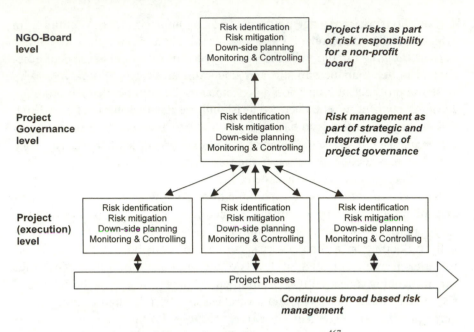

Figure 32. Organizational integration of risk management[467]

A systematic and cyclic approach, based on a system understanding as introduced with the categories of the St. Gallen Management Model, helps establish a (close to) *complete risk inventory.* The anchoring of risk management on the governance level underlines the importance of this inventory. An understanding of risks particular to development projects, as elaborated through numerous case examples and the proposed participative risk culture, support a process of continuous and *broad-based risk identification.* The resulting cyclic four-step process creates an integrated and *complete risk treatment process.* This cyclic function should help overcome the prevalent practice today, in which isolated risk assessments are common and risk monitoring is often lacking. This cyclic process creates continuity and manages to integrate the knowledge that has been gained from previous assessments. Finally, the *strategic anchoring* of risk management, once integrated into the concept of project governance, guarantees the presence of those support and communication channels which are particularly necessary for development projects, since it is in the very nature of such projects to run high risks.

---

[467] Adapted from Keiser 2005: 165.

4.6   Audit management

Audit management is the sixth key responsibility for effective project governance as identified in Chapter 3.

After outlining the objectives of audit management, the terminology and the link between audit and governance will be clarified. Then, the chapter will comment on the state-of-the-art in auditing and on the role of audit committees in *corporate* governance. Subsequently, the relevance of auditing for *development projects* will be examined. Then, the chapter describes the audit management tasks of the *project governance board*. Finally, thoughts on audit culture and the matter of structure conclude the chapter. As always, various case examples illustrate and substantiate the propositions.

4.6.1   Objectives of audit management

This book proposes that audit management is a part of project governance, with identical objectives to those known in corporate governance. These objectives are:[468]

1. Direction and control of internal auditing
2. Direction and control of external auditing
3. Assessment of financial reports and interim reports
4. Legal compliance
5. Liaise with audit-relevant key stakeholders.

Sometimes, risk management and ethical compliance are also included in audit functions. As seen earlier, both are crucial areas within development projects. That is why risk management constitutes its own key responsibility within project governance, and similarly why ethical compliance has become part of integrity management.

4.6.2   Terminology and importance for governance

Generally speaking, the *audit* function is part of the organizational control function. Control primarily belongs to the "fundamental tasks of each superior" when guiding his/her employees "so that the established goals

---

[468] See PwC 2005: 5ff, Hilb 2005: 158.

are met."[469] Auditing is a *complementary while "independent* [and] objective assurance and consulting activity designed to add value to and improve an organization's operations."[470] The main audit focus rests on the reliability of financial reporting, the effectiveness and efficiency of operations, and compliance with applicable laws and regulations.[471]

Organizationally speaking, three audit-related institutions can be distinguished: An external auditor, an internal audit unit (or assigned audit function in the case of smaller organizations), and the audit direction-and-control function of the (corporate or nonprofit) board. The internal auditing department usually reports directly to the highest organizational leadership, i.e. the board, in order to maintain a maximum of independence.

In contrast to internal audits, *external audits* are periodical, time-limited reviews, conducted by a specialized independent third-party. Mostly, they are mandatory by law and primarily serve to assure compliance with laws and regulatory processes.

Furthermore, there is a difference between (internal or external) audit and *internal control*: The latter is broadly defined as a continuous and ongoing process, resulting in an internal control system, assuring that the financial system for instance is reliable, i.e. *assuring the actuality of what the audit is going to examine.*

Auditing is also different from *controlling,* being an institutionalized and integrative part of management, and thereby constituting "an organizational combination of all managerial information provision, planning and control activities to a complete management service function."[472]

What is the relevance of the auditing function for governance? The (corporate) governance legislation, recently established in the aftermath of numerous corporate scandals and bankruptcies, has placed the main emphasis on managerial control.[473] Through this legislative reform, auditing

---

[469] Ulrich P. & Fluri 1995: 152 (translation Renz).

[470] IIA – Institute of Internal Auditor 2005a (emphasis Renz).

[471] See COSO Framework 1992, Hilb 2005: 164.

[472] Ulrich P. & Fluri 1995: 152 (translation Renz).

[473] While the control focus is certainly understandable, the current regulatory emphasis is also criticized as one-sided: For instance, Carter & Lorsch comment on whether the focus of the British Cadbury Committee was appropriate: "it may seem that Cadbury's focus should have been on recommendations for [...] auditors and accounting and financial information, but instead [...] the committee focused on boards in general" (2004: 2).

(specifically, the meaningful supervision of the execution of the audit function) has become "one of the cornerstones of corporate governance"[474]; in particular, the creation of specific audit committees[475] within the governing boards has become a frequently pursued measure.

4.6.3   Auditing within corporate governance

For a better understanding of the content of audit management, this chapter briefly summarizes the state of the art for auditing in the corporate world.

The rules for audit committees at the corporate governance level are mostly set by national legislation or recommended by best practice standards. In Switzerland, the "Swiss Code of Best Practice for Corporate Governance" describes the need and objective of the audit function, although in a summary fashion.[476]

Surprisingly, however, there is little in-depth or scientific literature on the audit function at the governance level.[477] This is reflected in a KPMG study of 2002 which reveals substantial differences in the organizational implementation of audit committees: While in the UK all respondents had audit committee charters, Switzerland (68%), France (58%) and Germany (40%) had substantially lower proportions.[478]

A recent (2005) and representative study conducted in Switzerland by PricewaterhouseCooper and the University of St. Gallen summarizes the current status of Swiss practice as follows: "Audit committees of companies quoted in Switzerland [are found to have reached] a high level with respect to composition, responsibility areas and competences."[479] However, the following areas for potential improvement were discovered, with respect to which "the size and the complexity of the enterprise plays an important role:

---

[474] IIA – Institute of Internal Auditor 2005b: 2.

[475] Hilb, for instance, suggests the creation of an "integrated Audit & Risk Management Committee for quoted companies" (2005: 157).

[476] See Economiesuisse 2002, paragraph 23, 24 and annex 8.

[477] In fact, the Center of Corporate Governance at the University of St. Gallen is currently running a research project on audit committees within corporate governance.

[478] KPMG 2002: 25.

[479] PwC 2005: 4 (translation Renz).

- risk management and internal control are only evaluated by two thirds of the audit committees

- only half of the committees feel responsible for compliance of [legal] norms

- the performance and efficiency of the [proper] audit committee is only evaluated and measured by 39% [of the responding enterprises].”[480]

In summary, then, the corporate sector has shown reasonable progress with audit committees, but still leaves important areas open to improvement.

4.6.4   Auditing within development – relevance to project governance

The field of international development is hardly free of scandals, as the following example shows:

Fraud in Pakistani project

On May 26, 2003, the Swiss Police Department released a press communiqué to the effect that an investigation had been started “in the context of embezzled government funds in the framework of a development project run in Pakistan.”[481] The Pakistani project manager appointed by a Swiss implementation NGO was “under major suspicion of having defrauded the Swiss Confederation of ca. 800’000 CHF’ by means of ‘fictitious overstated invoices.”

The recent revelations of widespread corrupt practices in the ‘oil-for-food’ program, which has been managed by the UN on behalf of Iraq, are another sad example.

For nonprofit-organizations, best-practice codes for nonprofit governance (i.e. at the level of foundation councils etc.) are only now in the process of taking shape. In October 2005, SwissFoundations published “as the first organization in Europe generally valid governance guidelines for modern

---

[480] PwC 2005: 4 (translation Renz).

[481] Schweiz. Bundesanwaltschaft 2003.

and professional foundation management" (SwissFoundations 2005). Simultaneously the 'Swiss NPO-Code' was developed and will be published in 2006 by the so-called 'Conference of presidents of large aid organizations in Switzerland.' A draft version of 2005 also mentions the importance of internal and external control, but it does so, however, only in a summary fashion.[482]

None the less, auditing, particularly external audits, is not new in the development field. Even though development *projects* often do not represent legal organizations on their own, it is normal practice for them to be audited by external auditors, as the next example illustrates:

The half-yearly external audit

SwissNGO has an established global audit contract with PricewaterhouseCoopers (PwC) for half-yearly external audits. The Swiss office of PwC would perform the group audit, and the local PwC branches or representatives would undertake the audits of local projects. In the case of DRIVER the audits were fine, "looking perfect" and "fine achievements" as the program director in Switzerland commented.

Are good-looking external audits a reason to relax – to declare "issues closed, and problem solved"? The development sector, being financed mostly through public funds, has certainly established numerous internal control processes and their corresponding guidelines, as can be understood from the next example, which illustrates the 'rules' in purchasing processes:

Transparency in purchasing decisions through three quotations

One of the quasi-standards for purchasing decisions is that transparency be guaranteed through the consideration of three independent offers, the most advantageous of which is expected to be chosen.[483]

---

[482] Swiss NPO-Code 2005: 16

[483] In the case of SwissNGO, this instruction is part of the so-called project manual, which is placed in the 'support rucksack' given to newly assigned project managers.

It is also an open secret that these three offers depend on the decision of the party who requests a proposal. It is also no news that competitors try to get hold of each others quotations.

I was, however, quite surprised when we were collecting quotations for purchase of a couple of thousand pens required for an awareness-creation campaign: One of the providers offered unexpectedly full service in that he could "provide us with two additional quotations which international organizations usually were needing for their purchasing decision."

'Best practices' reduce risks but protect operations only until 'smart people' (like the full-service provider in this example) have found another way to work around them. The results of the analysis of the audit-relevant case examples can be summarized as follows (further case examples are dispersed throughout the text):

- It seems that periodical external audits are widespread in development projects; there are, however, reservations regarding the 'business' understanding[484] of the external auditors as well as their independence.

- The idea of internal auditing (in terms of an "independent, objective assurance and consulting activity"[485]) is hardly recognizable within a given project.[486]

Development projects seem to be two steps behind auditing practices in the corporate sector (while acknowledging that further improvement is needed there also): The *auditing function per se* does seem to be *underdeveloped*, as well as the *attention from the governance bodies*. Audit management on the project-governance level offers a viable solution to both issues.

---

[484] See, for example, 'the development project expertise of external audit firms' below.

[485] IIA – Institute of Internal Auditors 2005a.

[486] An additional indication could be the existence of internal auditing offered by the head office and used by the projects as a service function. For SwissNGO, however, this was not the case, at least not under the conceptual heading of an independent function.

4.6.5   The tasks of audit management

This chapter explains the tasks behind the initially listed five objectives of audit management at the project-governance level. Again, various examples point out particular areas requiring closer attention.

4.6.5.1 Direction and control of internal auditing

First of all, a possible misunderstanding needs to be dealt with: The project governance board is neither the internal auditor nor the compliance officer. While the *internal or external auditor examine* the three areas of (a) reliability of financial reporting, (b) effectiveness and efficiency of operations, and (c) compliance with applicable laws and regulations,[487] the *governance board directs and controls* their work.

This responsibility needs to be put into the context of a development project, and in line with the challenges arising particularly at the start-up of a project. A project needs to build up its processes and internal control system, acquire local audit know-how, and establish audit processes and networks with local specialists for audit requirements. None of this is an easy task in a country like Bangladesh, where the case study took place, since Bangladesh notoriously ranks among the most corrupt countries:[488]

On the one hand, the board's *control* function has to assess the project internal audit system, assuring in particular that staff is continuously trained so that audit ideas remain inherent to both processes and culture. In this respect, the governance board has the "right to carry out any examination necessary in order to fulfill [this] task."[489] On the other hand, the direction function of the board also requires it to support the project's efforts in the establishment of such control infrastructure. Here is a concrete situation which illustrates the need of the project for support in building up its auditing capacity during start-up:

---

[487] See COSO Framework 1992, Hilb 2005: 164.

[488] Compare the corruption perception index as published yearly by Transparency International.

[489] Hilb 2005: 158.

Spontaneous checks of expenses

Terry, my expatriate manager in charge of supervising administration and finances, had received indications from a whistleblower that some of our employees were paid kick-backs by certain suppliers. At that moment, we had no proof, and no concrete data about specific suppliers. What to do? Could the whistleblower be trusted or did he have a hidden agenda? Searching for data, Terry spoke with the head administrator who tried to allay our concerns – with only partial success. Terry spoke with the head financial officer, seeking his advice. How can a kick-back be detected, if paid to an employee for a specific purchase? Any supplier would deny such allegations, particularly if raised by an 'over-powerful' expatriate! And the head administrator on his side may get his share from a corrupt purchasing employee. Whom could we trust? Terry wondered whether we could ask advice from our donor representatives on-site, but felt we would not find support among them: One of these donors had been pointing his finger at a case of fraud in an unrelated Pakistani project (see earlier example) since project start-up – a Damocles sword above us. An external auditor could be an option, but which one, without stirring up too much fuss? We hadn't dealt with any of them so far. No concrete support was anywhere in sight, while a negative and nagging feeling persisted.

Looking for creative solutions a couple of days later, Terry selected a number of receipts which he wanted to have verified. With the help of external, independent Bangladeshi businessmen whom he had known for a while, he visited four providers (imagine standard shops in a crowded market area). Price comparisons showed deviations within the acceptable range. About one of the suppliers, however, they came back saying that 'Something is going on there' – but again without being able to pin down a concrete fact. Another supplier offered to pay them a commission if they would bring a certain monthly volume of purchases. When confronted with our project inquiry, however, that supplier denied any such practice.

This example illustrates the fact that a project needs to be able to perform sporadic, spontaneous cross-checks; with internally dedicated resources or external 'rapid-response teams.' The particular difficulty lies in *building up* this capability given the specific nature or 'singularity' of projects: New staff, new infrastructure, a new location, and new processes –

all within the challenging setting of a development country. That is where project governance can facilitate the task substantially beyond the provision of financial resources: Often some of the key stakeholders, for instance local donor representatives, themselves have auditing practices which could be facilitated for certain functions during the project start-up phase, and through them references to audit specialists could be provided or tips could be supplied about particular practices on site. For this to happen, however, audit management also needs to be on the agenda of the governance board.

4.6.5.2 Direction and control of external auditing

Audit management has a direction and control function with respect to the external audit. Specifically, "the professionalism, integrity and independence of the external audit"[490] need to be carefully assessed. One of the requirements for auditors of development projects is whether they have an understanding of the particularities of the development business, as illustrated in the next example:

> **The development project expertise of external audit firms**
>
> During my assignment as project manager, we employed two different locally contracted auditors to perform the external audit, both representatives of global auditor firms. With both of them it was surprisingly difficult to make them understand certain particularities of development projects, for instance, practices such us complete write-offs at purchasing time, or limited income accounting (as the only income for projects comes mostly from fund-transfers from the administration of the head office).

Not only does the auditor's expertise need to be assessed, but also his or her independence. As the fall of Arthur Andersen underlines, 'external' does not imply neutrality. Conflicts of interest may appear where and when one least expects them, and they may also turn up with representatives of a globally contracted auditing firm, as illustrated below:

---

[490] Hilb 2005: 158.

Conflict of interest – external audit

I was in the final negotiations with the local PwC representative for the external audit to come, a task which was assigned to the project manager. While I had the final approval over all contracts, the middle managers had the authority to negotiate the numerous contracts within their mandate subject to normal reporting.

The big surprise came, however, when – on the same day that the signing of the audit contract was scheduled – the middle manager Parna asked me to review and sign a contract which he had negotiated with the same person to whom the audit was supposed to be contracted. Parna tried to contract her support for the promotion of accounting services among SMEs, while my finance manager and I were finalizing the audit contract. A closer analysis revealed the following: The auditor had (correctly) pointed out the possible conflict of interest, but instead of refraining from the opportunity she thought of handing over the audit assignment to a partner of hers. Parna on his side – himself an experienced CPA – had simply ignored her request to clear the issue with me before going ahead. After checking back with the SwissNGO head office, we kept the person as an auditor but not without previously asking her to certify that she had no other interests or appointments with us. The hopefully singular glitch was discussed with Parna in detail and the head office was informed of the incident.

The control exercised by 'several eyes,' as executed by the project governance body, can help to minimize such problematic appointments.

Finally, in line with the recent PwC study on audit committees,[491] the audit management of project governance also has the task of authorizing non-audit services by external auditors.

4.6.5.3 Assessment of (annual) financial reports and interim reports

From a financial perspective, audit management serves to assure and evaluate the quality of the financial reporting done by the project unit (including the applied accounting standards). Should several key stakeholders demand different reporting formats, it is the responsibility of the governance board to negotiate a balanced solution which takes effort and benefits into consideration.

---

[491] See PwC 2005.

4.6.5.4 Legal compliance

The governance audit management needs to assure the legal compliance of the project organization and its processes. Several countries have been changing or adapting their NGO legislation recently, not always in ways that favor development projects striving for integrity as understood within this book. To meet these circumstances, governance board involvement is crucial.[492]

4.6.5.5 Liaise with other audit-related key stakeholders

Finally, the governance board is responsible for the "assurance of effective communication"[493] not only with the project staff but between all key stakeholders on audit-related matters (for instance, the head-office of the implementing NGO, or the donor head-offices with their audit and governance bodies). This liaising assures an integrated audit system facilitating effective audit measures, thereby eliminating the governance gap.[494] It is also here that possibly divergent audit requirements stemming from various head-offices need to be sorted out and integrated.

With this, we turn to the organizational structure for audit management, and to the requirements for a parallel organizational culture.

4.6.6   The structure and culture of audit management

Audit management is among the key responsibilities of project governance. As such, it is an integral part of the project governance structure (see the discussion of board self-organization and processes in Chapter 4.2). One could imagine the creation of a specific 'audit committee' or,

---

[492] See also in Chapter 4.2 the example called 'An unimportant contract?' on the difficulty of achieving official project approval.

[493] Hilb 2005: 158.

[494] As seen above, the audit function isn't too well established on any level, either on the upper normative or the lower operational level. Hence, it could be argued that there is no audit gap to be filled (i.e. there is no gap between two non existing parts). This reflects only the implementation side, however. The requirements per se do exist (compare also the needs from the outlined examples). Project governance as a middle layer constitutes a conscious and strategically empowered enabler to a better fulfillment of this existing but not yet fully implemented audit requirement.

in line with Hilb, the creation of an "integrated audit and risk management committee."[495] The standard requirements for such a committee (at least three independent board members, no recent executive functions, and sufficient subject-matter knowledge) need to be considered. Whether such a specialized committee can be created depends mainly on the size of the project. The downside of such specialization would be that other board members may mentally disconnect from their holistic responsibility.[496]

Finally, the existence and/or promotion of an *audit-sensible organizational culture* reveals whether the outlined audit requirements are taken to heart. Just as risk management cannot simply be prescribed, so too an audit culture in the sense of 'checks and balances' needs to be *lived*, becoming a question of daily business. Project management therefore also has a pedagogical task to educate staff accordingly, and project governance needs to support (in fact spearhead!) this creation of cultural awareness. The fact that project members may try to elude audit-responsible behavior is illustrated in the next example:

---

[495] Hilb 2005: 157ff.

[496] Not within the scope of this text are possible organizational measures *within the project unit*. One might discuss how the project delivers on its own audit-related requirements, consisting principally of the *internal control* tasks with respect to financial and operational control. As for what project size justifies the hiring of a full time internal controller, who would report not to the financial manager but to the governance board (or to the project manager though less ideal). A benchmark study on internal control in Germany, Austria, and Switzerland (Füss 2004) mentions that in NPOs there is around 1 person per 160 employees, while in banks 1 per 60 employees works in internal control with a (mean value 6.3 respectively for 16.67 per 1000 employees). Obviously, the number of employees represents only a partial comparison criterion. If, however, development projects are considered high-risk endeavors (which from the political and ethical perspectives perspective is the case), then bigger development projects are justified to invest project internal resources into dedicated internal control staff. In the case example, in fact, one of the donors requested a full time external auditor. Unfortunately, it did not materialize – possibly because its value was not understood as *supporting* a strategic audit management within integrated project governance.

Streamlined expense reports

One of the processes established during start-up was a streamlined form for expense reports considering workflow and audit requirements. In particular three check boxes were introduced which the immediate superior was requested to mark when approving the expenditure, indicating whether (1) the amounts were accurate, (2) the receipts were complete and (3) the reason for the expense was business-appropriate.

When the new form was presented to the middle managers, Narad opposed it, arguing he would not be in any position to mark those boxes. The finance manager who had streamlined and presented the new form was quite puzzled, and I shared his surprise: How can a manager assume his budgeting responsibility if he isn't prepared to assure minimal 'checks and balances'? I explained that 'checks and balances' is an integral part of budget responsibility and that the new form primarily represented a help for the signing manager to assume his/her inherent responsibility.

Creating a culture sensitive to audit requirements is a long undertaking, maybe even longer than the project itself. This is no reason not to do it, however; on the contrary, it requires an honest, active, and visible commitment of management, starting at the top, from those in nonprofit governance, to those in project governance and project management.

4.6.7 Conclusion

Current arrangements without an audit function integrated into strategic project governance are simply inadequate. While in development projects certain achievements are recognizable with respect to periodic external audits, the area of internal audit capabilities seems to be an area in need of urgent improvements.

By merely assigning the task (as one among many) of "identifying risk areas and performing related audit steps"[497] to the project finance manager, one engages in self-appeasement rather than the honest intention to equip the project with all that is needed for a reliable internal control function.

The audit management procedure outlined herein constitutes a minimal set adapted from best practices to the context of development projects.

---

[497] As per project appraisal document of DRIVER.

Audit management needs to be understood as an enabling (governance) role that catalyzes and assures good audit practices for the project.[498] Institutionalized project governance with a committed governance board plays a pivotal role in actively and strategically supporting, checking, enabling, linking, and controlling the function of internal and external control.

Audit management as such can thereby become a key function for the effective and efficient implementation of projects.

---

[498] See Jans' comment on "internal control as a catalyst" (2003: 1).

5   Conclusions

5.1   Summary

> *Good governance doesn't fall from the sky; it must*
> *be learned, practiced and enforced.*[499]

This book is based on the hypothesis of a governance gap.

It presents a multi-dimensional view, from the perspectives of corporate governance, project management, and the development sector, including nonprofit governance, which substantiates this hypothesis. The hypothesis is further corroborated by ethical normative considerations whose particular intricacy and weight carry perhaps the most fruitful explorations in these chapters.

The book's case study, which follows the course of a major development project carried out over a period of 20 months, has *confirmed the hypothesis of the governance gap.* The analysis of around 400 examples has led to a multi-perspectival understanding of the kinds of problems and opportunities that come into focus once one begins to address governance issues. Based on this understanding, drawing on the governance roles framed in organizational theories and on several models developed by scholars at the University of St. Gallen, a solution for bridging this governance gap has been developed, the so-called Project Governance Model. Its application to the experience and understanding gained from this particular project has proven to be fundamental.

The governance gap, which this book has examined, is specific to the functioning of development projects in nonprofit organizations or NGOs. That gap has special interest if only because NGOs are in the business, finally, of promoting self-governance among the people with whom they carry out their projects.

---

[499] Jean-Daniel Gerber, Director of the Swiss State Secretariat for Economic Affairs, at a conference of Economiesuisse and Swisscontact on 'Poverty – what is the economy making,' Zürich, June 7, 2004.

Project governance is defined herein as a process-oriented system by which projects are strategically directed, integratively managed, and holistically controlled, in an entrepreneurial and ethically reflected way, appropriate to the singular, time-wise limited, interdisciplinary, and complex context of projects.

Six key responsibilities have been identified. Together, they constitute integrated modules of the Project Governance Model (and are italicized in the following paragraphs):

System management provides a systemic understanding of the environment and of influences. This book adapts the St. Gallen Management Model to the context of development projects, an application that allows one to set up a project in the first place. The same system understanding, and the lessons that come from it, allow all of the involved actors, from the manager to the donors and stakeholders, to steer the project in its environment and to guide it toward specific objectives.

The specific tasks of the governance board in directing and controlling the project and its mission are the subject of *mission management.*

Pursuing the development mission requires sensitivity to what development cooperation signifies. True development cooperation is made possible only through a discursive and recognition-based approach. The challenges inherent in development cooperation may pose threats to the integrity of the project – and indeed, the case study has identified 130 cases which have ethical relevance to that integrity. The study has yielded the need to resort to a universally valid normative foundation. Such a foundation is proposed in *integrity management* through an approach which combines discourse ethics and recognition ethics. Such a combined approach allows development actors to *understand and explicate* integrity challenges to the integrity of the project and its organizational elements, creating so-called tension-zones between the challenges and the elements themselves. A practical process model illustrates how such integrity challenges can be resolved.

Development cooperation ultimately relies on stakeholders. In order to go beyond lip-service to these parties, management tools and management commitment are needed. The proposed *extended stakeholder management* module provides a model with specific focus on the broad identification of stakeholders and a continuous monitoring of the expectations and claims which come to exist between the project and its stakeholders.

Risk management allows one to detect risks in an all-inclusive way once again through reliance on system understanding. This book has emphasized in particular the need for strategies capable of responding when risk down-sides occur with all of their troubling and messy consequences, as well as the need for monitoring risks on the level of project governance.

Finally, *audit management* expands on the audit roles of governance. Insights deriving from the case study propose that internal audit capabilities be strengthened in development projects and that audit needs are aligned on the governance level.

In summary, the proposed model for project governance allows one to close the governance gap in development projects, which was outlined in detail, and thereby contributes to bridging another gap as well, the famous one between theory and practice. The *importance* of such project governance, however, does not lie exclusively in its *support for a proper implementation* of development objectives; project governance as it is presented here also becomes an *implicit part of the objective of true and systemically understood development cooperation.*

5.2 Limitations

The main limitation of this study – that it possesses only a limited external validity – stems from the methodology inherent in a case study and the participant observation which that method entails. Both aspects were indispensable, however, precisely because they let a researcher in the field explore the complex issues and phenomena inherent in the nature of the governance tasks typically required for development projects. Research based on a representative sample can capture neither the particular cause-effect relationships that turn up in the management of such projects, nor the qualitative depth in such relationships and the context which surrounds them in a cross-cultural context. Case studies and the related participant observation methods consequently enable the researcher to dig deeply into the context, and consequently to arrive at qualitative explanations of issues, explanations which are often more meaningful than the statistical significance of data.

This methodological limitation or disadvantage has been taken into account in two ways: First, in selecting for rigorous case studies those criteria which can be *influenced*, in that way providing the best possible internal validity, construct validity, and reliability; and second, in the analysis of the data, in the sense that the model presented always builds and draws on existing theoretical models, such as the St. Gallen Management Model or the integrated business-ethics approach.

A second limitation may lie in the fact that the development project of the case study was one of major size. From one perspective, such gargantuan scale suggests that certain aspects of qualitative reality might be affected by the sheer mass and frequency of events and processes that go with such a large project. On the other hand, and by the same token, one can argue that the normally smaller projects offer fewer relevant case examples for reflection and comparative analysis. The range of circumstantial episodes encountered in this study is a matter not only of quantitative advantage (a large pool from which to draw examples), but also of qualitative richness (the ethical penetration available to a reader from the story of the BCC matter, for example). This reflection supports the reasonable supposition that, in spite of the large scale of the project in this case study, it is exactly the relatively large number of cases of qualitative depth which offer one a better chance of encountering the situations that smaller projects may also may to a lesser extent.

5.3   Implications and recommendations for practice

The governance gap illustrated applies to any development project, *independent of its size, type, or geographic location.* The governance gap does not suggest that currently there is no project oversight in common practice, but rather that such project oversight is probably not exercised in a strategically directed, integratively managed, and holistically controlled way that would foster a stably intermixed set of entrepreneurial and ethical considerations.

The project governance model proposed here, with its six key responsibilities, can be applied to *any* development project. Its implementation, however, may vary, particularly in the matter of structural self-organization, but the responsibilities and tasks *in any case* remain.

It is strongly recommended that international development organizations review their approach to the governance of development projects – and that in doing so, they would do well to focus on key projects first. Project governance requires top management commitment for maximal benefit. But where there is no such commitment, the project governance model can still at least serve managers of development projects on their own level of responsibility to very great effect. The particular circumstances of the project examined in this case study demonstrate exactly that fact, with respect to the level on which actual ad-hoc implementation and experimentation

were carried out, but it also illustrates the fact that without project governance such ideas are left to the good intentions of the project management.

Finally, the multi-organizational view of project governance suggests
that project governance could also be applied as a leadership tool in mandates with local NGOs, thereby allowing a more transparent and equalized
accountability.

5.4   Recommendations for further research

With its focus on closing the governance gap which it has identified, the
book at hand hopefully contributes to the debate around corporate and
nonprofit governance, particularly in its proposals for how to make the
implementation of such governance, that is to say, its operationalization
more meaningful on subordinate hierarchy-levels, specifically in project-
intense organizations. In accord with this aim, this book also contributes to
a more strategic orientation of the project-management theory. Not least
among its emphases, with its close attention to the ethical perspective, the
author also hopes to narrow the considerable knowledge gap in that domain between theory and practice.

The model of project governance is also theoretically applicable to *other
sectors* than that of development cooperation. Project-intense sectors like
construction, information technology, consulting, and so forth probably
face similar problems. Further research could test the applicability of the
Project Governance Model in other project-intense sectors.

The insights gained through the project-governance model proposed
here could also contribute to the further advancement of the emerging concepts of *nonprofit governance*. Further research along these lines could
enhance the nonprofit governance discussion by merging the project-
governance model with the nonprofit governance models that are currently
emerging, i.e. models on the level of foundation councils, association
committees, and so forth.

Finally, it is theoretically possible – and this has been confirmed by research cited in this book – that subsidiaries of multinational corporations
face similar problems and a similar governance gap, particularly when
operating in environments similar to those that are typical of development
projects. Further research may therefore very well contribute to the advancement of *subsidiary governance* by adapting the Project Governance
Model to subsidiary-specific conditions.

Annexes

Annex 1: The UN Millennium Development Goals (MDGs)

Following is an extract of the official UN website:[500]

"The eight Millennium Development Goals (MDGs) – which range from halving extreme poverty to halting the spread of HIV/AIDS and providing universal primary education, all by the target date of 2015 – form a blueprint agreed to by all the world's countries and all the world's leading development institutions. They have galvanized unprecedented efforts to meet the needs of the world's poorest.

The eight Millennium Development Goals are:

1. Eradicate extreme poverty and hunger;
2. Achieve universal primary education;
3. Promote gender equality and empower women;
4. Reduce child mortality;
5. Improve maternal health;
6. Combat HIV/AIDS, malaria and other diseases;
7. Ensure environmental sustainability;
8. Develop a global partnership for development."

In 2000, all 191 United Nations Member States have pledged to meet these goals by the year 2015.

Annex 2: Research methodology

First, the *general approach* describes the rationale for the most suitable research strategy, which is the case study approach. This methodology is further examined by discussing the chosen *data-collection* methodology, the participant observation, and by presenting the *data-analysis* methodology.

---

[500] See UN w/y (www.un.org/millenniumgoals/)

General approach

There are many ways of doing research in social science, just as there are also many taxonomies of research strategy. Apart from case studies, Yin mentions "experiments, surveys, histories and the analysis of archival information."[501] The difference between these research strategies lies accordingly in "(a) the type of research question posed, (b) the extent of control an investigator has over actual behavioral events, and (c) the degree of focus on contemporary as opposed to historical events."[502]

The *case study* research strategy has been selected for a number of reasons: (1) The type of research questions asked is exploratory in nature, where a primary need is to develop theory based on an understanding of 'how' and 'why'. Particularly helpful to this understanding is the inclusion of "extreme situations and polar types," one of the particularities of case studies specified by Eisenhardt;[503] in this way, the understanding of real-life events becomes deeper and more holistic. (2) The case at hand, a major development project in Bangladesh, a country which has hosted three decades of international development efforts, allows for a certain degree of control over behavioral events but never to the extent prevalent in the research strategy for experiments. (3) The focus falls on contemporary events, i.e. on an actual development project in a representative setting.

From a pragmatic perspective, an additional argument for the case study strategy is its flexibility during the data collection process, which allows for adjustments to the collection instruments and to the sources of data as another "key feature of theory-building case research," and as representing "controlled opportunism in which researchers take advantage of the uniqueness of a specific case and the emergence of new themes to improve resultant theory."[504] This flexibility has proved to be instrumental in capturing the relevant data during the process of data collection discussed in the next chapter.

Data collection

The research question calls for an exploratory and inductive data collection methodology with little upfront design, thereby allowing one – in the

---

[501] 2003: 1.

[502] Yin 2003: 5.

[503] 1989: 537.

[504] Eisenhardt 1989: 539.

words of Miles and Huberman[505] – to explore "exotic cultures, understudied phenomena, or very complex social phenomena." Additionally – for the best gathering of situational insights – it must be possible to alter and add data collection methods during the process.

The research at hand was conducted by way of *participant observation*, which "puts you where the action is and lets you collect data – any kind of data you want, qualitative or quantitative, narratives or numbers."[506] This method best responds to the requirement of *qualitative data depth*, as it also grants access to insight data such as interpretations, emotions, politics, and struggles which cannot be captured from an outside perspective or through standard interviews. This results in a high degree of internal validity, allowing studies of "cause and effect."[507]

Alternate data collection methods, according to Bernard,[508] are several types of interviews, and direct and indirect observation methods. Interviews, in particular unstructured interviews, allow for gathering data across a broader sample. Only with difficulty, however, would emotions, politics or ethical considerations be unveiled or discovered. In addition, interviews require a certain pre-understanding of the material; only then can exploration through interviews begin. This fact points to another weakness of interviews, their "reflexivity – [the] interviewee gives what [the] interviewer wants to hear."[509]

Finally, direct and indirect observation cannot deliver enough *insight* data, because they focus only on the *visible* aspects of people's behavior without capturing their thoughts. Cultural conflicts, power struggles and emotions can only be surmised.

The case study research accompanied the development project DRIVER during the project startup and during the first twenty months of project operation in the field. This was facilitated through the author's assignment as general or project manager to the project in Bangladesh. The data collection was hence performed in the form of a participant observation. The collected data consists of ca. 400 events or incidents which were collected in line with Eisenhardt's requirements for successful field notes:[510] Whatever occurred,

---

[505]   1994: 16.

[506]   Bernard 2000. See also Snow & Thomas 1994: 459.

[507]   Scandura & Williams 2000: 1252.

[508]   2000.

[509]   Yin, 2003: 86.

[510]   See 1989: 539.

the author's impressions were written down, i.e. through reacting to the whole feed rather than sifting out what might seem important; also, the thinking was pushed by asking questions such as "What am I learning?" and "How does this case differ from the last?" In fact, the making of field notes which included thoughts and alternative solutions often helped later in resolving the real project situation (which again was included in the field notes). With respect to variety in data sources, the 400 data records consist of observations, newspaper clippings, minutes, protocols, or emails.

As is usual with participant observation, and greatly to its advantage, several adjustments were made to the instruments during the data collection. While at the beginning field notes were kept in separate files, either in electronic format or paper-based, the final instrument is a database with date fields, keywords, comments and references.

With respect to the quality of key informants, specific events or incidents often included feedback loops with a number of project-external source persons or key informants who helped one to understand complex or difficult situations (such as how to react to the arbitrary arrest of three employees and the subsequent extortion spiral, for example). The respective conversations are also captured in the protocols. By assuring different perspectives, through various key informants and the variety of data sources named above, one constitutes a data triangulation, thereby increasing the construct validity and balancing possible observer bias.

During the data collection process, several preliminary classification schemes (for category building) were developed, and with reasonable success, as the content disparity of the data records was higher than expected (which, however, is a good sign for both broadness and depth of data).

From this description, it can also be inferred that the participant observations which the author carried out have fulfilled the measures stipulated by Bernard's "ethical imperative" for the participant observer: A reasonable number of key informants have been involved, data stems from various sources, and the data collection and data analysis have been separated into different phases.

Data analysis

Data analysis consists of "examining, categorizing, tabulating, testing [...] evidence to address the initial propositions of a study."[511] Case study analysis is still one of the most difficult research steps, i.e. "we still lack a bank of

---

[511] Yin, 2003: 109.

explicit methods to draw on" for which "we need to keep sharing our craft."[512] Yin therefore suggests choosing a *general analytic strategy.*[513]

This general analytic strategy can best be described by way of the three-process approach identified by Langley.[514] She advocates that "theory building involves three processes: (1) induction (data-driven generalization), (2) deduction (theory-driven hypothesis testing), and (3) inspiration (driven by creativity and insight)." The analysis of the case at hand has followed a modified circular process as illustrated in Figure 33.

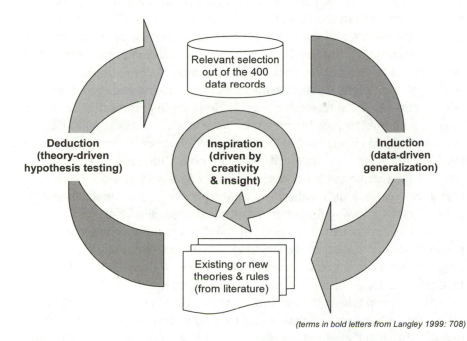

(terms in bold letters from Langley 1999: 708)

Figure 33. General analytic strategy applied to the case study research

On a specific level, the main technique used in support of the analytic strategy outlined above was the creation of a so-called hermeneutic unit based on the software tool Atlas.ti. It allowed the flexible qualitative analysis – principally based on grounded theory – of the large number of cases and associated documentation. Out of these cases, around 80 have

---

[512] Miles & Huberman 1994: 2.

[513] Yin 2003: 111.

[514] 1994: 708.

been included in this book. They are distributed among the chapters as illustrations, allowing the reader more clearly to follow the thought process (see table of case examples).

Discussion of the research approach

The vehicle of participant observation has yielded data of high quality and depth, resulting in a *high internal validity*. Bernard underlines the internal validity aspect of participant observation, in particular that it "lowers the reactivity problem in the collection of observational data"[515] as people get used to the presence of the participant observer and go about business as usual. Longitudinal studies (and with them the technique of participant observation) allow one to establish a "cause-and-effect relationship."[516]

One of the potential issues with participant observation, however, is a "distinct possibility of researcher bias."[517] In order to prevent this issue from arising, a number of possible measures were taken to support what Bernard calls the "ethical imperative" of the participant observer:[518] *Several* trustworthy key informants were involved, "who are observant, reflective and articulate,"[519] Data gathering proceeded by accessing a variety of sources (data triangulation), and data collection was separated from the data-analysis phase, thereby allowing for better distance and conceptualizing.

The increased potential for internal validity obviously comes at the expense of either statistical *generalizations* or external validity, a factor which in any case is one of the basic limitations of case studies. This may be one of the areas for further research (see Chapter 5.4).

As mentioned above, the construct validity of this study has been maximized through data triangulation and by following Ruigrok et al. with the use of participant observation *per se, which through its qualitative data depth allows that "a study investigates what it claims to investigate."*[520] Furthermore, over 80 examples in this book illustrate the sequential development of thinking and how the evidence was derived.

---

[515] Bernard 2000: 369.
[516] Scandura & Williams 2000: 1252.
[517] Miles & Huberman 1994: 2.
[518] Bernard 2000: 369. See also previous section on data collection.
[519] Bernard 2000: 370.
[520] Ruigrok et al. 2005: 7.

Reliability, finally, was considered in building a case-study database that included the hermeneutic unit in Atlas.ti. With the same aim, a protocol has been created that shows the logic by means of which the actors were rendered anonymous.

Annex 3: List of case examples

Bibliography

Aguilera, R.V. & Jackson, G. (2003). The cross-national diversity of corporate governance: dimension and determinants. In: *Academy of Management Review*. 28/3. pp. 447–465.

Albach, H. et. al. (2000). *Zeitschrift für Betriebswirtschaft. Corporate Governance.* Erg.-Heft 1. Wiesbaden: Gabler.

Alexander, J.A., Weiner, B.J. (1998). The adoption of the corporate governance model by Non-Profit Organizations. In: *Non-Profit Management & Leadership.* 8/3. pp. 223–242.

Aoki, M. (2001). *Towards a Comparative Institutional Analysis*. Cambridge: MIT Press.

Apel, K.-O. (1976). *Transformation der Philosophie*. 2 Bände. Frankfurt: Suhrkamp.

Apel, K.-O. (1984). Lässt sich ethische Vernunft von strategischer Zweckrationalisierung unterscheiden? Zum Problem der Rationalität sozialer Kommunikation und Interaktion. In: van Reijen, W. & Apel, K.-O. (Hrsg.). *Rationales Handeln und Gesellschaftstheorie*. Bochum: Germinal. pp. 23–79.

Argyris, C. & Schön, D. (1978). *Organizational learning: A theory of action perspective*. Reading: Addison-Wesley.

Arjoon, S. (2005). Corporate Governance: an ethical perspective. In: *Journal of business ethics.* 61. pp. 343–352.

Arvis, J.F. & Berenbeim, R.E. (2003). *Fighting corruption in East Asia*. Washington: The World Bank.

AusAID, of the Australian Government (2005). *AusGuideline – Activity design: 3.3 The Logical Framework Approach.* Accessed on Dec 10, 2005 on http://www.ausaid.gov.au/ausguide/pdf/ausguideline3.3.pdf.

Bachmann, H. (2002). *Psychological aspects of development co-operation. A comparison of thinking styles of Swiss and Nepali Experts.* Aachen: Shaker.

Bainey, K.R. (2004). *Integrated IT Project Management. A model centric approach*. Norwood MA: Artech.

Bayertz, K. (Hrsg.) (1998). *Solidarität. Begriff und Problem*. Frankfurt: Suhrkamp.

Bearle, A.A. & Means, G.C. (1932). *The modern corporation and private property*. New York: Macmillan.

Benhabib, S. (1995). *Selbst im Kontext: kommunikative Ethik im Spannungsfeld von Feminismus, Kommunitarismus und Postmoderne*. Frankfurt: Suhrkamp.

Bernard, R.H. (2000). *Social research methods. Qualitative and quantitative approaches*. Thousand Oaks: Sage.

Bickman, L. & Rog, D.J. (1998). *Handbook of Applied Social Research*. Thousand Oaks, CA: Sage.

Bleicher, K. (2004). *Das Konzept integriertes Management*. 7. überarbeitete und erweiterte Auflage. Frankfurt am Main: Campus.

Blickle, G. (1994). *Kommunikationsethik im Management. Argumentationsintegrität als personal- und organisationspsychologisches Leitkonzept*. Stuttgart: M&P.

Bodenmann, J.M. (2005). *Unternehmenssteuerung und -überwachung. Beitrag von Risikomanagement, interner und externer Revision zu einer effektiven Corporate Governance*. Bamberg: Difo.

Boutellier, R. & Gassmann, O. (2001). Flexibles Management von Entwicklungsprojekten. In: Gassmann, O., Kobe, C. & Voit, E. (Hrsg.). *High-Risk-Projekte*. Berlin: Springer. pp. 27–44.

Boutellier, R. & Kalia, V. (2004). *Risk management*. Under review.

Boutellier, R. & Kalia, V. (2005). Risk management in flux. In: KPMG. *Audit Committee News*. 9/March. pp. 5–9.

Brönnimann, T. (2003). *Corporate Governance und die Organisation des Verwaltungsrates*. Bern: Haupt.

Bruch, H., Krummaker, S. & Vogel, B (Hrsg.) (2006). *Leadership – Best Practices und Trends*. Wiesbaden: Gabler

Bruch, H., Vogel, B. & Krummaker, S. (2006). Leadership – Trends in Praxis und Forschung. In: Bruch, H., Krummaker, S. & Vogel, B (Hrsg.). *Leadership – Best Practices und Trends*. Wiesbaden: Gabler. pp. 301–308.

Buchta, D., Eul, M. & Schulte-Croonenberg, H. (2004). *Strategisches IT-Management*. Wiesbaden: Gabler.

Bynner, W. (1944). *The Way of Life according to Lao Tzu*. New York: John Day.

Caiden, G.E. (1988). Toward a General Theory of Official Corruption. In: *Asian Journal of Public Administration.* 10/1. pp. 3 – 26.

Caldwell, C. & Karri R. (2005). Organizational Governance and Ethical Systems: A Covenantal Approach to Building Trust. In: *Journal of Business Ethics.* 58. pp. 249 – 259.

Cambridge Advanced Learner's Dictionary. Online version. Accessed on http://dictionary.cambridge.org/.

Carter, C.B. & Lorsch, J.L. (2004). *Back to the drawing board. Designing corporate boards for a complex world.* Boston MA: Harvard.

Chandler, A. (1972). *Strategy and structure. Chambers in the history of industrial enterprises.* London: Cambridge.

Coase, R. (1988). *The firm, the market and the law.* Chicago: University of Chicago Press.

Conger, J.A., Lawler III, E.E. & Finegold, D.L. (2001). *Corporate Boards. New strategies for adding value at the top.* San Francisco: Joessey-Bass.

Cornforth, C. (2003). *The Governance of Public and Non-Profit Organizations, What do boards do?* London: Routledge.

COSO – Committee of sponsoring organizations of the Treadway Commission (1992). *Internal control – integrated framework.* COSO.

Crawford, K.J. (2002). *Project Management Maturity Model.* New York: Dekker.

Crocker, D. & Schwenke, S. (2005). *The relevance of development ethics for USAID.* Washington: MSI. Accessed on Jan 2, 2006 on http://www.sum.uio.no/dev_ethics/developmentethicsstudy.pdf.

Dailey, K. (2004). *The FMEA Pocket Handbook.* Mulberry: DW Publishing.

Davies, A. (1999). *A strategic approach to corporate governance.* London: Gower.

Davis, J.H., Schorman, F.D. & Donaldson, L. (1997). Toward a stewardship theory of management. In: *Academy of management review.* 22/1. pp. 20 – 47.

DFID, Department for International Development (1995). *Stakeholder Participation & Analysis.* London: Social Development Division, DFID.

Doh, J.P. & Stumpf, S.A. (eds.) (2005). *Handbook on responsible leadership and governance in global business.* Cheltenham: Elgar.

DRIVER project document (2002). The first project document or project appraisal document. Not published.

DRIVER project document (2004). The official project document accessible at the DRIVER website.

Drucker, P.F. (1981). The Bored Board. In: *Towards The Next Economics and Other Essays.* London: Heinemann. pp. 107-110.

Drucker, P.F. (1999). *The practice of management.* Reissue of first publication 1955. Woburn MA: Butterworth-Heinemann.

Drucker, P.F. (2005). We need Middle-Economics. In: Krieg, W., Galler, K. & Stadelmann, P. (eds.), *Richtiges und gutes Management: vom System zur Praxis.* Bern: Haupt. pp. 15–18.

Dubs, R., Euler, D., Rüegg-Stürm, J. & Wyss, C.E. (Hrsg.) (2004). *Einführung in die Managementlehre.* Band 1–5. Bern: Haupt.

Dyllick, T. & Meyer, A. (2004). Kommunikationsmanagement. In: Dubs, R., Euler, D., Rüegg-Stürm, J. & Wyss, C.E. (Hrsg.). *Einführung in die Managementlehre.* Band 4. Bern: Haupt. pp. 117–146.

Earley, P.C. & Erez, M. (eds.) (1996). *New perspectives on international industrial/organizational psychology.* San Francisco: New Lexington.

Economiesuisse (2002). *Swiss Code of best practice for corporate governance.* Dielsdorf: Lichtdruck AG. Accessed on Nov 2, 2005 on www.economiesuisse.ch.

Edwards, M. (2000). *NGO Rights and responsibilities: A new deal for global governance.* London: The Foreign Policy Centre.

Eigen, P. (2003). *Das Netz der Korruption.* Frankfurt: Campus.

Eisenhardt, K.M. (1989). Building theories from case study research. In: *Academy of Management Review.* 14/4. pp. 532–550.

Eldenburg, L., Hermalin B.E., Weisback, M.S. & Wosinska, M. (2001). *Hospital governance, performance objectives and organizational form.* National Bureau of economic research, NBER working paper No. 8201. Accessed on Oct 2, 2005 on www.nber.org/papers/w8201.

Engwall, L. (2003). Managerial Capitalism Revisited. In: Schwalbach, J. (ed.). *Corporate governance. Essays in honor of Horst Albach.* 2nd edition. Berlin: BWV. pp. 173–192.

Erfurt, R.A. (2004). *Corporate Governance in der Netzökonomie.* Berlin: Klünder.

Fassin, Y. (2005). The reasons behind non-ethical behavior in business and entrepreneurship. In: *Journal of Business Ethics.* 60. pp. 265–279.

Fest, J.C. (2005). The evil is a possibility of the human being. Interview with J.C. Fest in *NZZ (Neue Zürcher Zeitung)*. 17. Nov. 2005.

Fiedler, R. (2001). *Controlling von Projekten. Projektplanung, Projektsteuerung und Risikomanagement*. Braunschweig: Vieweg.

Forsgren, M., Holm, U. & Johanson, J. (1995). Division Headquarters go abroad – a step in the internationalization of the MNC. In: *Journal of Management Studies*. 32 July. pp. 475–491.

Forsgren, M., Holm, U. & Thilenius, P. (1997). Network infusion in the multinational corporation – business relationships and subsidiary influence. In: Björkman, I., Forsgren, M. (eds.). *The nature of international firm*. Copenhagen: Handelshojskolens Forlag. pp. 475–491.

Francis, R.D. (2000). *Ethics and Corporate Governance. An Australian handbook*. Sidney: University of New South Wales Press.

Freeman, R.E. (1984). *Strategic management: a stakeholder approach*. Marshfield: Pitman.

Fuchs, M. (1999). *Integriertes Projektmanagement für den Aufbau und Betrieb von Kooperationen*. Bern: Haupt.

Führer, A. & Züger, R.-M. (2005). *Projektmanagement – Management Basiskompetenz*. Zürich: Compendio.

Furubotn, E. & Richter, R. (1998). *Institutions and Economic Theory. The Contribution of the new Economics*. Michigan: The University of Michigan Press.

Füss, R. (2004). *Die interne Revision in Deutschland, Österreich und der Schweiz 2004*. Frankfurt: Dt. Institut für Interne Revision.

Fust, W. (2004a). Ethische Konflikte in der Entwicklungszusammenarbeit – wie gehen die Verantwortlichen der DEZA damit um. In: GEF (Gesellschaft für ethische Fragen). *Die Öffentlichkeit als ethischer Faktor*. Arbeitsblatt 45. pp. 43–55.

Fust, W. (2004b). Zu einer neuen Politik der DEZA gegenüber den NGOs. Interview with W. Fust. In: *Schweizerisches Jahrbuch für Entwicklungspolitik*. 23/2. Geneva: IUED. pp. 133–140.

Gandossy, R & Sonnenfeld, J.A. (2004). *Leadership and Governance from the inside out*. Hoboken: John Wiley & Sons.

Ganske, M. (2004). *Corporate Governance in öffentlichen Unternehmen*. Frankfurt: Lang.

García Echevarría, S. & del Val Núñez, T. (2000). The corporate dimension of human resources in a globalized economy. In: Albach, H. et. al. (2000). *Zeitschrift für Betriebswirtschaft. Corporate Governance.* Erg.-Heft 1. Wiesbaden: Gabler. pp. 127–141.

Gassmann, O., Kobe, C. & Voit, E. (eds). (2001). *High-Risk-Projekte.* Berlin: Springer.

Gioia, D.A. & Chittipeddi, K. (1991). Sensemaking and sensegiving in strategic change initiation. In: *Strategic Management Journal.* 12/6. pp. 433–448.

Global Compact (w/o year). *United Nations Global Compact.* Accessed on Dec. 12, 2005 on www.unglobalcompact.org.

Gomez, P. (1998). Ganzheitliches Wertmanagement – Von der Vision zur Prozessorganisation, Der VIP-Kreislauf als Klammer moderner Management-Konzepte. In: *IO Management.* 3. pp. 62–65.

Gomez, P. (2005). Die Kunst der optimalen Vereinfachung im Management – The law of requisite variety revisited. In: Krieg, W., Galler, K. & Stadelmann, P. *Richtiges und gutes Management: vom System zur Praxis. Festschrift für Fredmund Malik.* Bern: Haupt. pp. 23–34.

Gomez, P., Fasnacht, D., Wasserer, C. & Waldispühl, R. (2002). *Komplexe IT-Projekte ganzheitlich führen : ein praxiserprobtes Vorgehen.* Bern: Haupt.

Goulet, D. (1995). *Development ethics. A guide to theory and practice.* New York: Apex.

Grant, R.M. (1996). Toward a knowledge-based theory of the firm. In: *Strategic Management Journal.* 17/special issue: Knowledge and the firm. pp. 109–122.

Grimsey, D. & Lewis, M.K. (2004). *Public Private Partnerships.* Cheltenham UK: Elgar.

Groeben, N., Nüse, R. & Gauler, E. (1992). Diagnose argumentativer Unintegrität. Objektive und subjektive Tatbestandsmerkmale bei Werturteilen über argumentative Sprechhandlungen. In: *Zeitschrift für experimentelle und angewandte Psychologie.* 39. pp. 533–558.

Grün, O. (1992). Projektorganisation. In: Frese, E. (Hrsg.), *Handwörterbuch der Organisation.* 3. Ausgabe. Stuttgart: Poeschel. pp. 2102–2116.

Haberer, T. (2003). *Corporate Governance. Oesterreich – Deutschland – International.* Wien: Manz.

Habermas, J. (1981a). *Theorie des kommunikativen Handelns. Band 1. Handlungsrationalität und gesellschaftliche Rationalisierung.* Frankfurt: Suhrkamp.

Habermas, J. (1981b). *Theorie des kommunikativen Handelns. Band 2. Zur Kritik der funktionalistischen Vernunft.* Frankfurt: Suhrkamp.

Habermas, J. (1991). *Erläuterungen zur Diskursethik.* Frankfurt: Suhrkamp.

Habermas, J. (1996). *Die Einbeziehung des Anderen.* Frankfurt: Suhrkamp.

Haller, M. (2004). Risikomanagement. In: Dubs, R., Euler, D., Rüegg-Stürm, J. & Wyss C.E. (Hrsg.). *Einführung in die Managementlehre. Band 4.* Bern: Haupt. pp. 147–177.

Hamel, G. & Prahalad, C.K. (1997). *Wettlauf um die Zukunft: wie Sie mit bahnbrechenden Strategien die Kontrolle über Ihre Branche gewinnen und die Märkte von morgen schaffen.* Wien: Ueberreuter.

Harrison, F. & Lock, D. (2004). *Advanced Project Management. A structured approach.* Fourth edition. Burlington VT: Gower.

Herman, R.D. & Renz, D.O. (1998). Non-profit organizational effectiveness: Contrasts between especially effective and less effective organizations. In: *Non-profit Management & Leadership Journal*, 9/1.

Hickey, S. & Mohan, G. (2005). Relocating participation within a radical politics of development. In: *Development and Change.* 36/2. pp. 237–262.

Hilb, M. (1997). *Integrierte Erfolgsbewertung von Unternehmen. Zufriedenheit & Loyalität von Eigentümern, Kunden, Mitarbeitern, Öffentlichkeit.* Neuwied: Luchterhand.

Hilb, M. (2002). *Transnationales Management der Human-Resourcen. Das Modell des Glocalpreneuring.* Neuwied: Luchterhand.

Hilb, M. (2004). *Integriertes Personalmanagement. Ziele – Strategien – Instrumente.* 12th Edition. München: Luchterhand.

Hilb, M. (2005). *New Corporate Governance, Successful Board Management Tools.* Berlin: Springer.

Hitt, M.A., Ireland, R.D. & Rowe, G.W. (2005). Strategic leadership: strategy, resources, ethics and succession. In: Doh, J.P. & Stumpf, S.A. (eds.). *Handbook on responsible leadership and governance in global business.* Cheltenham: Elgar. pp. 19–53.

Hodge, M.M. & Piccolo, R.F. (2005). Funding source, board involvement techniques, and financial vulnerability in nonprofit organizations. A test of resource dependence. *Nonprofit management & leadership.* 16/2. pp. 171–190.

Hofstetter, K. & Sprecher, T. (2005). *Swiss foundation code. Empfehlungen zur Gründung und Führung von Förderstiftungen.* Basel: Helbing & Lichtenhahn.

Holmes, J.S., Gutiérrez de Piñeres, S.A. & Kiel, L.D. Reforming Government Agencies Internationally: Is There a Role for the Balanced Scorecard? In: *International Journal of Public Administration,* forthcoming.

Honderich, T. (ed.) (1995). *The Oxford Companion to Philosophy.* Oxford: Oxford University Press.

Honneth, A. (1997). Anerkennung und moralische Verpflichtung. In: *Zeitschrift für philosophische Forschung.* 51/1. pp. 25–41.

Honneth, A. (2000). Anerkennung oder Umverteilung? Veränderte Perspektiven einer Gesellschaftsmoral. In: Ulrich, P. & Maak, T. *Die Wirtschaft in der Gesellschaft.* Bern: Haupt. pp. 131–150.

Honneth, A. (2003). *Kampf um Anerkennung.* Erweiterte Ausgabe 2003. Frankfurt: Suhrkamp.

House, R.J., Wright, N.S. & Aditya, R.N. (1996). Cross-cultural research on organizational leadership. In: Earley, P.C. & Erez, M. (eds.). *New perspectives on international industrial/organizational psychology.* San Francisco: New Lexington. pp. 535–625.

Hung, H. (1998). A typology of the theories of the roles of governing boards. In: *Scholarly research and theory papers.* 6/2. April 1998. pp. 101–111.

IFAC – International Federation of Accountants (1999). *Enhancing Shareholder wealth by better managing business risks.* June 1999, Study 9. Accessed on Oct 17, 2005 on http://www.ifac.org/Members/Down Loads/FMA-Study_09.pdf.

IFAC – International Federation of Accountants (2004). *Enterprise governance: getting the balance right.* Accessed on Oct 17, 2005 on http://www.ifac.org.

IIA – Institute of Internal Auditor (2005a). *Definition of internal auditor.* Accessed on Nov 14, 2005 on www.theiia.org/index.cfm?doc_id=123.

IIA – Institute of Internal Auditor (2005b). *Audit committee briefing. Internal audit standards: why they matter.* Accessed on Nov 12, 2005 on www.theiia.org.

ILO – International Labor Organization (2002). *Safe Work – Violence at work.* Accessed on Dec 10, 2005 on http://www.ilo.org/public/english/protection/safework/violence/index.htm.

ILO – Website for small enterprise development. Accessed on Jan 15, 2006 on www.bdsknowledge.org/dyn/bds.

Jacoby, M., Kast, V. & Riedel, I. (1987). *Das Böse im Märchen.* 5. Auflage. Fellbach: Bonz.

Jans, V. (2003). Erfahrungen mit Control & Risk Self Assessement. *Der Schweizer Treuhänder.* 1-2/03.

Johnson, H.T. (1992). *Relevance Regained. From Top-Down Control to Bottom-up Empowerment.* New York: Free Press.

Kaplan, R.S. & Norton, D.P. (1992). Having Trouble with your Strategy? Then Map it. In: *Harvard Business Review.* 74/Jan,Feb. pp. 71 – 79.

Kappel, R. (2003). *Privatsektorförderung in der Entwicklungszusammenarbeit: Wie können sich Staat und Privatsektor gegenseitig unterstützen.* Manuskript zum Vortrag der Veranstaltung von Swisscontact und Economiesuisse. 2. April 2004. Zürich.

Kappel, R. & Zürcher, D. (2004). Erfolge in Empfängerländern rechtfertigen externe Hilfe. In: Eine Debatte über die schweizerische Entwicklungshilfe. In: *NZZ – Neue Zürcher Zeitung* 16.09.2004. p. 29.

Kaptein, M. (1998). *Ethics Management. Auditing and developing the ethical content of organizations.* Dordrecht: Kluwer.

Kaptein, M. & Wempe, J. (2002). *The balanced company. A theory of corporate integrity.* Oxford: Oxford University Press.

Kast, V. (1987). Zum Umgang der Märchen mit dem Bösen. Thematische Zugänge zum Märchen als dynamischer Prozess. In: Jacoby, M., Kast, V. & Riedel, I. *Das Böse im Märchen.* 5. Auflage. Fellbach: Bonz. pp. 24 – 45.

Keiser, O. (2005). Projektrisikomanagement. In: Schott, E. & Campana, C. (Hrsg.). *Strategisches Projektmanagement.* Berlin: Springer. pp. 154 – 173.

Kesselring, T. (2003). *Ethik der Entwicklungspolitik. Gerechtigkeit im Zeitalter der Globalisierung.* München: Beck.

Kirsch, W. (1997). *Wegweiser zur Konstruktion einer evolutionären Theorie der strategischen Führung.* 2. Auflage. München: Kirsch.

Kirsch, W. (2004). Gedanken zum organisationstheoretischen Kontext einer praktisch etwas "bewegenden" Wirtschaftsethik. In: Was bewegt die St. Galler Wirtschaftsethik? 14 Einschätzungen von aussen. *Bericht des Instituts für Wirtschaftsethik* Nr. 100. St. Gallen. pp. 22–23.

Kohlberg, L. (1981). *Essays on moral development. Vol. 1: The philosophy of moral development.* San Francisco: Harper.

KPMG (2002). *Corporate Governance in Europe.* KPMG.

KPMG (2003). *Corporate Governance Self Assessment.* Zürich: KPMG.

Kreitmeier, F. (2001). *Corporate Governance: Aufsichtsgremien und Unternehmensstrategien.* München: Kirsch.

Krieg, W., Galler, K. & Stadelmann, P. (2005). *Richtiges und gutes Management: vom System zur Praxis. Festschrift für Fredmund Malik.* Bern: Haupt.

Kupper, H. (2001). *Die Kunst der Projektsteuerung.* 9. Auflage. München: Oldenburg.

Lambert, K. (2003). *Project Governance.* Whitepaper of SMS Management & Technology. Accessed on July 15, 2005 on http://www.smsmt. com/pdf/whitepaper_klambert_270303.pdf.

Langley, A. (1998). Strategies for theorizing from process data. In: *Academy of Management Review.* 24/4. pp. 691–710.

Lattmann, C. (Hrsg.) (1990). *Unternehmenskultur.* Heidelberg: Physica.

Leavitt, H.J. (1955). Small groups in large organizations. In: *The journal of business.* 28/1. pp. 8–17.

Lee, J. (2004). *NGO accountability: Rights and responsibilities.* Accessed on Jan 15, 2004 on www.casin.ch.

Leisinger, K.M. (1995). Governanz oder: zu Hause muss beginnen, was leuchten soll im Vaterland. In: Leisinger, K.M. & Hoesle, V. (Hrsg.). *Entwicklung mit menschlichem Antlitz. Die Dritte und die Erste Welt im Dialog.* München: Beck. pp. 114–172.

Leisinger, K.M. (1997). *Unternehmensethik. Globale Verantwortung und modernes Management.* München: Beck.

Leisinger, K.M. (2003). *Whistleblowing und Corporate Reputation Management.* München : Hampp.

Leisinger, K.M. (2004). Nicht nur gut gemeint, auch gut gemacht. In: Was bewegt die St. Galler Wirtschaftsethik? 14 Einschätzungen von aussen. *Bericht des Instituts für Wirtschaftsethik* Nr. 100. St. Gallen. pp. 24–25.

Lencioni, P. (2002). *The five dysfunctions of a team. A leadership fable.* San Francisco: Jossey-Bass.

Lennertz, D. (2002). Projekt Management. In: Thommen, J.-P. (Hrsg.). *Management und Organisation: Konzepte, Instrumente, Umsetzung.* Zürich: Versus. pp. 307 – 347.

Lester, A. (2000). *Project planning and control.* 3rd edition. Oxford: Butterworth Heinemann.

Lucas, S.E. (2004). *The art of public speaking.* 8th edition. New York etc.: McGraw Hill. Accessed on Nov 18, 2005 on http://highered.mcgraw-hill.com/sites/007256296x.

Maak, T. (1999). *Die Wirtschaft der Bürgergesellschaft.* Bern: Haupt.

Mace, M.L. (1971). *Directors: Myths and reality.* Cambridge: Harvard University Press.

Mäkilouko, M. (2001). *Leading multinational project teams: formal, country specific perspective.* Tampere: TTKK-Paino.

Malik, F. (2002). *Die neue Corporate Governance.* 3. Auflage. Frankfurt: Frankfurter Allgemeine Buch.

Malik, F. & Probst, G. (1984). Evolutionary management. In: Ulrich, H. & Probst G.J.B. (eds.). *Self-organization and management of social systems.* Berlin: Springer. pp. 105 – 120.

Mann, A. (2003). *Corporate Governance Systems. Funktion und Entwicklung am Beispiel Deutschland und Grossbritannien.* Berlin: Dunker & Humboldt.

Matta, N.F. & Ashkenas, R.N. (2003). Why good projects fail anyway. In: *Harvard Business Review.* 9/2003. pp. 109 – 114.

McDermott, R.E, Mikulak, R.J. & Beauregard, M.R. (1996). *The Basics of FMEA.* New York: Productivity Press.

McDonnell, I. & Solignac Lecomte, H.-B. (2005). *MDGs, taxpayers and aid effectiveness. Policy insights No. 13.* OECD development centre. Accessed on Sep 1, 2005 on www.oecd.org/dev/insights.

Meyer, J.W. & Rowan, B. (1977). Institutional organizations: formal structure as myth and ceremony. In: *American Journal of sociology.* 83. pp. 304 – 363.

Michelman, F.I. (1986). The supreme court 1985 term. Foreword: Traces of self-government. In: *Harvard Law Review.* 100. pp. 4 – 77.

Miles, M.B. & A.M. Huberman (1994). *Qualitative data analysis: An expanded sourcebook,* Thousand Oaks: Sage.

Monks, R.A.G. & Minow, N. (2004). *Corporate Governance.* 3rd edition. Malden MA: Blackwell.

Mueller, R.K. (1993). *Building a power partnership: CEOs and their boards of directors.* New York: Amacom.

Müller-Stewens, G. & Lechner, C. (2005). *Strategisches Management, Wie strategische Initiativen zum Wandel führen, Der St.Galler Management Navigator.* 3. Auflage. Stuttgart: Schäffer-Poeschel.

Neiman, S. (2002). *Evil in modern thought. An alternative history of philosophy.* Princeton NJ: Princeton University Press.

Neumayer, E. (2003). *The pattern of aid giving: the impact of good governance on development assistance.* London and New York: Routledge.

Nussbaum, M. & Sen, A. (eds.) (1993). *The quality of life.* Oxford: Clarendon.

NZZ – Neue Zürcher Zeitung 09.07.2005. *Wie Afrika durch Geld gelähmt wird.* p. 29.

NZZ – Neue Zürcher Zeitung 23.08.2005. *Afrika braucht weder heisse Herzen noch volle Portemonnaies.* p. 7.

OECD, Organisation for Economic Co-operation and Development (2004). *OECD Principles of Corporate Governance.* Paris: OECD.

Örtengren, K. (2003). *A summary of the theory behind the LFA method. The logical framework approach.* A SIDA publication. Accessed on Dec 10, 2005 on www.sida.se/publications.

Oxford English Dictionary (1989) online version, 2nd edition with draft additions of September 2003. Accessed through Universität St. Gallen on http://dictionary.oed.com.

Oxford English Dictionary (1989, 2003) online version, 2nd edition with draft additions of September 2003. Accessed through Universität St. Gallen on http://dictionary.oed.com.

Paine, L.S. (1997). Integrity. In: Werhane, P. (ed.). *The Blackwell encyclopedic dictionary of business ethics.* Cambridge: Blackwell. pp. 335–337.

Palazzo, G. (2004). Identität versus Interessen. Die Governanceethik unter Dissensdruck. In: Wieland, J. (Hrsg.). *Governanceethik im Diskurs.* Marburg: Metropolis.

Paris declaration on aid effectiveness (2005). Accessed on Aug 15, 2005 on http://www.aidharmonization.org/.

Patry, E. (2005). Assessing Capability Change: A Case Study of the Impact of a North Indian NGO. In: *Social Change*. 35/ 2. June 2005. pp. 25 – 46.

PCM (2004). *Project Cycle Management Manual 2004*. Accessed on Dec 1, 2005 on http://europa.eu.int/comm/europeaid.

Peter, H.-B. (Hrsg.) (1999). *Globalisierung, Ethik und Entwicklung*. Bern: Haupt.

Peter, H.-B. (2000). *Entwicklungsethische Faustregeln. Entwicklungspolitik vor der Herausforderung durch Globalisierung – Erneuerung der ethischen Orientierung*. Bern: SDC (Swiss Agency for Development and Cooperation).

Peter, H.-B. (2003). *Dokumentation zur Werte Diskussion in der DEZA*. Beiheft zum Vademecum – Orientierung für die Werte-Diskussion in der DEZA. Bern: DEZA.

Peter, H.-P. & Kraut, M. (2000). *Entwicklungsethische Faustregel. Entwicklungspolitik vor der Herausforderung durch die Globalisierung – Erneuerung der ethischen Orientierung*. Bern: DEZA.

Peters, T.J. & Waterman R.H. Jr. (1982). *In search of excellence. Lessons from America's best run companies*. New York: Harper.

Pfeffer, J. (1982). *Organizations and Organization Theory*. Boston: Pitman.

Pfeffer, J. & Salancik, G.R. (1978). *The external control of organizations. A resource dependence perspective*. New York: Harper & Row.

Pless, N.M. & Maak, T. (2004). Building an inclusive diversity culture: Principles, processes and practice. In: *The Journal of Business Ethics*. 54. pp. 129 – 147.

PMI (2003). *The PMI Compendium of project management practices*. Newton Square, PA: Project Management Institute.

PMI (2004). *A guide to the project management body of knowledge*. 3rd edition. Newton Square, PA: Project Management Institute.

Post, J.E., Preston, L.E. & Sachs, S. (2002). *Redefining the corporation. Stakeholder Management and organizational wealth*. Stanford: Stanford University Press.

PWC (2005). *Audit committees in der Schweiz. Verantwortung, Fähigkeiten und Arbeitsweisen*. Bericht zur Studie von Prof. Dr. M. Hilb, Leiter des IFPM-HSG Center for Corporate Governance in Zusammenarbeit mit PricewaterhouseCooper. Accessed on Nov 2, 2005 on www.pwc.ch.

Rawls, J. (1971). *A theory of justice*. Revised edition. Oxford: Oxford University Press.

Rechkemmer, K. (2003). *Corporate Governance. Informations- und Früherkennungssystem*. München: Oldenburg.

Renz, P. & Pucetaite R. (2004). *The role of NGOs and challenges in operationalization*. Paper for doctoral seminar: Wirtschaftsethische Grundfragen der Entwicklungspolitik. St. Gallen.

Renz, P. & Weichsler, T. (2005). *Corporate Governance in Non-Governmental Organizations (NGOs). Results from a Board-Self-Evaluation conducted with Solidaritas*. Paper for doctoral seminar: From Good to Great Corporate Governance. St. Gallen.

Rhinow, R. (2004). Corporate Governance bei Nonprofit-Organisationen – ein dringendes Desideratum. In: Voggensperger, R.C., Bienek, R.J., Schneider, J. & Thaler, G.O. (Hrsg.). *Gutes besser tun. Corporate Governance in Nonprofit-Organisationen*. Bern: Haupt. pp. 11–23.

Rollins, S.C. & Lanza, R.B. (2005). *Essential project investment governance and reporting. Preventing Project Fraud and Ensuring Sarbanes-Oxley Compliance*. Boca Raton: J. Ross.

Roth, M. (2005). *Compliance, Integrität und Regulierung. Ein wirtschaftsethischer Ansatz in 10 Thesen*. Zürich: Schulthess.

Rüegg-Stürm, J. (2003). *Das neue St. Galler Management-Modell. Grundkategorien einer integrierten Managementlehre. Der HSG Ansatz*. Bern: Haupt.

Rüegg-Stürm, J. (2004). Das neue St. Galler Management-Modell. In: Dubs, R., Euler, D., Rüegg-Stürm, J. & Wyss, C.E. (Hrsg.). *Einführung in die Managementlehre*. Band 1. Bern: Haupt. pp. 65–142.

Rüegg-Stürm, J. (2005). *The new St. Gallen Management Model. Basic categories of an approach to integrated management*. New York: Palgrave Macmillan.

Ruigrok, W., Gibbert, M. & Kaes, B. (2004). *In search of rigorous case studies: Patterns of validity and reliability across ten management journals 1995-2000*. Currently under review.

Scandura, T.A. & Williams, E.A. (2000). Research methodology in management: Current practices, trends, and implications for future research. In: *Academy of Management Journal*. 43/6. pp. 1248–1264.

Schedler, K. (2003). '…and politics?' Public management developments in the light of two rationalities. In: *Public Management Review*. 5/4. pp. 533–550.

Schott, E. & Campana, C. (Hrsg.) (2005). *Strategisches Projektmanagement*. Berlin: Springer.

Schulman, P., Roe, E., van Eeten, M. & de Bruijne, M. (2004). High Reliability and the Management of Critical Infrastructures. In: *Journal of Contingencies and Crisis Management*. 12/1. March. pp. 14–28.

Schwaninger, M. (2001). System theory and cybernetics. In: *Kybernetes*. 30/9-10. pp. 1209–1222.

Schwaninger, M. (2005). Eine Theorie optimaler Organisation. In: Krieg, W., Galler, K. & Stadelmann, P. *Richtiges und gutes Management: vom System zur Praxis. Festschrift für Fredmund Malik*. Bern: Haupt. pp. 71–86.

Schwarz, P. (2005). *Organisation in Nonprofit-Organisationen. Grundlagen, Strukturen*. Bern, Stuttgart, Wien: Haupt.

Schwarz, P., Purtschert, R., Giroud, C. & Schauer, R. (2002). *Das Freiburger Management-Modell für Nonprofit-Organisationen (NPO)*. 4., weitgehend aktualisierte und ergänzte Auflage. Bern, Stuttgart, Wien: Haupt.

Schweiz. Bundesanwaltschaft (2003). *Bundesanwaltschaft und Bundeskriminalpolizei ermittelten wegen veruntreuten Bundesgeldern in Pakistan*. Press release accessed on Oct 10, 2005 on www.ba.admin.ch.

SDC, Swiss Agency for Development and Cooperation (1996). *PEMU – Ein Einstieg*. Bern: SDC.

SDC, Swiss Agency for Development and Cooperation (1997). *Monitoring*. Bern: SDC.

SDC, Swiss Agency for Development and Cooperation (1998). *Combating corruption. Guidelines*. Bern: SDC.

SDC, Swiss Agency for Development and Cooperation (1999). *Key questions and indicators*. Bern: SDC.

SDC, Swiss Agency for Development and Cooperation (2002). *English glossary / SDC. 27 most relevant terms related to evaluation and controlling in use in SDC*. Bern: SDC.

SDC, Swiss Agency for Development and Cooperation (2004). *Switzerland's international cooperation. Annual Report 2004*. Bern: SDC.

SDC, Swiss Agency for Development and Cooperation (w/o year). *Vademecum Werte. Orientierungshilfe im Werteprozess der DEZA*. Bern: SDC.

SDC, Swiss Agency for Development and Cooperation, & Intercooperation (1995). *Planning Pre-phases as an instrument in project planning)*. Bern: SDC

SECO, State Secretariat for Economic Affairs (2005). *Logframe User Manual*. Accessed on Dec 10, 2005 on www.seco-cooperation.ch.

Sen, A. (1999). *Development as freedom*. Oxford: Oxford University Press.

Shapiro, S.P. (2005). Agency theory. In: *Annual review of sociology*. 31. pp. 263–284.

Sharma, A. (1997). Professional as agent: knowledge asymmetry in agency exchange. In: *Academy of Management Review*. 22. pp. 758–798.

Snow, C.C. & Thomas, J.B. (1994). Field research methods in strategic management: Contributions to theory-building and testing. In: *Journal of Management Studies*. 31/4. pp. 457–480.

Sonnenfeld, J.A. (2002). What makes great boards great. In: *Harvard Business Review*. 80/9 pp. 106–113.

Spickers, J. (2004). *The Development of the «St.Gallen Management Model»*. Version 1.5 as of June 2. Accessed on Sep 13, 2005 on www.ifb.unisg.ch.

Steger, U. (ed.) (2004). *Mastering global corporate governance*. West Sussex: John Wiley & Sons.

Steinle, C. (2005). *Ganzheitliches Management. Eine Mehrdimensionale Sichtweise integrierter Unternehmensführung*. Wiesbaden: Gabler.

Steinmann, H. (2004). Zur Situation der Unternehmensethik. In: Was bewegt die St. Galler Wirtschaftsethik? 14 Einschätzungen von aussen. *Bericht des Instituts für Wirtschaftsethik* Nr. 100. St. Gallen. pp. 24–25.

Stiglitz, J. (2002). *Globalization and its discontent*. London: Penguin.

Stückelberger, C. (2001). *Ethischer Welthandel*. Bern: Haupt.

SustainAbility (2003). *The 21st century NGO*. London: SustainAbility.

Swiss NPO-Code (2005). *Corporate Governance für grosse gemeinnützige soziale und humanitäre Organisationen*. Vernehmlassungsentwurf Swiss NPO-Code vom 15. April 2005.

SwissFoundations (2005). *Erster europäischer Good Governance Code für Stiftungen*. Medienmitteilung 25. Okt. 2005. Accessed on Nov 3, 2005 on www.swissfoundations.ch.

SwissNGO (2005). *Strategy on Enabling Environment*. Internal paper of SwissNGO, made available to the author on Nov 7, 2005. Zürich.

Thommen, J.-P. (2000). *Lexikon der Betriebswirtschaft. Management-Kompetenz von A bis Z.* 2. Auflage. Zürich: Versus.

Thommen, J.-P. (2002). *Management und Organisation: Konzepte, Instrumente, Umsetzung.* Zürich: Versus.

Thomsett, R. (2004). *Project Management. Risk in Projects. The total tool set.* Accessed on Oct 5, 2005 on www.thomsett.com.au.

TI – Transparency International (2000). *Source Book 2000. Confronting corruption: the elements of a national integrity system.* Accessed on December 12, 2005 on www.transparency.org/publications/source-book.

TI – Transparency International (2002). *Business principles for countering bribery.* An initiative of Transparency International and Social Accountability international. Accessed on June 12, 2004 on www.transparency.org.

Tibi, B. (1991). *Die Krise des modernen Islams.* Frankfurt: Suhrkamp.

Tricker, R.I. (1984). *Corporate Governance. Practices, procedures and powers in British companies and their boards of directors.* Brookfield: Gower.

Tricker, R.I. (1994). Editorial. *Corporate Governance: an international review.* 2/1. pp. 55–58.

Trompenaars, F & Hampden-Turner, C. (2003, first edition published 1997). *Riding the waves of culture. Understanding cultural diversity in business.* London: Nicholas Brealey.

Ulrich, H. (1968/70). *Die Unternehmung als produktives soziales System.* Bern: Haupt.

Ulrich, H. (1978/1987). *Unternehmungspolitik.* 3. durchgesehene Auflage. Bern: Haupt.

Ulrich, H. (1984). *Management.* Bern: Haupt.

Ulrich, H. (2001). *Gesammelte Schriften, Band 2.* Bern: Haupt.

Ulrich, H. & Krieg, W. (1972). *Das St. Galler Management-Modell.* Bern: Haupt.

Ulrich, H. & Probst G.J.B. (eds.) (1984). *Self-organization and management of social systems.* Berlin: Springer.

Ulrich, H. & Probst G.J.B. (1995). *Anleitung zum ganzheitlichen Denken und Handeln. Ein Brevier für Führungskräfte.* Bern: Haupt.

Ulrich, P. (1999a). Führungsethik. In: *Handbuch der Wirtschaftsethik.* Herausgegeben im Auftrag der Görres-Gesellschaft von Wilhelm Korff et. al. Gütersloh: Gütersloher Verlagshaus.

Ulrich, P. (1999b). Grundrechte und Grundfähigkeiten. Gedanken zu einem Leitbild sozioökonomischer Entwicklung aus der Perspektive der integrativen Wirtschaftsethik. In: Peter, H.-B. (Hrsg.). *Globalisierung, Ethik und Entwicklung.* Bern: Haupt. pp. 55–76.

Ulrich, P. (2001a). *Integrative Wirtschaftsethik. Grundlagen lebensdienlicher Ökonomie.* 3., revidierte Auflage. Bern, Stuttgart, Wien: Haupt. (a manuscript for an English edition was used by the author for some of the translations).

Ulrich, P. (2001b). Weltethos und Weltwirtschaft – eine wirtschaftsethische Perspektive. In: Küng, H. & Kuschel, K.J. (Hrsg.). *Wissenschaft und Weltethos.* Durchgesehene Taschenbuchausgabe. München: Piper. pp. 40–60.

Ulrich, P. (2001c). Integritätsmanagement und „verdiente" Reputation. In: *io Management.* 1/2. pp. 42–47.

Ulrich, P. (2002). *Der entzauberte Markt. Eine wirtschaftsethische Orientierung.* Freiburg, Basel, Wien: Herder.

Ulrich, P. (2004). Was ist "gute" sozioökonomische Entwicklung? Eine wirtschaftsethische Perspektive. In: *Zeitschrift für Wirtschaft- und Unternehmensethik (zfwu).* 5/1. pp. 8–22.

Ulrich, P. (2005). *Zivilisierte Marktwirtschaft. Eine wirtschaftsethische Orientierung.* Freiburg: Herder.

Ulrich, P. & Fluri, E. (1995). *Management.* 7. Auflage. Bern: Haupt.

Ulrich, P., Lunau, Y. & Weber, T. (1999). Ethikmassnahmen in der Unternehmenspraxis. In: Ulrich, P. & Wieland, J. (Hrsg.). *Unternehmensethik in der Praxis. Impulse aus den USA, Deutschland und der Schweiz.* Bern: Haupt. pp. 121–194.

Ulrich, P. & Maak, T. (2000a). Business ethics – the founding principles. In: *European Business Forum.* Issue 3. pp. 19–23.

Ulrich, P. & Maak, T. (Hrsg.) (2000b). *Die Wirtschaft in der Gesellschaft.* Bern: Haupt.

Ulrich, P. & Wieland, J. (Hrsg.) (1999). *Unternehmensethik in der Praxis. Impulse aus den USA, Deutschland und der Schweiz.* Bern: Haupt.

UN (w/y). UN Millennium Development Goals. Accessed on May 3, 2006 on www.un.org/millenniumgoals.

UNO (1948). *Universal Declaration of Human Rights.* Accessed on Nov 30, 2005 on http://www.un.org/Overview/rights.html.

UNO (2000). *United Nations Millennium Declaration.* Resolution adopted by the General Assembly. A/Res/55/2 dated Sep 18, 2000. Accessed on Oct 3, 2005 on http://www.un.org/millennium/declaration/ares552e.pdf.

van Reijen, W. & Apel, K.-O. (Hrsg.) (1984). *Rationales Handeln und Gesellschaftstheorie.* Bochum: Germinal.

Voggensperger, R.C., Bienek, H.J., Schneider, J. & Thaler, G.O. (Hrsg.) (2004). *Gutes besser tun. Corporate Governance in Nonprofit-Organisationen.* Bern: Haupt.

Volcker, P.A., Goldstone, R.J. & Pieth, M. (2005). *The management of the United Nations Oil-for-Food programme. Vol. 1: The report of the committee.* Accessed on Dec 20, 2005 on www.iic-offp.org.

von Cranach, M. (2004). Integrative Wirtschaftsethik: Könnte sie praktischer werden? In: Was bewegt die St. Galler Wirtschaftsethik? 14 Einschätzungen von aussen. *Bericht des Instituts für Wirtschaftsethik* Nr. 100. St. Gallen. pp. 24–25.

Wallace, P. & Zinkin, J. (2005). *Mastering business in Asia. Corporate Governance.* Hoboken: John Wiley.

Waxenberger, B. (2001). *Integritätsmanagement. Ein Gestaltungsmodell prinzipiengeleiteter Unternehmensführung.* Bern: Haupt.

Waxenberger, B. (2003). Framework for ethically aware businesses: the integrity management model. In: Wieland, J. *Standards and audits for ethics management systems.* Berlin: Springer. pp. 233–251.

Wellmer, A. (1986). *Ethik und Dialog. Elemente des moralischen Urteils bei Kant und in der Diskursethik.* Frankfurt: Suhrkamp.

Werhane, P. (ed.) (1997). *The Blackwell encyclopedic dictionary of business ethics.* Cambridge: Blackwell.

Wieland, J. (2003). *Standards and audits for ethics management systems.* Berlin: Springer.

Wieland, J. (Hrsg.) (2004). *Governanceethik im Diskurs.* Marburg: Metropolis.

Wilbers, K. (2004). Anspruchsgruppen und Interaktionsthemen. In: Dubs, R., Euler, D., Rüegg-Stürm, J. & Wyss C.E. (Hrsg). *Einführung in die Managementlehre. Band 1.* Bern: Haupt. pp. 331–364.

Wittmann, S. (1998). *Ethik im Personalmanagement.* Bern: Haupt.

Woodley, S. (ed.) (2004). *Trends and developments in corporate governance. The comparative law yearbook of international business.* The Hague: Kluwer Law International.

World Bank (2003). *The Global Poll Multinational Survey of Opinion Leaders 2002.* Princeton Survey Research Associates for the World Bank. Washington D.C.

World Commission on Environment and Development. Accessed on www.un.org/esa/sustdev.

Wunderer, F.R. (1995). *Der Verwaltungsrats-Präsident: Gestaltungsansätze aus juristischer und managementorientierter Sicht.* Zürich: Schulthess.

Yin, R.K. (1998). The abridged version of case study research. In: Bickman, L. & Rog, D.J., *Handbook of Applied Social Research.* Thousand Oaks, CA: Sage. pp. 229–259.

Yin, R.K. (2003). *Case study research. Design and Methods.* 3rd Edition. Thousand Oaks, CA: Sage.

Index